Hands-On Neural Networks with TensorFlow 2.0

MW00837416

Understand TensorFlow, from static graph to eager execution, and design neural networks

Paolo Galeone

BIRMINGHAM - MUMBAI

Hands-On Neural Networks with TensorFlow 2.0

Commissioning Editor: Sunith Shetty
Acquisition Editor: Yogesh Deokar
Content Development Editor: Athikho Sapuni Rishana
Senior Editor: Sofi Rogers
Technical Editor: Utkarsha S. Kadam
Copy Editor: Safis Editing
Project Coordinator: Kirti Pisat
Proofreader: Safis Editing
Indexer: Tejal Daruwale Soni
Production Designer: Shraddha Falebhai

First published: September 2019

Production reference: 1170919

Published by Packt Publishing Ltd.
Livery Place
35 Livery Street
Birmingham
B3 2PB, UK.

ISBN 978-1-78961-555-5

www.packt.com

Packt.com

Subscribe to our online digital library for full access to over 7,000 books and videos, as well as industry leading tools to help you plan your personal development and advance your career. For more information, please visit our website.

Why subscribe?

- Spend less time learning and more time coding with practical eBooks and Videos from over 4,000 industry professionals

- Improve your learning with Skill Plans built especially for you

- Get a free eBook or video every month

- Fully searchable for easy access to vital information

- Copy and paste, print, and bookmark content

Did you know that Packt offers eBook versions of every book published, with PDF and ePub files available? You can upgrade to the eBook version at www.packt.com and as a print book customer, you are entitled to a discount on the eBook copy. Get in touch with us at customercare@packtpub.com for more details.

At www.packt.com, you can also read a collection of free technical articles, sign up for a range of free newsletters, and receive exclusive discounts and offers on Packt books and eBooks.

Contributors

About the author

Paolo Galeone is a computer engineer with strong practical experience. After getting his MSc degree, he joined the Computer Vision Laboratory at the University of Bologna, Italy, as a research fellow, where he improved his computer vision and machine learning knowledge working on a broad range of research topics. Currently, he leads the Computer Vision and Machine Learning laboratory at ZURU Tech, Italy.

In 2019, Google recognized his expertise by awarding him the title of Google Developer Expert (GDE) in Machine Learning. As a GDE, he shares his passion for machine learning and the TensorFlow framework by blogging, speaking at conferences, contributing to open-source projects, and answering questions on Stack Overflow.

About the reviewer

Luca Massaron is a data scientist, with over 15 years of experience in analytical roles, who interprets big data and transforms it into smart data by means of both the simplest and the most effective data mining and machine learning techniques. He is the author of 10 books on machine learning, deep learning, algorithms, and AI, and is a Google Developer Expert (GDE) in machine learning.

My sincerest thanks to my family, Yukiko and Amelia, for their support and loving patience.

Packt is searching for authors like you

If you're interested in becoming an author for Packt, please visit `authors.packtpub.com` and apply today. We have worked with thousands of developers and tech professionals, just like you, to help them share their insight with the global tech community. You can make a general application, apply for a specific hot topic that we are recruiting an author for, or submit your own idea.

Table of Contents

Preface

Technology leaders are adopting neural networks to enhance their products, making them smarter or, in marketing words, AI-powered. This book is a handy guide to TensorFlow, its inner structure, the new features of version 2.0 and how to use them to create neural-networks-based applications. By the end of this book, you will be well-versed in the TensorFlow architecture and its new features. You will be able to solve machine learning problems easily, using the power of neural networks.

This book starts with a theoretical overview of machine learning and neural networks, followed by a description of the TensorFlow library, in both its 1.x and 2.0 versions. Reading this book, you will become well-versed in the required theory for understanding how neural networks work, using easy-to-follow examples. Next, you will learn how to master optimization techniques and algorithms to build a wide range of neural network architectures using the new modules offered by TensorFlow 2.0. Furthermore, after having analyzed the TensorFlow structure, you will learn how to implement more complex neural network architectures such as CNNs for classification, semantic segmentation networks, generative adversarial networks, and others in your research work and projects.

By the end of this book, you will master the TensorFlow structure and will be able to leverage the power of this machine learning framework to train and use neural networks of varying complexities without much effort.

Who this book is for

This book is meant for data scientists, machine learning developers, deep learning researchers, and developers with a basic statistical background who want to work with neural networks and discover the TensorFlow structure and its new features. A working knowledge of the Python programming language is required to get the most out of the book.

What this book covers

Chapter 1, *What is Machine Learning?*, covers the fundamentals of machine learning: what supervised, unsupervised, and semi-supervised learning is and why these distinctions are important. Moreover, you will start to understand how to create a data pipeline, how to measure the performance of an algorithm, and how to validate your results.

Chapter 2, *Neural Networks and Deep Learning*, focuses on neural networks. You will learn about the strengths of machine learning models, how it is possible to make a network learn, and how, in practice, the model parameter update is performed. By the end of this chapter, you will understand the intuition behind backpropagation and network parameter updates. Moreover, you'll learn why deep neural network architectures are required to solve challenging tasks.

Chapter 3, *TensorFlow Graph Architecture*, covers the structure of TensorFlow – the structure that's shared between the 1.x and 2.x versions.

Chapter 4, *TensorFlow 2.0 Architecture*, demonstrates the difference between TensorFlow 1.x and TensorFlow 2.x. You'll start to develop some simple machine learning models using both these versions. You will also gain an understanding of all the common features of the two versions.

Chapter 5, *Efficient Data Input Pipelines and Estimator API*, shows how to define a complete data input pipeline using the `tf.data` API together with the use of the `tf.estimator` API to define experiments. By the end of this chapter, you'll be able to create complex and highly efficient input pipelines leveraging all the power of the `tf.data` and `tf.io.gfile` APIs.

Chapter 6, *Image Classification Using TensorFlow Hub*, covers how to use TensorFlow Hub to do transfer learning and fine-tuning easily by leveraging its tight integration with the Keras API.

Chapter 7, *Introduction to Object Detection*, shows how to extend your classifier, making it an object detector that regresses the coordinates of a bounding box, and also gives you an introduction to more complex object detection architectures.

Chapter 8, *Semantic Segmentation and Custom Dataset Builder*, covers how to implement a semantic segmentation network, how to prepare a dataset for this kind of task, and how to train and measure the performance of a model. You will solve a semantic segmentation problem using U-Net.

Chapter 9, *Generative Adversarial Networks*, covers GANs from a theoretical and practical point of view. You will gain an understanding of the structure of generative models and how the adversarial training can be easily implemented using TensorFlow 2.0.

Chapter 10, *Bringing a Model to Production*, shows how to go from a trained model to a complete application. This chapter also covers how to export a trained model to an indicated representation (SavedModel) and use it in a complete application. By the end of this chapter, you will be able to export a trained model and use it inside Python, TensorFlow.js, and also in Go using the tfgo library.

To get the most out of this book

You need to have a basic understanding of neural networks, but this is not mandatory since the topics will be covered from both a theoretical and a practical point of view. Working knowledge of basic machine learning algorithms is a plus. You need a good working knowledge of Python 3.

You should already know how to install packages using `pip`, how to set up your working environment to work with TensorFlow, and how to enable (if available) GPU acceleration. Moreover, a good background knowledge of programming concepts, such as imperative language versus descriptive language and object-oriented programming, is required.

The environment setup will be covered in `Chapter 3`, *TensorFlow Graph Architecture,* after the first two chapters on machine learning and neural network theory.

Download the example code files

You can download the example code files for this book from your account at `www.packt.com`. If you purchased this book elsewhere, you can visit `www.packtpub.com/support` and register to have the files emailed directly to you.

You can download the code files by following these steps:

1. Log in or register at `www.packt.com`.
2. Select the **Support** tab.
3. Click on **Code Downloads**.
4. Enter the name of the book in the **Search** box and follow the onscreen instructions.

Once the file is downloaded, please make sure that you unzip or extract the folder using the latest version of:

- WinRAR/7-Zip for Windows
- Zipeg/iZip/UnRarX for Mac
- 7-Zip/PeaZip for Linux

The code bundle for the book is also hosted on GitHub at `https://github.com/PacktPublishing/Hands-On-Neural-Networks-with-TensorFlow-2.0`. In case there's an update to the code, it will be updated on the existing GitHub repository.

We also have other code bundles from our rich catalog of books and videos available at `https://github.com/PacktPublishing/`. Check them out!

Download the color images

We also provide a PDF file that has color images of the screenshots/diagrams used in this book. You can download it here: `https://static.packt-cdn.com/downloads/9781789615555_ColorImages.pdf`.

Conventions used

There are a number of text conventions used throughout this book.

`CodeInText`: Indicates code words in text, database table names, folder names, filenames, file extensions, pathnames, dummy URLs, user input, and Twitter handles. Here is an example: "Mount the downloaded `WebStorm-10*.dmg` disk image file as another disk in your system."

A block of code is set as follows:

```
writer = tf.summary.FileWriter("log/two_graphs/g1", g1)
writer = tf.summary.FileWriter("log/two_graphs/g2", g2)
writer.close()
```

Any command-line input or output is written as follows:

```
# create the virtualenv in the current folder (tf2)
pipenv --python 3.7
# run a new shell that uses the just created virtualenv
pipenv shell
# install, in the current virtualenv, tensorflow
pip install tensorflow==2.0
#or for GPU support: pip install tensorflow-gpu==2.0
```

Bold: Indicates a new term, an important word, or words that you see onscreen. For example, words in menus or dialog boxes appear in the text like this. Here is an example: "The second peculiarity of the `tf.Graph` structure is its **graph collections**."

 Warnings or important notes appear like this.

 Tips and tricks appear like this.

Get in touch

Feedback from our readers is always welcome.

General feedback: If you have questions about any aspect of this book, mention the book title in the subject of your message and email us at customercare@packtpub.com.

Errata: Although we have taken every care to ensure the accuracy of our content, mistakes do happen. If you have found a mistake in this book, we would be grateful if you would report this to us. Please visit www.packt.com/submit-errata, selecting your book, clicking on the Errata Submission Form link, and entering the details.

Piracy: If you come across any illegal copies of our works in any form on the Internet, we would be grateful if you would provide us with the location address or website name. Please contact us at copyright@packt.com with a link to the material.

If you are interested in becoming an author: If there is a topic that you have expertise in and you are interested in either writing or contributing to a book, please visit authors.packtpub.com.

Reviews

Please leave a review. Once you have read and used this book, why not leave a review on the site that you purchased it from? Potential readers can then see and use your unbiased opinion to make purchase decisions, we at Packt can understand what you think about our products, and our authors can see your feedback on their book. Thank you!

For more information about Packt, please visit packt.com.

Section 1: Neural Network Fundamentals

This section provides a basic introduction to machine learning and the important concepts of neural networks and deep learning.

This section comprises the following chapters:

- Chapter 1, *What is Machine Learning?*
- Chapter 2, *Neural Networks and Deep Learning*

What is Machine Learning? 1

Machine learning (ML) is an artificial intelligence branch where we define algorithms, with the aim of learning about a model that describes and extracts meaningful information from data.

Exciting applications of ML can be found in fields such as predictive maintenance in industrial environments, image analysis for medical applications, time series forecasting for finance and many other sectors, face detection and identification for security purposes, autonomous driving, text comprehension, speech recognition, recommendation systems, and many other applications of ML are countless, and we probably use them daily without even knowing it!

Just think about the camera application on your smartphone— when you open the app and you point the camera toward a person, you see a square around the person's face. How is this possible? For a computer, an image is just a set of three stacked matrices. How can an algorithm detect that a specific subset of those pixels represents a face?

There's a high chance that the algorithm (also called a **model**) used by the camera application has been trained to detect that pattern. This task is known as face detection. This face detection task can be solved using a ML algorithm that can be classified into the broad category of supervised learning.

ML tasks are usually classified into three broad categories, all of which we are going to analyze in the following sections:

- Supervised learning
- Unsupervised learning
- Semi-supervised learning

Every group has its peculiarities and set of algorithms, but all of them share the same goal: learning from data. Learning from data is the goal of every ML algorithm and, in particular, learning about an unknown function that maps data to the (expected) response.

The dataset is probably the most critical part of the entire ML pipeline; its quality, structure, and size are key to the success of deep learning algorithms, as we will see in upcoming chapters.

For instance, the aforementioned face detection task can be solved by training a model, making it look at thousands and thousands of labeled examples so that the algorithm learns that a specific input corresponds with what we call a face.

The same algorithm can achieve a different performance if it's trained on a different dataset of faces, and the more high-quality data we have, the better the algorithm's performance will be.

In this chapter, we will cover the following topics:

- The importance of the dataset
- Supervised learning
- Unsupervised learning
- Semi-supervised learning

The importance of the dataset

Since the concept of the dataset is essential in ML, let's look at it in detail, with a focus on how to create the required splits for building a complete and correct ML pipeline.

A **dataset** is nothing more than a collection of data. Formally, we can describe a dataset as a set of pairs, (e_i, l_i), where e_i is the *i*-th example and l_i is its label, with a finite cardinality, k :

$$\text{Dataset} = \{(e_i, l_i)\}_{i=1}^{k}$$

A dataset has a finite number of elements, and our ML algorithm will loop over this dataset several times, trying to understand the data structure, until it solves the task it is asked to address. As shown in `Chapter 2`, *Neural Networks and Deep Learning*, some algorithms will consider all the data at once, while other algorithms will iteratively look at a small subset of the data at each training iteration.

A typical supervised learning task is the classification of the dataset. We train a model on the data, making it learn that a specific set of features extracted from the example e_i (or the example, e_i, itself) corresponds to a label, l_i.

It is worth familiarizing yourself with the concept of datasets, dataset splits, and epochs from the beginning of your journey into the ML world so that you are already familiar with these concepts when we talk about them in the chapters that follow.

Right now, you already know, at a very high level, what a dataset is. But let's dig into the basic concepts of a dataset split. A dataset contains all the data that's at your disposal. As we mentioned previously, the ML algorithm needs to loop over the dataset several times and look at the data in order to learn how to solve a task (for example, the classification task).

If we use the same dataset to train and test the performance of our algorithm, how can we guarantee that our algorithm performs well, even on unseen data? Well, we can't.

The most common practice is to split the dataset into three parts:

- **Training set**: The subset to use to train the model.
- **Validation set**: The subset to measure the model's performance during the training and also to perform hyperparameter tuning/searches.
- **Test set**: The subset to never touch during the training or validation phases. This is used only to run the final performance evaluation.

All three parts are disjoint subsets of the dataset, as shown in the following Venn diagram:

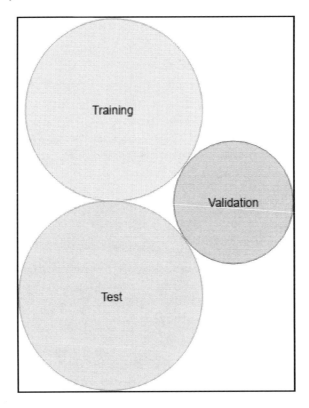

Venn diagram representing how a dataset should be divided no overlapping among the training, validation, and test sets is required

The training set is usually the bigger subset since it must be a meaningful representation of the whole dataset. The validation and test sets are smaller and generally the same size—of course, this is just something general; there are no constraints about the dataset's cardinality. In fact, the only thing that matters is that they're big enough for the algorithm to be trained on and represented.

We will make our model learn from the training set, evaluate its performance during the training process using the validation set, and run the final performance evaluation on the test set: this allows us to correctly define and train supervised learning algorithms that could generalize well, and therefore work well even on unseen data.

An epoch is the processing of the entire training set that's done by the learning algorithm. Hence, if our training set has 60,000 examples, once the ML algorithm uses all of them to learn, then an epoch is passed.

One of the most well-known datasets in the ML domain is the MNIST dataset. MNIST is a dataset of labeled pairs, where every example is a 28 x 28 binary image of a handwritten digit, and the label is the digit represented in the image.

However, we are not going to use the MNIST dataset in this book, for several reasons:

- MNIST is too easy. Both traditional and recent ML algorithms can classify every digit of the dataset almost perfectly (> 97% accuracy).
- MNIST is overused. We're not going to make the same applications with the same datasets as everyone else.
- MNIST cannot represent modern computer vision tasks.

The preceding reasons come from the description of a new dataset, called **fashion-MNIST**, which was released in 2017 by the researchers at Zalando Research. This is one of the datasets we are going to use throughout this book.

Fashion-MNIST is a drop-in replacement for the MNIST dataset, which means that they both have the same structure. For this reason, any source code that uses MNIST can be started using fashion-MNIST by changing the dataset path.

It consists of a training set of 60,000 examples and a test set of 10,000 examples, just like the original MNIST dataset; even the image format (28 x 28) is the same. The main difference is in the subjects: there are no binary images of handwritten digits; this time, there's grayscale images of clothing. Since they are grayscale and not binary, their complexity is higher (binary means only 0 for background and 255 for the foreground, while grayscale is the whole range [0,255]):

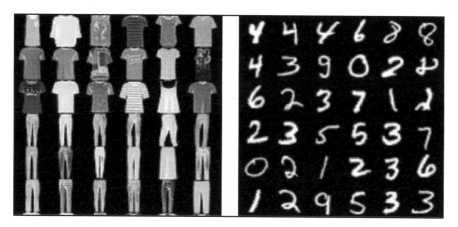

Images sampled from the fashion-MNIST dataset on the left and from the MNIST dataset on the right. It's worth noting how the MNIST dataset is simpler since it's a binary images dataset, while the fashion-MNIST dataset is more complex because of the grayscale palette and the inherent complexity of the dataset elements.

A dataset such as fashion-MNIST is a perfect candidate to be used in supervised learning algorithms since they need annotated examples to be trained on.

Before describing the different types of ML algorithms, it is worth becoming familiar with the concept of n-dimensional spaces, which are the daily bread of every ML practitioner.

n-dimensional spaces

n-dimensional spaces are a way of modeling datasets whose examples have n attributes each.

Every example, e_i, in the dataset is entirely described by its n attributes, $x_{j=0,\cdots,n-1}$:

$$e_i = (x_0, x_1, \cdots, x_{n-1})$$

Intuitively, you can think about an example such as a row in a database table where the attributes are the columns. For example, an image dataset like the fashion-MNIST is a dataset of elements each with 28 x 28 = 284 attributes—there are no specific column names, but every column of this dataset can be thought of as a pixel position in the image.

The concept of dimension arises when we start thinking about examples such as points in an n-dimensional space that are uniquely identified by their attributes.

It is easy to visualize this representation when the number of dimensions is less than or equal to 3, and the attributes are numeric. To understand this concept, let's take a look at the most common dataset in the data mining field: the Iris dataset.

What we are going to do here is explorative data analysis. Explorative data analysis is good practice when you're starting to work with a new dataset: always visualize and try to understand the data before thinking about applying ML to it.

The dataset contains three classes of 50 instances each, where each class refers to a type of Iris plant. The attributes are all continuous, except for the label/class:

- Sepal length in cm
- Sepal width in cm
- Petal length in cm
- Petal width in cm
- Class—Iris Setosa, Iris Versicolor, Iris Virginica

In this small dataset, we have four attributes (plus the class information), which means we have four dimensions that are already difficult to visualize all at once. What we can do to explore the dataset is pick pairs of features (sepal width, sepal length) and (petal width, petal length) and draw them in a 2D plane in order to understand how a feature is related (or not) with another and maybe find out whether there are some natural partitions in the data.

Using an approach such as visualizing the relation between two features only allows us to do some initial consideration on the dataset; it won't help us in a more complex scenario where the number of attributes is way more and not always numerical.

In the plots, we assign a different color to every class, (Setosa, Versicolor, Virginica) = (blue, green, red):

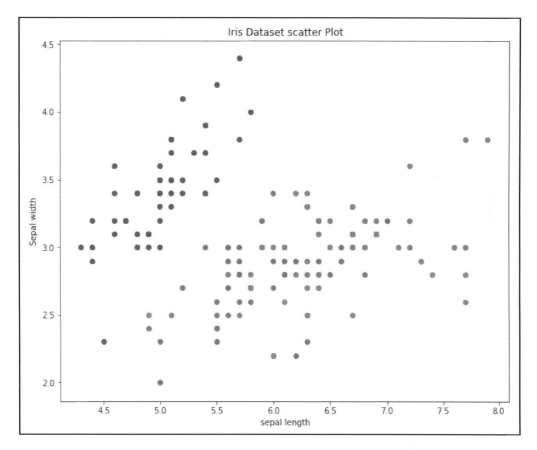

Scatter plot of the Iris dataset; every class has a different color and the two dimensions represented are sepal length (x axis) and sepal width (y axis)

As we can see, in this 2D space identified by the attributes (sepal width, sepal length) the blue dots are all close together, while the two other classes are still blended. All we can conclude by looking at this graph is that there could be a positive correlation between the sepal length and width of the Iris setosa, but nothing else. Let's look at the petal relation:

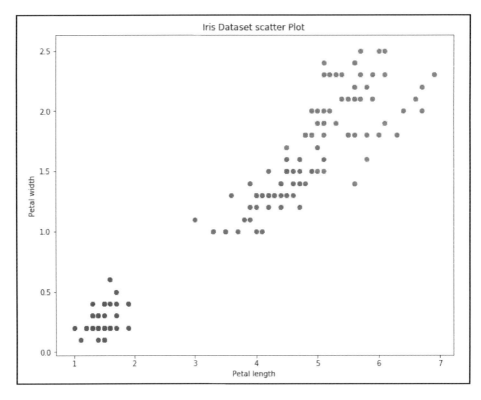

Scatter plot of the Iris dataset; every class has a different color and the two dimensions represented are petal length (x axis) and petal width (y axis).

This plot shows us that there are three partitions in this dataset. To find them, we can use the petal width and length attributes.

The goal of classification algorithms is to get them to learn how to identify what features are discriminative in order to learn a function so that they can correctly separate elements of different classes. Neural networks have proven to be the right tool to use to avoid doing feature selection and a lot of data preprocessing: they're so robust to the noise that they almost removed the need for data cleaning.

Warning: This is only valid on massive datasets, where the noise is overwhelmed by the correct data—for small datasets, it is always better to look at the features by plotting them and helping the ML algorithm by giving only the significant features as input.

The Iris dataset is the most straightforward dataset we could have used to describe an *n*-dimensional space. If we jump back to the fashion-MNIST dataset, things become way more interesting.

A single example has 784 features: how can we visualize a 784-dimensional space? We can't!

The only thing we can do is perform a dimensionality reduction technique in order to reduce the number of dimensions that are needed for visualization and have a better understanding of the underlying data structure.

One of the simplest data reduction techniques—and usually meaningless on high-dimensional datasets—is the visualization of randomly picked dimensions of the data. We did it for the Iris dataset: we just chose two random dimensions among the four available and plotted the data in the 2D plane. Of course, for low-dimensional space, it could be helpful, but for a dataset such as fashion-MNIST, it is a complete waste of time. There are better dimensionality reduction techniques, such as **Principal Component Analysis (PCA)** or **t-distributed Stochastic Neighbor Embedding (t-SNE)**, that we won't cover in detail in this book, since the data visualization tool we are going to use in the upcoming chapters, that is, TensorBoard, already implements these algorithms for us.

Moreover, there are specific geometrical properties that don't work as we expect them to when we're working in high-dimensional spaces: this fact is called the **curse of dimensionality**. In the next section, we'll see how a simple geometrical example can be used to show how the Euclidean distances work differently as the number of dimensions increases.

The curse of dimensionality

Let's take a hypercube unitary $[0,1]^D$ with a center of $c = \left(\frac{1}{2}, \frac{1}{2}, ..., \frac{1}{2}\right)$ in a D-dimensional space.

Let's also take a D-dimensional hypersphere, with S^D centered on the origin of the space, $o = (0, 0, \ldots, 0)$. Intuitively, the center of the hypercube, c, is inside the sphere. Is this true for every value of D?

We can verify this by measuring the Euclidean distance between the hypercube center and the origin:

$$L_2(c, o) = \sqrt{\sum_{i=1}^{D} (\frac{1}{2} - 0)^2} = \sqrt{D \cdot (\frac{1}{2})^2} = \frac{1}{2} \cdot \sqrt{D}$$

Since the radius of the sphere is 1 in any dimension, we can conclude that, for a value of D greater than 4, the hypercube center is outside the hypersphere.

With the curse of dimensionality, we refer to the various phenomena that arise only when we're working with data in high-dimensional spaces that do not occur in low-dimensional settings such as the 2D or 3D space.

In practice, as the number of dimensions increases, some counterintuitive things start happening; this is the curse of dimensionality.

Now, it should be clearer that working within high-dimensional spaces is not easy and not intuitive at all. One of the greatest strengths of deep neural networks—which is also one of the reasons for their widespread use—is that they make tractable problems in high dimensional spaces, thereby reducing dimensionality layer by layer.

The first class of ML algorithms we are going to describe is the supervised learning family. These kinds of algorithms are the right tools to use when we aim to find a function that's able to separate elements of different classes in an n-dimensional space.

Supervised learning

Supervised learning algorithms work by extracting knowledge from a **knowledge base (KB)**, that is, the dataset that contains labeled instances of the concept we need to learn about.

Supervised learning algorithms are two-phase algorithms. Given a supervised learning problem—let's say, a classification problem—the algorithm tries to solve it during the first phase, called the **training phase**, and its performance is measured in the second phase, called the **testing phase**.

The three dataset splits (train, validation, and test), as defined in the previous section, and the two-phase algorithm should sound an alarm: why do we have a two-phase algorithm and three dataset splits?

Because the first phase (should—in a well-made pipeline) uses two datasets. In fact, we can define the stages:

- **Training and validation**: The algorithm analyzes the dataset to generate a theory that is valid for the data it has been trained on, but also for items it has never seen.
  The algorithm, therefore, tries to discover and generalize a concept that bonds the examples with the same label, with the examples themselves.
  Intuitively, if you have a labeled dataset of cats and dogs, you want your algorithm to distinguish between them while being able to be robust to the variations that the examples with the same label can have (cats with different colors, positions, backgrounds, and so on).
  At the end of every training epoch, a performance evaluation using a metric on the validation set should be performed to select the model that reached the best performance on the validation set and to tune the algorithm hyperparameters to achieve the best possible result.
- **Testing**: The learned theory is applied to labeled examples that were never seen during the training and validation phases. This allows us to test how the algorithm performs on data that has never been used to train or select the model hyperparameters—a real-life scenario.

Supervised learning algorithms are a broad category, and all of them share the need for having a labeled dataset. Don't be fooled by the concept of a label: it is not mandatory for the label to be a discrete value (cat, dog, house, horse); in fact, it can also be a continuous value. What matters is the existence of the association (example, value) in the dataset. More formally, the example is a predictor variable, while the value is the dependent variable, outcome, or target variable.

Depending on the type of the desired outcome, supervised learning algorithms can be classified into two different families:

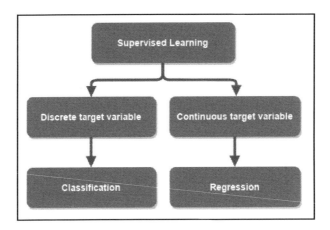

The supervised learning family—the target variable defines the problem to solve

- **Classification**: Where the label is discrete, and the aim is to classify the example and predict the label. The classification algorithm's aim is to learn about classification boundaries. These boundaries are functions that divide the space where the examples live into regions.
- **Regression**: Where the target variable is continuous, and the aim is to learn to regress a continuous value given an example.
  A regression problem that we will see in the upcoming chapters is the regression of the bounding box corner coordinates around a face. The face can be anywhere in the input image, and the algorithm has learned to regress the eight coordinates of the bounding box.

Parametric and non-parametric algorithms are used to solve classification and regression problems; the most common non-parametric algorithm is the k-NN algorithm. This is used to introduce the fundamental concepts of distances and similarities: concepts that are at the basis of every ML application. We will cover the k-NN algorithm in the next section.

Distances and similarities – the k-NN algorithm

The k-NN algorithm's goal is to find elements similar to a given one, rank them using a similarity score, and return the top-k similar elements (the first k elements, sorted by similarity) found.

To do this, you need to measure the similarity that's required for a function that assigns a numerical score to two points: the higher the score, the more similar the elements should be.

Since we are modeling our dataset as a set of points in an *n*-dimensional space, we can use any L_p norm, or any other score function, even if it's not a metric, to measure the distance between two points and consider similar elements that are close together and dissimilar elements that are far away. The choice of the norm/distance function is entirely arbitrary, and it should depend on the topology of the *n*-dimensional space (that is why we usually reduce the dimensionality of the input data, and we try to measure the distances in lower dimensional space—so the curse of dimensionality gives us less trouble).

Thus, if we want to measure the similarity of elements in a dataset with dimensionality *D*, given a point, *p*, we have to measure and collect the distance from *p* to every other point, *q*:

$$||p - q_i|| = \left(\sum_{j=0}^{D-1} |p - q_{i,j}|^p \right)^{\frac{1}{p}}$$

The preceding example shows the general scenario of computing the generic *p* norm on the distance vector that connects *p* and *q*. In practice, setting *p=1* gives us the Manhattan distance, while setting *p=2* gives us the Euclidean distance. No matter what distance is chosen, the algorithm works by computing the distance function and sorting by closeness as a measure of similarity.

When k-NN is applied to a classification problem, the point, *p*, is classified by the vote of its k neighbors, where the vote is their class. Thus, an object that is classified with a particular class depends on the class of the elements that surround it.

When k-NN is applied to regression problems, the output of the algorithm is the average of the values of the k-NN.

k-NN is only one among the various non-parametric models that has been developed over the years; however, parametric models usually show better performance. We'll look at these in the next section.

Parametric models

The ML models we are going to describe in this book are all parametric models: this means that a model can be described using a function, where the input and output are known (in the case of supervised learning, it is clear), and the aim is to change the model parameters so that, given a particular input, the model produces the expected output.

Given an input sample, $x = (x_0, x_1, \cdots, x_{n-1})$, and the desired outcome, y, an ML model is a parametric function, f_θ, where θ is the set of model parameters to change during the training in order to fit the data (or in other words, generating a hypothesis).

The most intuitive and straightforward example we can give to clarify the concept of model parameters is linear regression.

Linear regression attempts to model the relationship between two variables by fitting a linear equation to observed data.

Linear regression models have the following equation:

$$y = mx + b$$

Here, x is the independent variable and y is the dependent one. The parameter, m, is the scale factor, coefficient, or slope, and b is the bias coefficient or intercept.

Hence, the model parameters that must change during the training phase are $\theta = \{m, b\}$.

We're talking about a single example in the training set, but the line should be the one that fits all the points of the training set the best. Of course, we are making a strong assumption about the dataset: we are using a model that, due to its nature, models a line. Due to this, before attempting to fit a linear model to the data, we should first determine whether or not there is a linear relationship between the dependent and independent variables (using a scatter plot is usually useful).

The most common method for fitting a regression line is the method of least squares. This method calculates the best-fitting line for the observed data by minimizing the sum of the squares of the vertical deviations from each data point to the line (if a point lies on the fitted line exactly, then its vertical deviation is 0). This relationship between observed and predicted data is what we call the *loss function*, as we will see in Chapter 2, *Neural Networks and Deep Learning*.

The goal of the supervised learning algorithm is, therefore, to iterate over the data and to adjust the θ parameters iteratively so that f_θ correctly models the observed phenomena.

However, when using more complex models (with a considerable number of adjustable parameters, as in the case of neural networks), adjusting the parameters can lead to undesired results.

If our model is composed of just two parameters and we are trying to model a linear phenomenon, there are no problems. But if we are trying to classify the Iris dataset, we can't use a simple linear model since it is easy to see that the function we have to learn about to separate the different classes is not a simple line.

In cases like that, we can use models with a higher number of trainable parameters that can adjust their variables to almost perfectly fit the dataset. This may sound perfect, but in practice, it is not something that's desirable. In fact, the model is adapting its parameters only to fit the training data, almost *memorizing* the dataset and thus losing every generalization capability.

This pathological phenomenon is called **overfitting**, and it happens when we are using a model that's too complex to model a simple event. There's also an opposite scenario, called **underfitting**, that occurs when our model is too simple for the dataset and therefore is not able to capture all the complexity of the data.

Every ML model aims to learn, and will adapt its parameters so that it's robust to noise and generalize, which means to find a suitable approximate function representing the relationship between the predictors and the response:

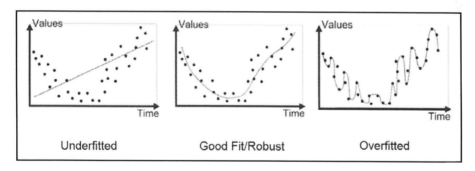

The dashed line represents the model's prediction. Underfitting, on the left, is a model with very poor generalization performance and therefore is unable to learn a good dataset approximation. The center image represents a good model that can generalize well in contrast to the model on the right that memorized the training set, overfitting it.

Several supervised learning algorithms have been developed over the years. This book, however, will focus on the ML model that demonstrated to be more versatile and that can be used to solve almost any supervised, unsupervised, and semi-supervised learning task: neural networks.

During the explanation of the training and validation phases, we talked about two concepts we haven't introduced yet—hyperparameters and metrics:

- **Hyperparameters**: We talk about hyperparameters when our algorithm, which is to be fully defined, requires values to be assigned to a set of parameters. We call the parameters that define the algorithm itself hyperparameters. For example, the number of neurons in a neural network is a hyperparameter.
- **Metrics**: The functions that give the model prediction. The expected output produces a numerical score that measures the goodness of the model.

Metrics are crucial components in every ML pipeline; they are so useful and powerful that they deserve their own section.

Measuring model performance – metrics

Evaluating a supervised learning algorithm during the evaluation and testing phases is an essential part of any well-made ML pipeline.

Before we describe the various metrics that are available, there's one last thing that's worth noting: measuring the performance of a model is something that we can always do on every dataset split. During the training phase, usually at the end of every training epoch, we can measure the performance of the algorithm on the training set itself, as well as the validation set. Plotting how the curves change during the training and analyzing the relationships between the validation and training curve allow us to quickly identify the previously described pathological conditions of an ML model—overfitting and underfitting.

Supervised learning algorithms have the significant advantage of having the expected outcome of the algorithm inside the dataset, and all the metrics hereby presented use the label information to evaluate "how well" the model performs.

There are metrics to measure the performance of classifiers and metrics to measure the performance of regressors; it is clear that it wouldn't make any sense to treat a classifier in the same way as a regressor, even if both are members of the supervised learning algorithm family.

The first metric and the most used metric for evaluating a supervised learning algorithm's performance is accuracy.

Using accuracy

Accuracy is the ratio of the number of correct predictions made to the number of all predictions made.

Accuracy is used to measure classification performance on multiclass classification problems.

Given y_i as the label and $\hat{y}_i$ as the prediction, we can define the accuracy of the i-th example as follows:

$$\text{accuracy}(\hat{y}, y) = \begin{cases} 1 & \text{if } \hat{y}_i = y_i \\ 0 & \text{otherwise} \end{cases}$$

Therefore, for a whole dataset with N elements, the mean accuracy over all the samples is as follows:

$$\text{accuracy}(D) = \frac{1}{N} \sum_{i=1}^{N} \text{accuracy}(\hat{y}_i, y_i)$$

We have to pay attention to the structure of the dataset, D, when using this metric: in fact, it works well only when there is an equal number of samples belonging to each class (we need to be using a balanced dataset).

In the case of an unbalanced dataset or when the error in predicting that an incorrect class is higher/lower than predicting another class, accuracy is not the best metric to use. To understand why, think about the case of a dataset with two classes only, where 80% of samples are of class 1, and 20% of samples are of class 2.

If the classifier predicts only class 1, the accuracy that's measured in this dataset is 0.8, but of course, this is not a good measure of the performance of the classifier, since it always predicts the same class, no matter what the input is. If the same model is tested on a test set with 40% of samples from class 1 and the remaining ones of class 2, the measurement will drop down to 0.4.

Remembering that metrics can be used during the training phase to measure the model's performance, we can monitor how the training is going by looking at the validation accuracy and the training accuracy to detect if our model is overfitting or underfitting the training data.

If the model can model the relationships present in the data, the training accuracy increases; if it doesn't, the model is too simple and we are underfitting the data. In this case, we have to use a complex model with a higher learning capacity (with a more significant number of trainable parameters).

If our training accuracy increases, we can start looking at the validation accuracy (always at the end of every training epoch): if the validation accuracy stops growing or even starts decreasing, the model is overfitting the training data and we should stop the training (this is called an **early stop** and is a regularization technique).

Using the confusion matrix

The confusion matrix is a tabular way of representing a classifier's performance. It can be used to summarize how the classifier behaved on the test set, and it can be used only in the case of multi-class classification problems. Each row of the matrix represents the instances in a predicted class, while each column represents the instances in an actual class. For example, in a binary classification problem, we can have the following:

Samples: 320	Actual: YES	Actual: NO
Predicted: YES	98	120
Predicted: NO	150	128

It is worth noting that the confusion matrix is **not a metric**; in fact, the matrix alone does not measure the model's performance, but is the basis for computing several useful metrics, all of them based on the concepts of true positives, true negatives, false positives, and false negatives.

These terms all refer to a **single class**; this means you have to consider a multiclass classification problem as a binary classification problem when computing these terms. Given a multiclass classification problem, whose classes are A, B, ..., Z, we have, for example, the following:

- (TP) **True positives of A**: All A instances that are classified as A
- (TN) **True negatives of A**: All non-A instances that are not classified as A
- (FP) **False positives of A**: All non-A instances that are classified as A
- (FN) **False negatives of A**: All A instances that are not classified as A

This, of course, can be applied to every class in the dataset so that we get these four values for every class.

The most important metrics we can compute that have the TP, TN, FP, and FN values are precision, recall, and the F1 score.

Precision

Precision is the number of correct positives results, divided by the number of positive results predicted:

$$precision = \frac{TP}{TP + FP}$$

The metric name itself describes what we measure here: a number in the [0,1] range that indicates how accurate the predictions of the classifier are: the higher, the better. However, as in the case of accuracy, the precision value alone can be misleading. High precision only means that, when we predict the positive class, we are precise in detecting it. But this does not mean that we are also accurate when we're not detecting this class.

The other metric that should always be measured to understand the complete behavior of a classifier is known as recall.

Recall

The recall is the number of correct positive results, divided by the number of all relevant samples (for example, all the samples that should be classified as positive):

$$recall = \frac{TP}{TP + FN}$$

Just like precision, recall is a number in the [0,1] range that indicates the percentage of correctly classified samples over all the samples of that class. The recall is an important metric, especially in problems such as object detection in images.

Measuring the precision and recall of a binary classifier allows you to tune the classifier's performance, making it behave as needed.

Sometimes, precision is more important than recall, and vice versa. For this reason, it is worth dedicating a short section to the classifier regime.

Classifier regime

Sometimes, it can be worth putting a classifier in the high-recall regime. This means that we prefer to have more false positives while also being sure that the true positives are detected.

The high-recall regime is often required in computer vision industrial applications, where the production line needs to build a product. Then, at the end of the assembly process, a human controls whether the quality of the complete product reaches the required standard.

The computer vision applications that control the assembly robots usually work in a high-recall regime since the production line needs to have high throughput. Setting the computer vision applications in a high-precision regime would have stopped the line too often, reducing the overall throughput and making the company lose money.

The ability to change the working regime of a classifier is of extreme importance in real-life scenarios, where the classifiers are used as production tools that should adapt themselves to the business decisions.

There are other cases where a high-precision regime is required. In industrial scenarios, there are also processes commanded by computer vision applications that are critical and for this reason, require high accuracy.

In an engine production line, classifiers could be used to decide on which part the camera sees is the correct one to pick and to assemble in the engine. In critical cases like this one, a high-precision regime is required and a high-recall regime is discouraged.

A metric that combines both precision and recall is the F1 score.

F1 score

The F1 score is the harmonic mean between precision and recall. This number, which is in the [0,1] range, indicates how precise the classifier is (precision) and how robust it is (recall).

The greater the F1 score, the better the overall performance of the model:

$$F1 = 2 \cdot \cfrac{1}{\cfrac{1}{\text{precision}} + \cfrac{1}{\text{recall}}}$$

Using the area under the ROC curve

The area under the **Receiving Operating Characteristic (ROC)** curve is one of the most used metrics for the evaluation of binary classification problems.

Most classifiers produce a score in the [0,1] range and not directly as a classification label. The score must be thresholded to decide the classification. A natural threshold is to classify it as positive when the score is higher than 0.5 and negative otherwise, but this is not always what our application wants (think about the identification of people with a disease).

Varying the threshold will change the performance of the classifier, varying the number of TPs, FPs, TNs, and FNs, and thereby the overall classification performance.

The results of the threshold variations can be taken into account by plotting the ROC curve. The ROC curve takes into account the false positive rate (specificity) and the true positive rate (sensitivity): binary classification problems are a trade-off between these two values. We can describe these values as follows:

- **Sensitivity**: The true positive rate is defined as the proportion of positive data points that are correctly considered positive, with respect to all the positive data points:

$$TPR = \frac{TP}{FN + TP}$$

- **Specificity**: The false positive rate is defined as the proportion of negative data points that are considered positive, with respect to all the negative data points:

$$FPR = \frac{FP}{FP + TN}$$

The **AUC** is the area under the ROC curve, and is obtained by varying the classification threshold:

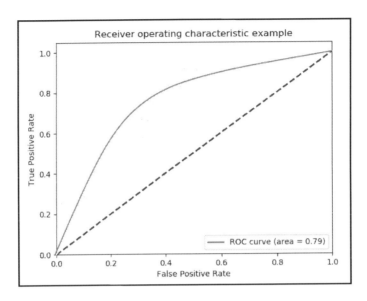

ROC curve obtained by varying the classification threshold. The dashed lines represent the expectation for random guessing.

It is clear that both TPR and FPR have values in the [0,1] range, and the graph is drawn by varying the classification threshold of the classifier in order to get different pairs of TPR and FPR for every threshold value. The AUC is in the [0,1] range too and the greater the value, the better the model is.

If we are interested in measuring the performance of a regressor's precision and recall and all the data that was gathered from the confusion matrix is useless, then we have to use other metrics to measure the regression error.

Mean absolute error

Mean absolute error (**MAE**) is the average of the absolute difference between the original and the predicted values. Since we are now interested in the measurement of the performance of a regressor, we have to take into account that the y_i and $\hat{y}_i$ values are numerical values:

$$\text{MAE} = \frac{1}{N} \sum_{i=1}^{N} |y_i - \hat{y}_i|$$

The MAE value has no upper bound, and its lower bound is 0. It should be evident that we want the MAE value to be as close as possible to 0.

MAE gives us an indication of how far the predictions are from the actual output; this metric is easily interpretable since its value is also on the same scale as the original response value.

Mean squared error

Mean squared error (MSE) is the average of the squared difference between the original and the predicted values:

$$\text{MSE} = \frac{1}{N} \sum_{i=1}^{N} (y_i - \hat{y}_i)^2$$

Just like MAE, MSE has no upper bound and its lower bound is 0.

On the contrary, the presence of the square terms makes the metric less easy to interpret.

A good practice to follow is to consider both metrics so that you get as much information as possible about the distribution of the errors.

The $\text{MAE} \leq \text{MSE}$ relation holds, and so the following is true:

- If MSE is close to MAE, the regressor makes small errors
- If MSE is close to MAE^2, the regressor makes large errors

Metrics are probably the most important part of the ML model selection and performance measurement tools: they express relations between the desired output and model output. This relation is fundamental since it is what we want to optimize our model for, as we will see in `Chapter 2`, *Neural Networks and Deep Learning*, where we will introduce the concept of the *loss function*.

Moreover, since the models we are treating in this book are all parametric models, we can measure the metrics during/at the end of the training process and save the model parameters (and by definition, the model) that reached the best validation/test performance.

Using parametric models allows us this kind of flexibility— we can freeze the status of a model when it reaches the desired performance and go ahead with training, changing hyperparameters, and experimenting with different configurations/training strategies, while also having the certainty of having stored a model that already has good performance.

Having metrics and the ability to measure them during the training process, together with the usage of parametric models that can be saved, gives us the power to evaluate different models and save only the one that fits our needs best. This process is called **model selection** and is fundamental in every well-made ML pipeline.

We've focused on the supervised learning family algorithm a lot, but of course, ML is much more than this (even tough supervised learning algorithms have the best performance when it comes to solving real-life problems).

The next family of algorithms we are briefly going to describe are from the unsupervised learning family.

Unsupervised learning

In comparison to supervised learning, unsupervised learning does not need a dataset of labeled examples during the training phase–labels are only needed during the testing phase when we want to evaluate the performance of the model.

The purpose of unsupervised learning is to discover natural partitions in the training set. What does this mean? Think about the MNIST dataset—it has 10 classes, and we know this because every example has a different label in the [1,10] range. An unsupervised learning algorithm has to discover that there are 10 different objects inside the dataset and does this by looking at the examples without prior knowledge of the label.

It is clear that unsupervised learning algorithms are challenging compared to supervised learning ones since they cannot rely on the label's information, but they have to discover features and learn about the concept of labels by themselves. Although challenging, their potential is huge since they discover patterns in data that humans can struggle to detect. Unsupervised learning algorithms are often used by decision-makers that need to extract meaning from data.

Just think about the problem of fraud detection: you have a set of transactions, a huge volume of money exchanged between people, and you don't know if there are fraudulent transactions inside them because there are no labels in the real world!

In this scenario, the application of unsupervised learning algorithms could help you find the big natural partition of normal transactions and help you discover the outliers.

Outliers are the points outside, and usually far away, from any partition (also called a cluster) found in the data, or a partition itself with some particular characteristic that makes it different from the normal ones.

Unsupervised learning is, for this reason, used frequently in anomaly detection tasks, and in many different domains: not only fraud detection, but also quality control in images, video streams, streams of datasets coming from sensors in production environments, and much more.

Unsupervised learning algorithms are two-phase algorithms as well:

- **Training and validation**: Since there are no labels inside the training set (and they should be discarded if present), the algorithm is trained to discover the existing patterns in the data. If there's a validation set, that should contain labels; the model's performance can be measured at the end of every training epoch.
- **Testing**: A labeled dataset is given in the input to the algorithm (if such a dataset exists) and its results are compared with the label's information. In this phase, we measure the performance of the algorithm using the label's information in order to verify that the algorithm learned to extract patterns from data that humans have also been able to detect.

Working on these examples only, unsupervised learning algorithms are not classified on the basis of the label type (as the supervised learning algorithms), but on what they aim to discover.

Unsupervised learning algorithms can be classified as follows:

- **Clustering**: The aim is to discover clusters, that is, natural partitions of the data.
- **Association**: In this case, the aim is to discover rules that describe data and associations between them. These are usually used to give recommendations:

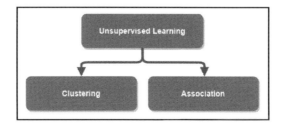

The unsupervised learning family—there are two main families of algorithms

The association learning algorithms are powerful tools of the data mining world: they're used to discover rules, such as "if a person is buying butter and bread, they will probably also buy milk". Learning about these rules can be a huge competitive advantage in business. By recalling the previous example, we can say that a store can place butter, bread, and milk together on the same shelf to maximize selling!

During the training phase of a clustering algorithm, we are interested in measuring the performance of the model, just like we do in the supervised learning case. Metrics, in the case of unsupervised learning algorithms, are more complex and task-dependent. What we usually do is exploit additional labels present in the dataset, but that aren't used during the training, and thus reconduct the problem to a supervised learning problem and use the usual metrics.

As in the case of supervised learning, there are parametric and non-parametric models.

Most non-parametric algorithms work by measuring the distance between a data point and every other data point in the dataset; then, they use the distance information to cluster the data space in different regions.

Like in the supervised learning case, a lot of algorithms have been developed over the years to find natural partitions and/or rules in non-labeled datasets. However, neural networks have been applied to solve unsupervised learning tasks and have achieved superior performance and shown to be very flexible. This is another reason why this book only focuses on neural networks.

Unsupervised learning algorithms explicitly require to do not have any label information during the training phase. However, since labels could be present in the datasets, why not take advantage of their presence while still using a ML algorithm to discover other patterns in the data?

Semi-supervised learning

Semi-supervised learning algorithms fall between supervised and unsupervised learning algorithms.

They rely upon the assumption that we can exploit the information of the labeled data to improve the result of unsupervised learning algorithms and vice versa.

Being able to use semi-supervised learning algorithms depends on the available data: if we have only labeled data, we can use supervised learning; if we don't have any labeled data, we must go with unsupervised learning methods. However, let's say we have the following:

- Labeled and unlabeled examples
- Examples that are all labeled with the same class

If we have these, then we can use a semi-supervised approach to solve the problem.

The scenario in which we have all the examples labeled with the same class could look like a supervised learning problem, but it isn't.

If the aim of the classification is to find a boundary that divides at least two regions, how can we define a boundary among regions if we only have a single region?

We can't!

An unsupervised or semi-supervised learning approach is the way to go for these kinds of problems: the algorithm will learn how the input space is partitioned (hopefully, in one single cluster), its shape, and how the data is distributed in the space.

An unsupervised learning approach could be used to learn that there is a single cluster in the data. By using the labels, and thereby switching to a semi-supervised learning approach, we can enforce some additional constraints on the space so that we lean toward a better representation of the data.

Once the unsupervised/semi-supervised learning algorithm has learned about a representation of the data, we can test whether a new example—one that we have never seen during the training process—falls inside the cluster or not. Alternatively, we can calculate a numerical score that tells us "how much" the new example fits inside the learned representation.

Just like the unsupervised learning algorithms, the semi-supervised algorithm has two phases.

Summary

In this chapter, we went through the ML algorithm families from a general and theoretical point of view. It is essential to have good knowledge of what machine learning is, how algorithms are categorized, what kind of algorithms are used given a certain task, and how to become familiar with all the concepts and the terminology that's used among machine learning practitioners.

In the next chapter, `Chapter 2`, *Neural Networks and Deep Learning*, we will focus on neural networks. We will understand the strengths of machine learning models, how is it possible to make a network learn, and how, in practice, a model parameter update is performed.

Exercises

Answering the following questions is of extreme importance: you are building your ML foundations—do not skip this step!

1. Given a dataset of 1,000 labeled examples, what do you have to do if you want to measure the performance of a supervised learning algorithm during the training, validation, and test phases, while using accuracy as the unique metric?
2. What is the difference between supervised and unsupervised learning?
3. What is the difference between precision and recall?
4. A model in a high-recall regime produces more or less false positives than a model in a low recall regime?
5. Can the confusion matrix only be used in a binary classification problem? If not, how can we use it in a multiclass classification problem?
6. Is one-class classification a supervised learning problem? If yes, why? If no, why?
7. If a binary classifier has an AUC of 0.5, what can you conclude from this?
8. Write the formula of precision, recall, F1-score, and accuracy. Why is F1 important? Is there a relationship between accuracy, precision, and recall?
9. The true positive rate and false positive rate are used to plot the ROC curve. What is the ROC curve's purpose, and is there a relationship among the true positive rate/false positive rate and precision/recall? Hint: write the math.
10. What is the curse of dimensionality?
11. What are overfitting and underfitting?

12. What is the learning capacity of a model? Is it related to the condition of overfitting/underfitting?
13. Write the *Lp* norm formula—is this the only way to measure the distance among points?
14. How can we say that a data point is similar to another data point?
15. What is model selection? Why is it important?

2
Neural Networks and Deep Learning

Neural networks are the main machine learning models that we will be looking at in this book. Their applications are countless, as are their application fields. These range from computer vision applications (where an object should be localized in an image), to finance (where neural networks are applied to detect frauds), passing trough trading, to reaching even the art field, where neural networks are used together with the adversarial training process to create models that are able to generate new and unseen kinds of art with astonishing results.

This chapter, which is perhaps the richest in terms of theory in this whole book, shows you how to define neural networks and how to make them learn. To begin, the mathematical formula for artificial neurons will be presented, and we will highlight why a neuron must have certain features to be able to learn. After that, fully connected and convolutional neuronal topologies will be explained in detail since these are the building blocks of almost every neural network architecture. At the same time, the concept of deep learning and deep architectures will be introduced. Introducing this concept is a must since it is because of deep architectures that, nowadays, neural networks are used to solve challenging problems with super-human performance.

To conclude, the optimization process that's required to train a parametric model, together with some regularization techniques that are used to improve the model's performance, will be shown. Gradient descent, the chain rule, and the graphical representation of the computations all have their own dedicated sections since it is extremely important for any machine learning practitioner to know what happens when a framework is used to train a model.

If you are already familiar with the concepts presented in this chapter, you can jump directly to the next chapter, Chapter 3, *TensorFlow Graph Architecture*, which is dedicated to the TensorFlow graph architecture.

In this chapter, we will cover the following topics:

- Neural networks
- Optimization
- Convolutional neural networks
- Regularization

Neural networks

The definition of a neural network, as provided by the inventor of one of the first neurocomputers, *Dr. Robert Hecht-Nielson*, in *Neural Network Primer—Part I*, is as follows:

> *"A computing system made up of a number of simple, highly interconnected processing elements, which process information by their dynamic state response to external inputs."*

In practice, we can think of artificial neural networks as a computational model that is based on how the brain is believed to work. Hence, the mathematical model is inspired by biological neurons.

Biological neurons

The main computational units of the brain are known as neurons; in the human nervous system, approximately 86 billion neurons can be found, all of which are connected by synapses. The following diagram shows a biological neuron and the mathematical model that draws inspiration from it:

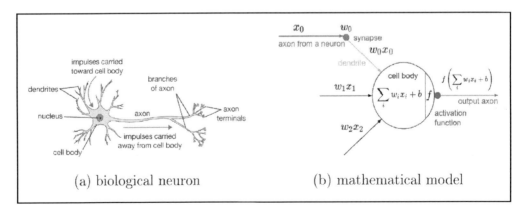

Representation of the biological neuron, (a), on the left and its mathematical model, (b), on the right. Source: Stanford cs231n

Biological neurons are made up of the following:

- **Dendrites**: Minor fibers that carry information, in the form of an electric signal, from the outside to the nucleus.
- **Synapses**: These are the connection points among neurons. Neurons receive input signals on the synapses that are connected to the dendrites.
- **Nucleus**: This receives the signals from the dendrites, elaborates on them, and produces a response (output signal) that it sends to the axon.
- **Axon**: The output channel of the neuron. It can be connected to other neuron synapses.

Each neuron receives input signals from its dendrites and transports them to the nucleus where they are processed; dendrites process the signals, thereby integrating (adding up or combining) excitation and inhibition from every input synapse. The nucleus receives the integrated signals and adds them. If the final sum is above a certain threshold, the neuron fires and the resulting information is carried down through the axon and thus to any other connected neuron.

The amount of signal that's transmitted among neurons depends on the strength of the connections. It is the arrangement of the neurons and the strength of these synapses that establish the function of the neural network.

The learning phase of biological neurons is based on the modification of the output signal generated by the nucleus over time, as a function of certain types of input signals. Neurons specialize themselves in recognizing certain stimuli during their lifetime.

Artificial neurons

Artificial neurons are based on the structure of the biological neuron and use mathematical functions with real values to simulate their behavior. Such artificial neurons are called **perceptrons**, a concept that was developed in the 50s and 60s by the scientist Frank Rosenblatt. Taking this mathematical analogy into account, we can talk about the biological neurons as follows:

- **Dendrites**: The number of inputs the neuron accepts. It can also be seen as the number of dimensions, D, of the input data.

- **Synapses**: $w_i, \quad i = 0, 1, \ldots, D-1$ weights associated with the dendrites. These are the values that change during the training phase. At the end of the training phase, we say the neuron is specialized (it learned to extract particular features from the input).

  If x is a D-dimensional input vector, the operation that's executed by the synapses is $x_i w_i \quad \forall i \in [0, D-1]$.

- **Nucleus** (body cell): This is a function that bonds the values coming from the synapses, thereby defining the behavior of the neuron. To simulate the action of the biological neuron, that is, firing (activating) only when there are certain stimuli in the input, the nucleus is modeled with **non-linear** functions.
  If $f : \mathbb{R} \to \mathbb{R}$ is a non-linear function, the output of the neuron, which takes into account all input stimuli, is given by the following equation:

$$O = f\left(\sum_{i=0}^{D-1} x_i w_i + b\right),$$

- Here, b is the **bias term**, which is of fundamental importance. It allows you to learn about a decision boundary that's not centered on the origin of the D-dimensional space.

If we remove the non-linear (also called **activation**) function for a moment, we can easily see that the synapses define a hyper-plane with the following equation:

$$\sum_{i=0}^{D-1} x_i w_i + b$$
.

A single neuron is able to perform *only* binary classification because the D-dimensional vector, x, can just be over or under the hyperplane it defines.
A perceptron can correctly classify samples in a D-dimensional space if—and only if—those samples are linearly separable.

The nucleus, with its non-linearity, maps the hyperplane defined by the dendrites in a more general hypersurface, which is the learned decision boundary. Non-linearity, in the best-case scenario, transforms the hyperplane into a hypersurface that's able to correctly classify points in a D-dimensional space. However, it only does this if those points are separable in two regions by a single hypersurface.

This is the main reason we need multi-layer neural networks: if the input data is not separable by a single hypersurface, adding another layer on top that works by transforming the learned hypersurface into a new hypersurface with an additional classification region allows it to learn complex classification boundaries that are capable of separating the regions correctly.

Moreover, it is worth noting that feed-forward neural networks, such as neural networks with connections among neurons that do not form a cycle, are universal function approximators. This means that, if a way to separate regions exists, a well-trained neural network with enough capacity will learn to approximate that function.

- **Axon**: This is the output value of the neuron. It can be used as input by other neurons.

It's important to stress that this model of a biological neuron is very coarse: for example, there are many different types of neuron, each with different properties. The dendrites in biological neurons perform complex nonlinear computations. The synapses are not just a single weight; they are a complex non-linear dynamical system. There are many other simplifications in the model because the reality is way more complicated and tougher to model than this. Hence, this biological inspiration is just a nice way to think about neural networks, but don't be fooled by all of these similarities: artificial neural networks are only loosely inspired by biological neurons.

"Why we should use neural networks and not other machine learning models?"

Traditional machine learning models are powerful but usually not as flexible as neural networks. Neural networks can be arranged in different topologies, and the geometry changes what the neural networks see (the input stimuli). Moreover, it's straightforward to create layers upon layers of neural networks with different topologies, creating deep models.

One of the greatest strengths of neural networks is their ability to become feature extractors: other machine learning models need the input data to be processed, have their meaningful features extracted, and only on those features (manually defined!) can the model be applied.

Neural networks, on the other hand, can extract meaningful features from any input data by themselves (depending on the topology of the layers that are used).

The single perceptron illustrates how it is possible to weigh and add different types of input to make a simple decision; a complex network of perceptrons could make a quite subtle decision. A **neural network architecture**, therefore, is made up of neurons, all of which are connected through synapses (biologically) where the information flows through them. During training, the neurons fire when they learn specific patterns from the data.

This fire rate is modeled using an activation function. More precisely, the neurons are connected in an acyclic graph; c

ycles are not allowed since that would imply an infinite loop in the forward pass of the network (these types of networks are called **feed-forward neural networks**). Instead of amorphous blobs of connected neurons, neural network models are often organized into distinct layers of neurons. The most common layer type is the fully connected layer.

Fully connected layers

The fully connected configuration is a particular network topology in which neurons between two adjacent layers are fully pairwise-connected, but neurons within a single layer share no connections.

Organizing networks into layers allows us to create stacks of fully connected layers, with a different number of neurons per layer. We can think about a multi-layer neural network as a model with visible and hidden layers. The visible layers are just the input and output layers; the hidden layers are the ones that aren't connected to the outside:

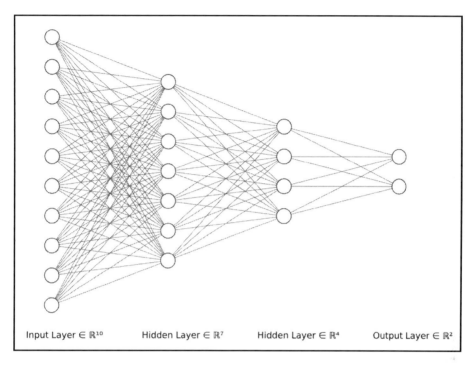

Input Layer $\in \mathbb{R}^{10}$ Hidden Layer $\in \mathbb{R}^{7}$ Hidden Layer $\in \mathbb{R}^{4}$ Output Layer $\in \mathbb{R}^{2}$

A typical representation of a fully connected neural network, with two hidden layers. Every layer reduces the dimensionality of its input with the aim of producing two different outputs given the ten input features.

The number of neurons in the hidden layers is entirely arbitrary, and it changes the learning capacity of the network. The input and output layers, instead, have a fixed dimension due to the task we are going to solve (for example, if we want to solve an n-classes classification on D-dimensional inputs, then we need an input layer with D inputs and an output layer with n outputs).

Mathematically, it is possible to define the output of a fully connected layer as the result of a matrix product. Let's say we have the following equation:

$$x = \begin{pmatrix} x_0 \\ \vdots \\ x_{D-1} \end{pmatrix}, \quad W \in \mathbb{M}_{M \times D-1}, \quad b = \begin{pmatrix} b_0 \\ \vdots \\ b_{M-1} \end{pmatrix},$$

The output, O, is given by the following formula:

$$O = f(Wx + b), \quad |O| = M$$

Here, M is the arbitrary number of neurons in the layer.

While the design of the input and output layers of a neural network is straightforward, the design of the hidden layers is not so simple. There are no rules; neural networks researchers have developed many design heuristics for hidden layers which help to get the correct behavior (for example, when there's a trade-off between the number of hidden layers and the time to train the network).

In general, increasing the number of neurons per layer and/or the number of layers in a neural network means having to increase the network capacity. This means that the neural network can express more complicated functions and that the space of representable functions grows; however, this is good and bad at the same time. It's good because we can learn more complicated functions, but it's bad because having more trainable parameters increases the risk of overfitting the training data.

In general, smaller neural networks should be preferred if the data is not complex or we are working with small datasets. Fortunately, there are different techniques that allow you to prevent overfitting the data when you're using high-capacity models. These techniques are called regularization techniques (L2 penalties on the parameters, dropout, batch normalization, data augmentation, and so on). We will dig into them in upcoming chapters.

The activation function is another important part of the design of every neural network. It is applied to every single neuron: nobody forces us to use the same non-linear function on every neuron, but it is a convention to pick a form of nonlinearity and use it for every neuron in the same layer.

If we are building a classifier, we are interested in evaluating the output layer of the network and being able to interpret the output values to understand what the network predicted. Let's say we have a linear activation function that's been applied to every single neuron of the output layer, where every neuron is associated with a particular class (looking at the preceding image, we have a 3-dimensional input and two output neurons, one for each class) – how can we interpret those values, since their codomain is the whole set of real numbers? It's hard to interpret values that are expressed in this way.

The most natural way is to constrain the sum of the output values to the [0,1] range so that we can consider the output values as sampled from the probability distribution over the predicted classes and we can consider the neuron with the highest value as the predicted class. Alternatively, we could choose to apply a thresholding operation on the values in order to simulate the biological neurons firing: if the output of a neuron is greater then a certain threshold value, we can output a value of 1, or 0 otherwise.

Another thing we can do is squash every single neuron's output in the [0,1] range if, for instance, we are solving a multi-class classification task where the classes are not mutually exclusive.

It's easy to understand why a certain non-linearity in the output layer is important – it can change the behavior of the network since the way we interpret the network's output depends on it. However, understanding why non-linearity is important in every single layer is mandatory for a complete understanding of neural networks.

Activation functions

As we already know, the output value of the i-th neuron in a layer is computed as follows:

The activation function, f, is important for several reasons:

- As stated in the previous section, depending on the layer we are applying the non-linearity to, it allows us to interpret the result of the neural network.
- If the input data is not linearly separable, it's non-linearity allows you to approximate a non-linear function that's capable of separating data in a non-linear way (just think about the transformation of a hyperplane into a generic hypersurface).
- Without non-linearities among adjacent layers, multi-layer neural networks are equivalent to a single neural network with a single hidden layer, and so they are able to separate only two regions of the input data. In fact, given:

$$f : \mathbb{R} \to \mathbb{R} \text{ linear}$$

And two perceptrons stacked:

$$O_1 = f(W_1 x + b_1) \quad O_2 = f(W_2 O_1 + b_2),$$

We know that the output of the second perceptron is equivalent to the output of a single perceptron:

$$O_2 = f\left(W_2\left(W_1 x + b_1\right) + b_2\right) = f\left(W_{eq} + b_{eq}\right),$$

- Where W_{eq} and b_{eq} are the matrix of weights and the bias vector is equivalent to the product of the single weight matrices and bias vectors.

This means that, when f is linear, a multi-layer neural network is always equal to a single layer neural network (hence, it has the same learning capacity). If not, the last equation doesn't hold.

- Non-linearities make the network robust to noisy input. If the input data contains noise (the training set contains values that are not perfect – it happens, and it happens often), the non-lineary avoids its propagation to the output. This can be demonstrated as follows:

$$O(x + \Delta_e) = f\left(\sum_{i=0}^{D-1} w_i\left(x_i + \Delta_e\right) + b\right) \neq f(x) + f(\Delta_e).$$

Two of the most frequently used activation functions are the sigmoid (σ)and the hyperbolic tangent ($\tanh$).

The first is used as the activation function of the output layer in almost every classification problem since it squashes the output in the [0,1] range and allows you to interpret the prediction as a probability:

$$f(x) = \sigma(x) = \frac{1}{1 + e^{-x}}.$$

The hyperbolic tangent, instead, is used as the activation function of the output layer of almost every generative model that's trained to generate images. Even in this case, the reason we use it is to correctly interpret the output and to create a meaningful bond among the input images and the generated images. We are used to scaling the input values from [0,255] to [-1,1], which is the range of the $\tanh$ function.

However, using functions such as $\tanh$ and σ as activations in the hidden layer isn't the best choice for reasons related to training via backpropagation (as we will see in the following sections, saturating nonlinearities can be a problem). Many other activation functions have been developed in order to overcome the problems that have been introduced by saturating nonlinearities. A short visual overview of the most common nonlinearities that have been developed is shown in the following diagram:

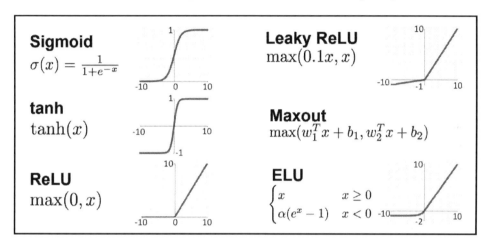

A list of the most common activation functions. Source: Stanford cs231n.

Once the network structure has been defined, as well as the activation functions to use in the hidden and the output layers, it's time to define the relation among the training data and the network's output in order to be able to train the network and make it solve the task at hand.

In the upcoming sections, we will talk about a discrete classification problem that follows on from Chapter 1, *What is Machine Learning?* We're talking about the fact that everything that holds for a classification problem also holds for continuous variables since we are using neural networks as a tool to solve a supervised learning problem. Since a neural network is a parametric model, training it means that we need to update the parameters, W, to find the configuration that solves the problem in the best possible way.

Training a neural network is mandatory if we wish to define a relationship among the input data and the desired output: an objective function—or loss function, since we want to minimize the loss as our objective.

Loss function

After defining the network architecture, the model must be trained. It's now time to define the relationship between the model's output and the real data. To do so, a loss function must be defined.

The loss function is used to assesses the goodness-of-fit of a model.

There are several loss functions, each one expressing a relationship among the network output and the real data, and their form completely influences the quality of the model's prediction.

For a discrete classification problem over M classes, we can model the defined neural network that accepts a D-dimensional input vector, x, and produces an M-dimensional vector of predictions as a function of its parameters, W, like so:

$$\hat{y} = F(W, x) : \mathbb{R}^D \to \mathbb{R}^M.$$

The model produces an M-dimensional output vector that contains the probabilities the model assigns to the input, x, for every possible class (if we applied the sigmoid activation to the output layer, we can interpret the output in this way).

It's easy to extract the position of the neuron in the output layer that produced the highest value. The equation for the predicted class is as follows:

$$\hat{l} = \operatorname*{argmax}_{0 \le i \le M-1} \hat{y}_i$$

By using this, we can find the index of the neuron that produced the highest classification score. Since we know the label associated with the input, x, we are almost ready to define the relationship between the prediction and the label. The last problem we will face is the label format: the label is a scalar value, whereas the network output is an M-dimensional vector. Although we can find the position of the neuron with the highest probability value, we are interested in the whole output layer, since we want to increase the probability of the correct class and penalize the incorrect ones.

For this reason, the label must be converted into an M-dimensional representation so that we can create a bond between every output neuron and the label.

The most natural conversion from a scalar value to an M-dimensional representation is called **one-hot** encoding. This encoding consists of the creation of an M-dimensional vector that has a value of 1 in the position of the label and 0 in every other position. Therefore, we can consider the one-hot encoded-label as follows:

$$y = \begin{pmatrix} y_0 \\ \vdots \\ y_M \end{pmatrix} : y_i = \begin{cases} 1, & \text{if } i = \text{position assiged to } l \\ 0, & \text{otherwise} \end{cases}$$

It's now possible to define the general formulation of the loss-function for the *i*-th training set instance as a real-valued function that creates a bond between the ground truth (the label that's been correctly encoded) and the predicted value:

$$\mathcal{L}_i(y, \hat{y}) : \mathbb{N}^M \times \mathbb{R}^M \to \mathbb{R}.$$

The general formulation of a loss function that's applied to the complete training set of cardinality, *k*, can be expressed as the mean of the loss that's computed on the single instances:

$$\mathcal{L}(F; \text{dataset}) = \frac{1}{k} \sum_{i=0}^{k} \mathcal{L}_i(y, \hat{y}).$$

The loss must be chosen (or defined) based on the problem at hand. The simplest and most intuitive loss function for a classification problem (of mutually exclusive classes) is the L2 distance among the one-hot encoded representation of the label and the network output. The aim is to minimize the distance between the network output and the one-hot encoded label, thereby making the network predict an M-dimensional vector that looks like the correct label:

$$\mathcal{L} = \frac{1}{k} \sum_{i=1}^{k} \|\hat{y}_i - y_i\|_2.$$

The minimization of the loss function occurs through small iterative adjustments of the model's parameter values.

Parameter initialization

The initial model parameter values are the solution to the problem the training phase iteratively refines: there's no unique way of initializing the network parameters, and perhaps the only working suggestions regarding the parameter's initialization are as follows:

- **Do not initialize the network parameters to zero**: It is impossible to find a new solution using gradient descent (as we will see in the next section) since the whole gradient is 0 and therefore there's no indication of the update direction.
- **Break symmetry between different units**: If two hidden units with the same activation function are connected to the same input, then these two inputs must have a different initial parameter value. This is required because almost every solution requires a set of different parameters to be assigned to each neuron to find a meaningful solution. If we start with all the parameters with the same value instead, every update step will update all the network parameters by the same amount since the updated value depends on the error, which is equal for every neuron in the network. Due to this, we will be unable to find a meaningful solution.

Usually, the initial solution to the problem is sampled by a random normal distribution with zero mean and unary variance. This distribution ensures that network parameters are small and equally distributed around the zero value while being different among them, therefore breaking the symmetry.

Now that we have defined the network architecture, correctly formatted the input labels, and defined the input-output relation with the loss function, how can we minimize the loss? How can we iteratively adjust the model parameters to minimize the loss and thus solve the problem?

It's all a matter of optimization and optimization algorithms.

Optimization

Operation research gives us efficient algorithms that we can use to solve optimization problems by finding the global optimum (the global minimum point) if the problems are expressed as a function with well-defined characteristics (for instance, convex optimization requires the function to be a convex).

Artificial neural networks are universal function approximators; therefore, it is not possible to make assumptions about the shape of the function the neural network is approximating. Moreover, the most common optimization methods exploit geometric considerations, but we know from `Chapter 1`, *What is Machine Learning?*, that geometry works in an unusual way when dimensionality is high due to the curse of dimensionality.

For these reasons, it is not possible to use operation research methods that are capable of finding the global optimum of an optimization (minimization) problem. Instead, we have to use an iterative refinement method that, starting from an initial solution tries, to refine it (by updating the model parameters that represent the solution) with the aim of finding a good, local optimum.

We can think about the model parameters, W, as the initial solution to a minimization problem. Therefore, we can start evaluating the loss function at the training step, 0 $\mathcal{L}_{s=0}$, so that we have an idea about the value it assumes with the actual initial configuration of parameters, $W_{s=0}$. Now, we have to decide on how to update the model parameters. To do this, we need to perform the first update step, which we do by following the information that the loss gives us. We can proceed in two ways:

- **Random perturbations**: We can apply a random perturbation, ΔW, to the current set of parameters and compute the loss value on the obtained new set of parameters, $W_s = W_{s-1} + \Delta W_{s-1}$.

  If the loss value at the training step, s, is less than the value at the previous one, we can accept the found solution and move on with a new random perturbation that's applied to the new set of parameters. Otherwise, we have to repeat the random perturbation until a better solution is found.

- **Estimation of the update direction**: Instead of generating a new set of parameters randomly, is it possible to guide the local optimum research process toward the direction of the maximum descent of the function.

The second approach is the de facto standard for training parametric machine learning models that are expressed as differentiable functions.

To properly understand this gradient descent method, we have to think about the loss function as a way of defining a surface in the parameter space—our objective, that is, minimizing the loss, means that we need to find the lowest point on this surface.

Gradient descent

Gradient descent is a method that's used to calculate the best direction to move in when we're searching for the solution to a minimization/maximization problem. This method suggests the direction to follow when we're updating the model parameters: the direction that's found, depending on the input data that's used, is the direction of the steepest descent of the loss surface. The data that's used is of extreme importance since it follows the evaluation of the loss function and therefore the surface that's used to evaluate the update direction.

The update direction is given by the gradient of the loss function. It's known from calculus that the derivative operation for a single variable differentiable function, $f(x)$, in point x is given by the following formula:

$$\frac{df(x)}{dx} = \lim_{h \to 0} \frac{f(x+h) - f(x)}{h}.$$

This operation gives us a description of the behavior of the function in x: it shows us how much the function varies with respect to the x variable in an infinitely small region centered in x.

The generalization of the derivative operation for an n-variables function is given by the gradient, that is, the vector of the partial derivatives (the vector of the derivatives of the function with respect to a single variable considering constants any other variable). In the case of our loss function, it is as follows:

$$\nabla \mathcal{L}(W) = (\frac{\partial \mathcal{L}}{\partial w_1}, \cdots, \frac{\partial L}{\partial w_n}).$$

$\nabla \mathcal{L}(W)$ indicates the direction along which the function is growing. Hence, since our objective is to find the minimum, we have to move along the direction indicated by the anti-gradient, like so:

$$d = -\nabla \mathcal{L}(W),$$

Here, the anti-gradient represents the direction to follow when performing the parameter update. The parameter update step now looks as follows:

$$W_s = W_{s-1} - \eta \nabla \mathcal{L}(\text{dataset}; W_{s-1}).$$

The η parameter is the learning rate and is a hyperparameter of the training phase with gradient descent. Choosing the correct value for the learning rate is more of an art than a science, and the only thing we can do is use our intuition to choose a value that works well for our model and dataset. We have to keep in mind that the anti-gradient only tells us the direction to follow; it doesn't give us any information about the distance from the current solution to the minimum point. The distance, or the strength of the update, is regulated by the learning rate:

- A learning rate that's too high could make the training phase unstable due to jumps around the local minima. This causes oscillations of the loss function's value. To remember this, we can just think about a U shaped surface. If the learning rate is too high, we jump from the left to the right of the U, and vice versa in the next update step, without ever descending the valley (because the distance from the two peaks of the U is greater than η).

- A learning rate that's too small could make the training phase suboptimal since we never jump out of a valley that is not the point of the global minimum. Hence, there's a risk of being stuck in a local minimum. Moreover, another risk with a learning rate that's too small is never finding a good solution – not because we are stuck in a local minimum, but because we are moving too slowly toward the direction at hand. Since this is an iterative process, the research could take too long.

In order to face the challenge of choosing the learning rate value, various strategies have been developed that change its value during the training phase, usually reducing it in order to find a trade-off between the exploration of the landscape using a big learning rate and the refinement of the found solution (descending the valley) using a smaller learning rate value.

So far, we've looked at updating parameters by considering a loss function that's computed using the complete dataset, all at once. This method is called **batch gradient descent**. This method, in practice, can never be applied to a real scenario since modern applications of neural networks deal with huge amounts of data that rarely fit inside the computer's memory.

Several variants of batch gradient descent have been developed to overcome its limitations, together with different strategies for updating the model parameters, that will help us solve face some challenges related to the gradient methods themselves.

Stochastic gradient descent

Stochastic gradient descent updates the model parameter for every element of the training dataset—one example, one update step:

$$W_s = W_{s-1} - \eta \nabla \mathcal{L}((x_i, y_i); W_{s-1}).$$

If the dataset has high variance, stochastic gradient descent causes huge fluctuations of the loss value during the training phase. This can be both an advantage and a disadvantage:

- It can be an advantage because, due to the fluctuations of the loss, we jump into unexplored zones of the solution space that could contain a better minimum.
- It is a method suited for online training. This means training with new data during the whole lifetime of the model (which means we can continue to train the model with new data, usually coming from a sensor).
- The convergence is slower and finding a good minimum is more difficult since the updates have high variance.

The de facto method for training neural networks that try to keep the advantages of both batch and stochastic gradient descent is known as mini-batch gradient descent.

Mini-batch gradient descent

Mini-batch gradient descent keeps the best parts of the batch and stochastic gradient descent methods. It updates the model parameters using a subset of cardinality, b, of the training set, which is a mini-batch:

$$W_s = W_{s-1} - \eta \nabla \mathcal{L}((x_{[j,j+b]}, y_{[j,j+b]}); W_{s-1}).$$

This is the most widely used approach due to the following reasons:

- Using mini-batches reduces the parameter's update variance, and so it causes faster convergence in the training process
- Using a mini-batch of cardinality allows you to reuse the same method for online training

It's possible to write down a generic formula for gradient descent at the update step, *s*, as follows:

$$W_s = W_{s-1} - \eta \frac{1}{b} \sum_{j=1}^{b} \mathcal{L}_{[j,j+b]}\left((x_{[j,j+b]}, y_{[j,j+b]}); W_{s-1}\right)$$

- For $b = 1$, the method is stochastic gradient descent
- For $b = |\text{dataset}|$, the method is batch gradient descent
- For $1 < b < |\text{dataset}|$, the method is mini-batch gradient descent

The three methods that have been shown here update the model parameters in a so-called **vanilla** way that only considers the current parameter's value and the anti-gradient that's computed by applying the definition. They all use a fixed value for the learning rate.

Other parameter optimization algorithms exist, and all of them have been developed with the aim of finding better solutions, exploring the parameter space in a better way, and overcoming all the problems that a vanilla approach can face when searching for a good minimum:

- **Choose the learning rate**: The learning rate is probably the most important hyperparameter of the whole training phase. These reasons were explained at the end of the *Gradient descent* section.
- **Constant learning rate**: The vanilla update strategy doesn't change the learning rate value during the training phase. Moreover, it uses the same learning rate to update every parameter. Is this always desirable? Probably not, since treating parameters associated with input features with a different frequency of appearance in the same manner is not reasonable. Intuitively, we want to update the parameters associated with low appearance frequency features and the others with smaller steps.
- **Saddle points and plateau**: The loss functions that are used to train neural networks are a function of a huge number of parameters and thus are non-convex functions. During the optimization process, it is possible to run into saddle points (points in which the value of the function increases along one dimension, but decreases along other dimensions) or plateaus (locally constant regions of the loss surface).

In these cases, the gradient is almost zero along every dimension, and so the direction that's pointed to by the anti-gradient is nearly 0. This means we are stuck, and the optimization process can't go on. We have been fooled by the constant value that was assumed by the loss function during several training steps; we think we have found a good minimum, but in reality, we are stuck inside a meaningless region of the solution space.

Gradient descent optimization algorithms

Several optimization algorithms have been developed to improve the efficiency of vanilla optimization. In the upcoming sections, we will recap on vanilla optimization and show the two most common optimization algorithms: momentum and ADAM. The former will be discussed because it shows how a physical interpretation of the loss surface can lead to successful results, while the latter will be discussed because it is the most widely adaptive optimization method that's used.

Vanilla

As we saw previously, the update formula only requires an estimation of the direction, which it gets by using the anti-gradient and the learning rate:

$$W_s = W_{s-1} - \eta \nabla \mathcal{L}(W_{s-1}).$$

Momentum

The momentum optimization algorithm is based on a physical interpretation of the loss surface. Let's think about the loss surface as a messy landscape where a particle is moving around, with the aim of finding the global minimum.

The vanilla algorithm updates the position of the particle as a function of the direction that was found by calculating the anti-gradient, making the particle jump from one position to another without any physical meaning. This can be seen as an unstable system rich in energy.

The basic idea that was introduced in the momentum algorithm is to update the model parameters by considering the interaction between the surface and the particle, just like you would in a physical system.

In the real world, a system that teleports a particle from one point to a new point in zero time and without loss of energy does not exist. The initial energy of the system is lost due to external forces and because the velocity changes over time.

In particular, we can use the analogy of an object (the particle) that slides over a surface (the loss surface) and is subject to a kinetic friction force that reduces its energy and speed over time. In machine learning, we call friction coefficient momentum, but in practice, we can reason exactly like we do in physics. Hence, given a friction coefficient, μ (a hyperparameter with values in the [0,1] range but usually in the [0.9, 0.999] range), the update rule of the Momentum algorithm is given by the following equation:

$$v_s = \mu v_{s-1} - \eta \nabla \mathcal{L}(W_{s-1})$$
$$W_s = W_{s-1} + v_s$$

Here, v is the vectorial velocity of the particle (every component if the vector is the velocity in a particular dimension). The analogy of velocity is natural since, in one dimension, the derivative of the position with respect to time is the velocity.

This method takes into account the vectorial velocity that's reached by the particle at the previous step and reduces it for those components that go in a different direction, while increasing it for points that go in the same direction for subsequent updates.

In this way, the overall energy of the system is reduced, which in turn reduces the oscillations and gets faster convergence, as we can see from the following diagram, which shows the difference between the vanilla (on the left) and the momentum (on the right) optimization algorithms:

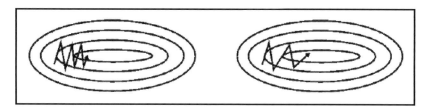

Visual representation of the vanilla (left) and momentum (right) optimization algorithms. Momentum causes fewer loss oscillations and reaches the minimum faster.

ADAM

The vanilla and the momentum optimization algorithms consider the η parameter as being constant: the strength of the update (the step size) is the same for every parameter in the network; there's no distinction among parameters associated with high or low occurrence features. To face this problem and increase the efficiency of the optimization algorithms, a whole set of new algorithms has been developed, known as **adaptive learning rate optimization methods**.

The idea behind these algorithms is to associate a different learning rate to every parameter of the network and thus update them using a learning rate that adapts itself to the type of feature the neuron is specialized to extract (or in general, to adapt itself to the different features the neuron sees as input): small updates associated with a high frequency of occurrence features, bigger otherwise. **Adaptive Moment Estimation (ADAM)** wasn't the first adaptive method to be developed, but it is the most commonly used because it outperforms almost every other adaptive and non-adaptive algorithm on many different tasks: it increases the model's generalization capabilities while speeding up its convergence.

Being an adaptive method, it creates a learning rate for every parameter in the model, like so:

$$\eta_i, \quad i = 0, 1, \ldots, |W|$$

The algorithm's authors decided to take into account how the (square of the) gradients changes, as well as their variance:

$$m_s = \beta_1 m_{s-1} + (1 - \beta_1)\nabla\mathcal{L}(W_{s-1})$$
$$v_s = \beta_2 v_{s-1} + (1 - \beta_2)\nabla\mathcal{L}(W_{s-1})^2.$$

The first term is the exponential moving average of the gradients (estimation of the first-order momentum), while the second term is the exponential moving average of the square of the gradients (estimation of the second-order momentum). Both m_s and v_s are vectors with $|W|$ components, and both have been initialized to 0.

β_1 and β_2 are the decaying factors of the exponential moving average and are hyperparameters of the algorithm.

The zero initializations of the m_s and v_s vectors make their value close to 0, especially if the decaying factors are close to 1 (hence a low decay rate).

This is a problem since we are estimating values close to zero, and without any influence from any possible update rule. To solve this, the authors suggested to correct the first and second-order momentums by computing them in the following way:

$$\hat{m}_s = \frac{m_s}{1 - \beta_1^s}$$

$$\hat{v}_s = \frac{v_s}{1 - \beta_2^s}.$$

Finally, they suggested an update rule that was inspired by other adaptive algorithms (Adadelta and RMSProp, which are not explained in this book):

$$W_s = W_{s-1} - \frac{\eta}{\sqrt{\hat{v}_s} + \epsilon} \hat{m}_s$$

They suggested that we use decaying rates close to 1 and a very small value for the epsilon parameter (it's only there to avoid divisions by zero).

Why should using the first and second-order moment estimation and this update rule to update every single parameter of the network improve the model's speed convergence and improve the generalization capabilities of the model?

The effective learning rate, $\frac{\eta}{\sqrt{\hat{v}_s} + \epsilon}$, adapts itself during training for every single parameter and takes the frequency of occurrence of the input features for every neuron into account. The denominator will increase if the computed partial derivatives associated with the current parameter are different from zero, such as if the input feature associated with that neuron occurs frequently. The higher the occurrence frequency, the smaller the update steps becomes during training.

If, instead, the partial derivatives are almost zero every time, the update steps are almost constant and never change their size during training.

Every gradient descent optimization algorithm that we've presented thus far requires that we compute the gradient of the loss function. Since neural networks can approximate any function and their topology can be very complex, how can we compute the gradient of a complex function efficiently? Representing the computation using data flow graphs and the backpropagation algorithm is the solution.

Backpropagation and automatic differentiation

Computing partial derivatives is a process that's repeated thousands upon thousands of times while training a neural network and for this reason, this process must be as efficient as possible.

In the previous sections, we showed you how, by using a loss function, is it possible to create a bond between the model's output, the input, and the label. If we represent the whole neural network architecture using a graph, it's easy to see how, given an input instance, we are just performing a mathematical operation (input multiplied by a parameter, adding those multiplication results, and applying the non-linearity function to the sum) in an ordinate manner. At the input of this graph, we have the input samples from the dataset. The output nodes of the graph are the predictions; the graph can be seen as a set of compound functions of the type:

$$f(g(x))$$

The output of a neuron with two inputs, x_1 and x_2, that uses the ReLU activation function is as follows:

$$\hat{y} = max(0, w_1 x_1 + w_2 x_2 + b)$$

The functions that are used in the previous equations are as follows:

- $p_{w_i}(x) = w_i x$ is the product function of an input for a parameter
- $s(x, y) = x + y$ is the sum function of two values
- $ReLu(x) = max(0, x)$ is the rectified linear unit activation function

Hence, we can represent the output neuron as a composition of these functions:

$$\hat{y} = ReLU(s(s(p_{w_1}(x_1), p_{w_2}(x_2)), b))$$

Keep in mind that the variables are not the input values of the functions, but the model parameters w_i. We are interested in computing the partial derivatives of the loss function in order to train the network. We do this using the gradient descent algorithm. As a simple example, we can just consider a simple loss function:

$$\mathcal{L}(y, \hat{y}) = y - \hat{y} = s(y, -ReLU(s(s(p_{w_1}(x_1), p_{w_2}(x_2)), b)))$$

To compute the loss gradient with respect to the variables ($w_{1,2}, b$), it is possible to apply the chain rule (the rule of the derivatives of compound functions):

$$(f \circ g)'(x) = f'(g(x))g'(x).$$

Using the Leibniz notation, it is easier to see how the chain rule can be applied to compute the partial derivatives of any differentiable function, which is represented as a graph (and thus represented as a set of compound functions):

$$\frac{df}{dx} = \frac{df}{dz}\frac{dz}{dx}.$$

In the end, it is just a matter of expressing the operations as compound functions, and using a graph is a natural way to do this. We can associate a graph node with a function: its inputs are the function inputs; the node performs the function computation and outputs the result. Moreover, a node can have attributes, such as a formula to apply when calculating the partial derivative with respect to its inputs.

Moreover, a graph can be traversed in both directions. We can traverse it in the forward direction (forward pass of the backpropagation algorithm), and thus compute the loss value. We can also traverse it in the backward direction, applying the formula of the derivative of the output with respect to the input associated with every node and multiplying the value coming from the previous node with the current to compute the partial derivative. This is the application of the chain rule.

Representing computations as graphs allow us to perform automatic differentiation by computing the gradient of complex functions. We only consider operations singularly, and just look at the node's inputs and outputs.

There are two different ways of applying the chain rule on a graph – forward and backward mode. A detailed explanation of the automatic differentiation in both forward and backward mode is beyond the scope of this book; however, in upcoming chapters, we will see how TensorFlow implements automatic differentiation in backward mode and how it applies the chain rule to compute the loss value and then traverse the graph in a backward fashion D times. Automatic differentiation in backward mode depends on the input cardinality and not on the number of parameters of the network, compared to implementing it in forwarding mode (it's now easy to imagine why TensorFlow implements automatic differentiation in backward mode; neural networks can have millions of parameters).

So far, we've described optimization algorithms and strategies that can be applied to compute the loss function so that it fits the training data. We do this by using a generic function that's been approximated by our neural network. In practice, we only introduced one neural network architecture: the fully connected architecture. However, there are several different neural network architectures that can be applied to solve different problems, depending on the dataset type.

One of the strengths of neural networks is their ability to be able to perform different tasks, depending on the neuron topology that's used.

The fully connected configuration is a global view on the input—every neuron sees everything. However, there are certain types of data that do not require a complete view to be correctly used by a neural network, or that are computationally intractable with a fully connected configuration. Think about a high-resolution image with millions of pixels; we have to connect every neuron to every single pixel, creating a network with a number of parameters equal to the number of pixels times the number of neurons: a network with only two neurons will lead to $2 * \text{number of pixels}$ parameters—that is completely intractable!

The architecture that's been developed to work with images, and maybe the most important neuronal layer that's been developed in the past years, is the convolutional neural network.

Convolutional neural networks

Convolutional Neural Networks (CNNs) are the fundamental building blocks of modern computer vision, speech recognition, and even natural language processing applications. In this section, we are going to describe the convolution operator, how it is used in the signal analysis domain, and how convolution is used in machine learning.

The convolution operator

Signal theory gives us all the tools we need to properly understand the convolution operation: why it is so widely used in many different domains and why CNNs are so powerful. The convolution operation is used to study the response of certain physical systems when a signal is applied to their input. Different input stimuli can make a system, *S*, produce a different output, and the behavior of a system can be modeled using the convolution operation.

Let's start from the one-dimensional case by introducing the concept of the **Linear Time-Invariant (LTI)** system.

A system, S, that accepts an input signal and produces an output signal, $y(t)$, is an LTI system if the following properties hold:

- **Linearity**: $S[\alpha x_1(t) + \beta x_2(t)] = \alpha y(x_1(t)) + \beta y(x_2(t)) \, \alpha, \beta \in \mathbb{R}$
- **Time invariance**: $S[x(t + t_0)] = y(t + t_0)$

Is it possible to analyze the behavior of an LTI system by analyzing its response to the Dirac Delta function, δ(t). δ(t) is a function with a value of zero in every point of its domain, except in $t = 0$. In $t = 0$, it assumes a value that makes its definition true:

$$\int_{-\infty}^{+\infty} \delta(t) \, \phi(t) \, \mathrm{d}t = \phi(0).$$

Intuitively, applying δ(t) to a function, φ(t), means sample the φ(t) in 0. Hence, if we put δ(t) as the input of a system, S, we get its response to a unitary impulse centered on zero. The system output when the input is the Dirac Delta function is called the system impulse response, and is noted with the following equation:

$$h(t) = S[\delta(t)].$$

The system impulse response is of fundamental importance since it allows us to compute the response of an LTI system to any input.

A generic signal, $x(t)$, can be seen as the sum of the value it assumes on every instant, t. This can be modeled as the application of δ(t) that's translated in every point of the x domain:

$$x(t) = \int_{-\infty}^{+\infty} x(t)\delta(t - \tau)d\tau = x(t) * \delta(t),$$

This formula is the definition of convolution among two signals.

So, why is the convolution operation important for the study of LTI systems? Given $x(t)$ as a generic input signal and $h(t)$ as the impulse response of an LTI system, we get the following:

$$y(t) \stackrel{\mathrm{def}}{=} x(t) * h(t) = (x * h)(t) = \int_{-\infty}^{+\infty} x(t)h(t - \tau)d\tau$$

The result of the convolution represents the behavior of the LTI system that's modeled by its impulse response, *h(t)*, when *x(t)* is its input. This is an important result since it shows us how the impulse response completely characterizes the system and how the convolution operation can be used to analyze the output of an LTI system when given any input signal.

The convolution operation is commutative and the result of the operation is a function (a signal).

So far, we've only considered the continuous case, but there's a natural generalization on the discrete domain. If $g[n]$ and $x[n]$ are defined on $\mathbb{Z}$, the convolution is computed as follows:

$$(x * g)[n] \stackrel{\text{def}}{=} \sum_{m=-\infty}^{\infty} x[m]\, g[n-m].$$

2D convolution

The generalization of the 1D convolution we've introduced in terms of the 2D case is natural. Images, in particular, can be seen as 2D discrete signals. In the 2D case, the counterpart of the Dirac Delta function is the Kronecker Delta function, and it can be expressed independently from the dimensionality of the space it is used in. It's seen as a tensor, δ, with components:

$$\delta_{i,j} \stackrel{\text{def}}{=} \begin{cases} 1 & \text{if} \quad i = j \\ 0 & \text{otherwise} \end{cases}$$

Images can be thought as 2D versions of LTI systems. In this case, we are talking about **Linear Space-Invariant (LSI)** systems.

In the bi-dimensional discrete case, the convolution operation is defined as follows:

$$O(i,j) = \sum_{u=-\infty}^{\infty} \sum_{v=-\infty}^{\infty} F(u,v)I(i-u, j-v).$$

Images are finite dimension signals with a well-defined spatial extent. This means that the previously introduced formula becomes the following:

$$O(i,j) = \sum_{u=-k}^{k} \sum_{v=-k}^{k} F(u,v)I(i-u, j-v)$$

Here, we have the following:

- I is the input image
- F is the convolutional filter (also called the kernel) itself and $2k$ is its side
- $O(i,j)$ is the output pixel, in the (i,j) position

The operation that we've described is performed for every *(i,j)* position of the input image that has a complete overlap with the convolutional filter, as it slides over the input image:

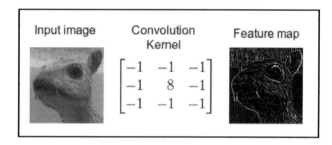

The convolution operation between the input image (on the left) and the convolution kernel produces the feature map on the right

As shown in the preceding diagram, different convolutional filters extract different features from the input image. In fact, in the preceding diagram, we can see how that rectangular filter (Sobel filter) is able to extract the edges of the input image. Convolving an image with a different convolutional filter means having to extract different input features that the kernel can capture. Before the introduction of convolutional neural networks, as we will see in the next section, we would had to manually design convolutional kernels that were able to extract the features needed that were to solve the task at hand.

There are two additional parameters that aren't shown in the preceding formula that control how the convolution operation is performed. These parameters are the horizontal and vertical stride; they tell the operation how many pixels to skip when we move the kernel over the input image over the horizontal and vertical directions. Usually, the horizontal and vertical strides are equal, and they are noted with the letter S.

If the input image has side $I_w = I_h$, then the resolution of the output signal resulting from the convolution with a kernel of size k can be computed as follows:

$$O_w = O_h = \frac{I_w - 2k}{S} + 1.$$

2D convolutions among volumes

So far, we've only considered the case of a grayscale image, that is, an image with a single channel. The images we are used to seeing in real life are all RGB images, which are images with three color channels. The convolution operation also works well when the input image has more than one channel; in fact, its definition has been slightly changed in order to make the convolution operation span every channel.

This extended version requires the convolution filter to have the same number of channels as the input image; in short, if the input image has three channels, the convolutional kernel must have three channels too. This way, we are treating images as stacks of 2D signals; we call these volumes.

As a volume, every image (or convolutional kernel) is identified by the triple (W, H, D), where W, H, and D are the width, height, and depth, respectively.

By considering images and kernels as volumes, we can treat them as unordered sets. In fact, the order (RGB, BGR) of the channels only changes how the software interprets the data, while the content remains the same:

$$I = \{I_1, \cdots, I_D\}, \quad F = \{F_1, \cdots, F_D\}$$

This reasoning allows us to extend the previous formula, thereby making it take the input depth into account:

$$O(i, j) = \sum_{d=1}^{D} \sum_{u=-k}^{k} \sum_{v=-k}^{k} F_d(u, v) I_d(i - u, j - v).$$

The result of this convolution operation is called a feature map. Even though the convolution is performed among volumes, the output is a feature map with unitary depth since the convolution operation sums the feature maps that have been produced to take into account all the information of the pixels that share the same spatial (x,y) location. In fact, summing the resulting D feature maps is a way to treat a set of 2D convolutions as a single 2D convolution.

This means that every single position of the resulting activation map, *O*, contains the information that was captured from the same input location through its complete depth. This is the intuitive idea behind the convolution operation.

Alright; we now have a grasp of the convolution operation in 1 and two spatial dimensions; we also introduced the concept of convolutional kernel highlighting whereby defining the kernel value is a manual operation where different kernels can extract different features from the input image/volume.

The process of kernel definition is pure engineering, and defining them is not easy: different tasks can require different kernels; some of them have never been defined, and most of them can be simply impossible to design since certain features can only be extracted by processing a processed signal, which means we would have to apply the convolution operation on the result of another convolution operation (a cascade of convolution operations).

Convolutional neural networks solve this problem: instead of manually defining the convolutional kernels, we can just define convolutional kernels made of neurons.

We can extract features from the input volume by convolving it with multiple volumes of filters and combining them while considering the feature maps that extract new input for a new convolutional layer.

The deeper the network becomes, the more abstract the extracted feature becomes. One of the greatest strengths of CNNs is their ability to combine features that have been extracted, ranging from raw, basic features that were extracted by the first convolutional layers to high-level abstract features that were extracted by the last layers and learned as a combination of the low-level features that were extracted by the other layers:

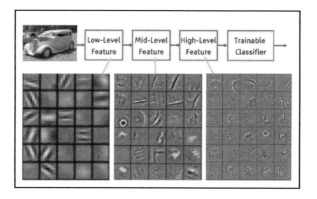

CNNs learn to extract low-level features in the first layers; as the networks become deeper, the abstraction level of the extracted features increases. Image from Zeiler and Fergus, 2013.

Another advantage of convolutional layers with respect to fully connected layers is their local-view nature.

To process an image, a fully connected layer has to linearize the input image and create a connection from every pixel value to every neuron of the layer. The memory requirements are huge, and making every neuron see the whole input isn't the ideal way to extract meaningful features.

There are certain features that, due to their nature, are not global like the ones that are captured by a fully connected layer. Instead, they are local. For example, the edges of an object are local features to a certain input region, not the whole image. Therefore, CNNs can learn to extract only local features and combine them in the following layers. Another advantage of convolutional architectures is their low number of parameters: they don't need to see (and thus create connections) the whole input; they only need to have a view of their local receptive field. Convolution operations requires fewer parameters to extract meaningful feature maps, all of which capture the local features of the input volume.

CNNs are usually used with another layer, known as the pooling layer. Without digging too much into the details of this operation (it tends to be avoided in today's architectures), we can just think about it as an operation with the same structure as the convolution operation (hence a window that moves in the horizontal and vertical direction of the input) but without a learnable kernel. In every region of the input, a non-learnable function is applied. The aim of this operation is to reduce the size of the feature maps that are produced by a convolution operation in order to reduce the number of parameters of the network.

So that we have an idea of what the common convolutional neural network architecture looks like, the following diagram presents the LeNet 5 architecture that uses a convolutional layer, max-pooling (a pooling operation where the non-learnable function is the max operation over the window), and fully connected layers with the aim of classifying images of handwritten digits in 10 classes:

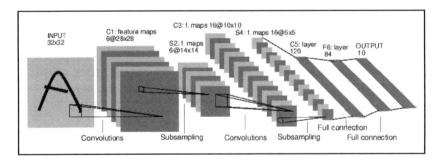

LeNet 5 architecture – each plane is a feature map. Source: Gradient-Based Learning Applied to Document Recognition, Yann LeCun at al—1998

Defining network architectures such as LeNet 5 is an art – there are no precise rules on the number of layers you can use, the number of convolutional filters to learn, or the number of neurons in the fully connected layers. Moreover, even picking the right activation function for the hidden layer is another hyperparameter to search for. Complex models are not only rich in terms of learnable parameters, but also rich in terms of hyperparameters to tune, making the definition of deep architectures non-trivial and challenging.

Convolutions among volumes allow us to do fancy things such as replace every fully connected layer with a 1 x 1 x D convolutional layer and use a 1 x 1 x D convolution inside the network to reduce the dimensionality of the input.

1 x 1 x D convolutions

$1 \times 1 \times D$ convolutions are important building blocks of state-of-the-art models because they can be used for different goals.

One goal is the use them as a dimensionality reduction technique. Let's understand this by going through an example.

If the convolution operation is applied to an input volume of $100 \times 100 \times 512$ and it is convolved with a set of D filters, each one being $1 \times 1 \times 512$ in size, the number of features is reduced from 512 to D. The output volume now has a shape of $100 \times 100 \times D$.

A $1 \times 1 \times D$ convolution is also equivalent to a fully connected layer. The main difference lies in the nature of the convolution operator and the architectural structure of the fully connected layer: while the latter requires the input to have a fixed size, the former accepts every volume with a spatial extent greater than or equal to 1×1 as input. A $1 \times 1 \times D$ convolution can therefore substitute any fully connected layer because of this equivalence.

Additionally, the $1 \times 1 \times D$ convolutions not only reduce the features in the input to the next layer but also introduce new parameters and new non-linearity into the network that could help increase the model's accuracy.

When a $1 \times 1 \times D$ convolution is placed at the end of a classification network, it acts exactly like a fully connected layer, but instead of thinking about it as a dimensionality reduction technique, it's more intuitive to think about it as a layer that will output a tensor with a shape of $W \times H \times \text{num\_classes}$. The spatial extent of the output tensor (identified by W and H) is dynamic and is determined by the locations of the input image that the network analyzed.

If the network has been defined with an input of 200 x 200 x 3 and we give it an image with this size as input, the output will be a map with $W = H = 1$ and $\text{depth} = \text{num\_classes}$. However, if the input image has a spatial extent greater than 200×200, then the convolutional network will analyze different locations of the input image (just like a standard convolution does, since it's not possible to consider the whole convolutional architecture as a convolution operation with its own kernel side and stride parameters) and will produce a tensor with $W > 1$ and $H > 1$. This is not possible with a fully connected layer that constrains the network to accept a fixed-size input and produce a fixed-size output.

$1 \times 1 \times D$ convolutions are also the fundamental building blocks of semantic segmentation networks, as we will see in the upcoming chapters.

Convolutional, pooling, and fully connected layers are the building blocks of almost every neural network architecture that's used nowadays to solve computer vision tasks such as image classification, object detection, semantic segmentation, image generation, and many others!

We will implement all of these neural network architectures using TensorFlow 2.0 in the upcoming chapters.

Although CNNs have a reduced number of parameters, even this model can suffer from the problem of overfitting when used in a deep configuration (a stack of convolutional layers).

Hence, another fundamental topic any ML practitioner should be aware of is regularization.

Regularization

Regularization is a way to deal with the problem of overfitting: the goal of regularization is to modify the learning algorithm, or the model itself, to make the model perform well—not just on the training data, but also on new inputs.

One of the most widely used solutions to the overfitting problem—and probably one of the most simple to understand and analyze—is known as **dropout**.

Dropout

The idea of dropout is to train an ensemble of neural networks and average the results instead of training only a single standard network. Dropout builds new neural networks, starting from a standard neural network, by dropping out neurons with p probability.

When a neuron is dropped out, its output is set to zero. This is shown in the following diagram:

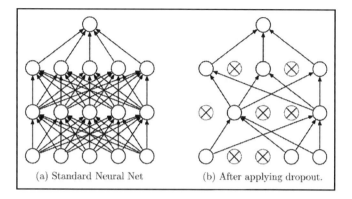

(a) Standard Neural Net   (b) After applying dropout.

On the left, a standard fully connected architecture. On the right, a possible network architecture that's been obtained by dropping out neurons, which means it used dropout during the training phase. Source: Dropout: A simple way to Prevent Neural Networks from Overfitting - N. Srivastava—2014

The dropped neurons do not contribute to the training phase. Since neurons are dropped randomly at each new training iteration, using dropout makes the training phase different every time. In fact, using dropout means that every training step is performed on a new network—and even better, a network with a different topology.

 N. Srivastava et al. in *Dropout: A simple way to Prevent Neural Networks from Overfitting* (*the* paper that introduced this regularization technique) explained this concept very well:

> *"In a standard neural network, the derivative that's received by each parameter tells it how it should change, so the final loss function is reduced, given what all the other units are doing. Therefore, units may change in a way that they fix the mistakes of the other units.*
> *This may lead to complex co-adaptations. This, in turn, leads to overfitting because these co-adaptations do not generalize to unseen data. We hypothesize that, for each hidden unit, dropout prevents co-adaptation by making the presence of other hidden units unreliable. Therefore, a hidden unit cannot rely on other specific units to correct its mistakes."*

Dropout works well in practice because it prevents the co-adaption of neurons during the training phase. In the upcoming sections, we will analyze how dropout works and how it is implemented.

How dropout works

We can analyze how dropout works by looking at its application on a single neuron. Let's say we have the following:

- $h(x) = xW + b$ as a linear neuron
- $a(h)$ as an activation function

By using these, it is possible to model the application of dropout – in the training phase only – as a modification of the activation function:

$$f(h) = D \odot a(h)$$

Here,

$$D = (X_1, \cdots, X_{d_h})$$

Is a d_h-dimensional vector of Bernoulli random variables, X_i.

A Bernoulli random variable has the following probability mass distribution:

$$f(k; p) = \begin{cases} p & \text{if} \quad k = 1 \\ 1 - p & \text{if} \quad k = 0 \end{cases}$$

Here, k is the possible outcomes. The Bernoulli random variable correctly models the dropout application on a neuron since the neuron is turned off with the probability of $p = P(k = 1)$ and kept on otherwise. It can be useful to see the application of dropout on the generic *i*-th neuron of a fully-connected layer (but the same holds for the application on a single neuron of a convolutional layer):

$$O_i = X_i a\left(\sum_{k=1}^{d_i} w_k x_k + b\right) = \begin{cases} a(\sum_{k=1}^{d_i} w_k x_k + b) & \text{if} \quad X_i = 1 \\ 0 & \text{if} \quad X_i = 0 \end{cases}$$

Here, $P(X_i = 0) = p$.

During training, a neuron is kept on with probability q. Therefore, during the test phase, we have to emulate the behavior of the ensemble of networks that were used in the training phase. To do this, we need to scale the neuron's output by a factor of q d.

Thus, we have the following:

$$\cdot \textbf{ Train phase:} \quad O_i = X_i a(\sum_{k=1}^{d_i} w_k x_k + b)$$

$$\cdot \textbf{ Test phase:} \quad O_i = qa(\sum_{k=1}^{d_i} w_k x_k + b)$$

Inverted dropout

A slightly different approach—and the one that's used in practice in almost every deep learning framework – is to use inverted dropout. This approach consists of scaling the activations during the training phase, with the obvious advantage of not having to change the network architecture during the test phase.

The scale factor is the inverse of the keep probability, $\frac{1}{1-p} = \frac{1}{q}$, and so we have the following:

$$\cdot \textbf{ Train phase:} \quad O_i = \frac{1}{q} X_i a(\sum_{k=1}^{d_i} w_k x_k + b)$$

$$\cdot \textbf{ Test phase:} \quad O_i = a(\sum_{k=1}^{d_i} w_k x_k + b)$$

Inverted dropout is how dropout is implemented in practice because it helps us define the model and just change a parameter (the keep/drop probability) to train and test on the same model.

Direct dropout, which is the version that was presented in the previous section, forces you to modify the network during the test phase because, if you don't multiply by q, the neuron will produce values that are higher with respect to the one expected by the successive neurons (thus the following neurons can saturate or explode). This is why inverted dropout is the more common implementation.

Dropout and L2 regularization

Dropout is often used with L2 normalization and other parameter constraint techniques, but this is not always the case.

Normalization helps keep model parameter values low. In this way, a parameter can't grow too much. In brief, the L2 normalization is an additional term to the loss, where $\lambda \in [0, 1]$ is a hyperparameter called regularization strength, $F(W; x)$ is the model, and ε is the error function between the real y and the predicted $\hat{y}$ value:

$$\mathcal{L}(y, \hat{y}) = \mathcal{E}(y, F(W; x)) + \frac{\lambda}{2} W^2$$

It's easy to understand that this additional term, when we're doing back-propagation via gradient descent, reduces the update amount. If η is the learning rate, the update amount of the parameter $w \in W$ is as follows:

$$w \leftarrow w - \eta \left(\frac{\partial F(W; x)}{\partial w} + \lambda w \right)$$

Dropout alone does not have any way of preventing parameter values from becoming too large during this update phase.

There are two other solutions that are extremely easy to implement that do not even require the model to be changed or for the loss to have additional terms. These are known as data augmentation and early stopping.

Data augmentation

Data augmentation is a simple way to increase the dataset's size. This is done by applying a set of transformations on the train data. Its aim is to make the model aware that certain input variations are possible and thus make it perform better on a variety of input data.

The set of transformations highly depends on the dataset itself. Usually, when working with an image dataset, the transformations to apply are as follows:

- Random flip left/right
- Random flip up/down
- Adding random noise to the input image

- Random brightness variation
- Random saturation variation

However, before applying any of these transformations to our training set, we have to ask: *is this transformation meaningful for this data type, for my dataset, and for the task at hand?*

Just think about the random flip left/right of the input image: if our dataset is a dataset of drawn arrows, each labeled with its direction, and we are training a model to predict the arrow's direction, mirroring the image will just break our training set.

Early stopping

As we introduced in `Chapter 1`, *What is Machine Learning?*, measuring the performance of the model during the training phase on both the validation and training sets is a good habit. This good habit can help us prevent overfitting and save us a lot of training time since the measured metrics tell us whether the model is starting to overfit the training data and thus if it is time to stop the training process.

Let's think about a classifier—we measure the validation accuracy, the training accuracy, and the loss value.

Looking at the loss value, we can see that, as the training process goes on, the loss decreases. Of course, this is true only for healthy training. Training is healthy when the loss trend decreases. It is possible to just observe the fluctuation that was introduced by mini-batch gradient descent or the usage of the stochastic regularization process (dropout).

If the training process is healthy and the loss trend decreases, the training accuracy will increase. Training accuracy measures how well the model learns the training set—it does not capture its generalization capabilities. Validation accuracy, on the other hand, is the measure of how good the predictions of your model are on unseen data.

If the model is learning, the validation accuracy increases. If the model is overfitting, the validation accuracy stops increasing and can even start to decrease, while the accuracy measured on the training set reaches the maximum value.

If you stop training the model as soon as the validation accuracy (or whatever the monitored metric is) stops increasing, then you are facing the overfitting problem easily and effectively.

Data augmentation and early stopping are two ways of reducing overfitting without changing the model's architecture.

However, similar to dropout, there is another common regularization technique, known as batch normalization, that requires that we change the model architecture that we use. This helps speed up the training process and lets us achieve better performance.

Batch normalization

Batch normalization is not only a regularization technique—it is also a good way to speed up the training process. To increase the stability of the learning process, and thus reduce the oscillation of the loss function, batch normalization normalizes the output of a layer by subtracting the batch mean and dividing it by the batch standard deviation.

After this normalization, which is not a learned process, batch normalization adds two trainable parameters: the standard deviation parameter (gamma) and the mean parameter (beta).

Batch normalization not only helps speed up convergence by reducing the training oscillations, it also helps in reducing overfitting since it introduces stochasticity in the training process in a way that's similar to dropout. The difference is that, while dropout adds noise in an explicit manner, batch normalization introduces stochasticity by computing the mean and the variance over the batch.

The following image, which was taken from the original paper, *Batch Normalization – Accelerating Deep Network Training*, by Reducing Internal Covariate Shift (Ioffe et al. 2015), shows the algorithm that's applied during the training process:

Input: Values of x over a mini-batch: $\mathcal{B} = \{x_{1\ldots m}\}$;
Parameters to be learned: γ, β
Output: $\{y_i = BN_{\gamma,\beta}(x_i)\}$

$$\mu_\mathcal{B} \leftarrow \frac{1}{m} \sum_{i=1}^{m} x_i \qquad \text{// mini-batch mean}$$

$$\sigma_\mathcal{B}^2 \leftarrow \frac{1}{m} \sum_{i=1}^{m} (x_i - \mu_\mathcal{B})^2 \qquad \text{// mini-batch variance}$$

$$\widehat{x}_i \leftarrow \frac{x_i - \mu_\mathcal{B}}{\sqrt{\sigma_\mathcal{B}^2 + \epsilon}} \qquad \text{// normalize}$$

$$y_i \leftarrow \gamma \widehat{x}_i + \beta \equiv BN_{\gamma,\beta}(x_i) \qquad \text{// scale and shift}$$

Algorithm 1: Batch Normalizing Transform, applied to activation x over a mini-batch.

The batch normalization algorithm. Source: *Batch Normalization – Accelerating Deep Network Training by Reducing Internal Covariate Shift*, Ioffe et al. 2015

At the end of the training process, it is required that you apply the same affine transformation that was learned during the training process. However, instead of computing the mean and the variance over the input batch, the mean and the variance that accumulated during the training process are used. In fact, batch normalization, just like dropout, has a different behavior during the training and inference phases. During the training phase, it computes the mean and variance over the current input batch, while it accumulates the moving mean and variance use during the inference phase.

Fortunately, since this is a very common operation, TensorFlow has a BatchNormalization layer ready to use, so we don't have to worry about the accumulation of statistics during the training and having to change the layer's behavior during the inference phase.

Summary

This chapter is probably the most theory intensive of this whole book; however, it is required that you have at least an intuitive idea of the building blocks of neural networks and of the various algorithms that are used in machine learning so that you can start developing a meaningful understanding of what's going on.

We have looked at what a neural network is, what it means to train it, and how to perform a parameter update with some of the most common update strategies. You should now have a basic understanding of how the chain rule can be applied in order to compute the gradient of a function efficiently.

We haven't explicitly talked about deep learning, but in practice, that is what we did; keep in mind that stacking layers of neural networks is like stacking different classifiers that combine their expressive power. We indicated this with the term deep learning. In practice, we can say that deep neural networks (a deep learning model) are just neural networks with more than one hidden layer.

Later in this chapter, we introduced a lot of important concepts about parametric model training, the origin of neural networks, as well as their mathematical formulation. It is of extreme importance to have at least an intuitive idea of what happens when we define a fully connected (among others) layer when we define the loss and use a certain optimization strategy to train a model using a machine learning framework such as TensorFlow.

TensorFlow hides the complexity of everything we've described in this chapter, but having an understanding of what happens under the hood will allow you to debug a model just by looking at its behavior. You will also have an idea of why certain things happen during the training phase and how to solve certain problems. For instance, knowledge of optimization strategies will help you understand why your loss function value follows a certain trend and assumes certain values during the training phase, and will give you an idea of how to choose the right hyperparameters.

In the next chapter, Chapter 3, *TensorFlow Graph Architecture*, we will see how all the theoretical concepts presented in this chapter, using the graph representation of the computation, can be effectively implemented in TensorFlow.

Exercises

This chapter was filled with various theoretical concepts to understand so, just like the previous chapter, don't skip the exercises:

1. What are the similarities between artificial and biological neurons?
2. Does the neuron's topology change the neural network's behavior?
3. Why do neurons require a non-linear activation function?
4. If the activation function is linear, a multi-layer neural network is the same as a single layer neural network. Why?
5. How is an error in input data treated by a neural network?
6. Write the mathematical formulation of a generic neuron.
7. Write the mathematical formulation of a fully connected layer.
8. Why can a multi-layer configuration solve problems with non-linearly separable solutions?
9. Draw the graph of the sigmoid, tanh, and ReLu activation functions.
10. Is it always required to format training set labels into a one-hot encoded representation? What if the task is regression?
11. The loss function creates a bond between the desired outcome and the model output: why is this required for the loss function to be differentiable?
12. What does the gradient of the loss function indicate? What about the anti-gradient?
13. What is a parameter update rule? Explain the vanilla update rule.
14. Write the mini-batch gradient descent algorithm and explain the three possible scenarios.

15. Is random perturbation a good update strategy? Explain the pros and cons of this approach.

16. What's the difference between a non-adaptive and adaptive optimization algorithm?

17. What's the relationship between the concept of velocity and momentum update? Describe the momentum update algorithm.

18. What is an LTI system? How is it related to the convolution operation?

19. What is a feature vector?

20. Are CNNs feature extractors? If yes, can a fully connected layer be used to classify the output of a convolutional layer?

21. What are the guidelines for model parameter initialization? Is assigning a constant value of 10 to every parameter of the network a good initialization strategy?

22. What are the differences between direct and inverted dropout? Why does TensorFlow implement the inverted version?

23. Why is the L2 normalization of network parameters useful when using dropout?

24. Write the formula of convolution among volumes: show how it behaves in the case of a 1 x 1 x D convolutional kernel. Why is there an equivalence between the fully connected layer and a 1 x 1 x D convolution?

25. If, while training a classifier, the validation accuracy stops increasing, what does this mean? Can adding dropout or increasing the drop probability if dropout layers are already present make the network improve the validation accuracy again? Why or why not?

2
Section 2: TensorFlow Fundamentals

This section shows how TensorFlow 2.0 works and the differences compared with version 1.x. This section also covers how to define a complete machine learning pipeline, from data acquisition, passing through the model definition, and how the graph of TensorFlow 1.x is still present in TensorFlow 2.0.

This section comprises the following chapters:

- Chapter 3, *TensorFlow Graph Architecture*
- Chapter 4, *TensorFlow 2.0 Architecture*
- Chapter 5, *Efficient Data Input Pipelines and Estimator API*

TensorFlow Graph Architecture

3

The most concise and complete explanation of what TensorFlow is can be found on the project home page (`https://www.tensorflow.org/`) and it highlights every important part of the library. TensorFlow is an open source software library for high-performance numerical computation. Its flexible architecture allows easy deployment of computation across a variety of platforms (CPUs, GPUs, and TPUs), from desktops to clusters of servers, to mobile and edge devices. Originally developed by researchers and engineers from the Google Brain team within Google's AI organization, it comes with strong support for machine learning and deep learning, and the flexible numerical computation core is used across many other scientific domains.

TensorFlow's strengths and most important features can be summarized in the following three points:

- **High-performance numerical computation library**: TensorFlow can be used in many different applications just by importing it. It is written in C++ and it offers bindings for several languages. The most complete, high-level, and widely used binding is the Python one. TensorFlow is a high-performance computational library that can be used in several domains (not only machine learning!) to execute numerical computation efficiently.
- **Flexible architecture**: TensorFlow has been designed to work on different hardware (GPUs, CPUs, and TPUs) and different network architectures; its abstraction level is so high that (almost) the same code can train a model on a single computer or a cluster of machines in a data center.
- **Production-oriented**: TensorFlow has been developed by the Google Brain team as a tool for developing and serving machine learning models at scale. It was designed with the idea of simplifying the whole design-to-production pipeline; the library already comes with several APIs ready to be used in a production environment.

TensorFlow, thus, is a numerical computational library—keep that in mind. You can use it to perform any mathematical operation it offers, leveraging the power of all the hardware you have at your disposal, without doing anything ML-related.

In this chapter, you'll learn everything you need to know about the TensorFlow architecture: what TensorFlow is, how to set up your environment to test both versions 1.x and 2.0 to see the differences, and you will learn a lot about how a computational graph is built; in the process, you will also learn how to use TensorBoard to visualize graphs.

In this chapter, you'll (finally!) start reading some code. Please don't just read the code and the related explanations; write all the code you read and try to execute it. Follow the instructions on how to set up the two virtual environments we need and get your hands dirty with the code. At the end of this chapter, you'll be familiar with the fundamentals of TensorFlow that are valid for every TensorFlow version.

In this chapter, we will cover the following topics:

- Environment setup
- Dataflow graphs
- Model definition and training
- Interacting with the graph using Python

Environment setup

In order to understand the structure of TensorFlow, all the examples presented in this chapter will use the latest TensorFlow 1.x release: 1.15; however, we will also set up everything needed to run TensorFlow 2.0 since we are going to use it in the next chapter, `Chapter 4`, *TensorFlow 2.0 Architecture*.

All the examples presented in this book specify the version of TensorFlow to use when running it. Being a library, we can just install it specifying the version we need. Of course, having two different versions of the same library installed on one system would be a mistake. In order to be able to switch between versions, we are going to use two different *Python virtual environments*.

An explanation of what a **virtual environment** (**virtualenv**) is and why it perfectly fits our needs follows here, from the official introduction to virtual environments (`https://docs.Python.org/3/tutorial/venv.html#introduction`):

> *Python applications will often use packages and modules that don't come as part of the standard library. Applications will sometimes need a specific version of a library, because the application may require that a particular bug has been fixed or the application may be written using an obsolete version of the library's interface.*
>
> *This means it may not be possible for one Python installation to meet the requirements of every application. If application A needs version 1.0 of a particular module, but application B needs version 2.0, then the requirements are in conflict and installing either version 1.0 or 2.0 will leave one application unable to run.*
>
> *The solution to this problem is to create a virtual environment, a self-contained directory tree that contains a Python installation for a particular version of Python, plus a number of additional packages.*
>
> *Different applications can then use different virtual environments. To resolve the earlier example of conflicting requirements, application A can have its own virtual environment with version 1.0 installed, while application B has another virtual environment with version 2.0. If application B requires a library to be upgraded to version 3.0, this will not affect application A's environment.*

In order to create virtual environments in the easiest way, we use `pipenv`: the definitive tool for `virtualenv` creation and management; follow the installation guide at `https://github.com/pypa/pipenv`. Being a cross-platform tool, using Windows, Mac, or Linux makes no difference. Having installed `pipenv`, we just need to create these two separate virtual environments for the two different TensorFlow versions.

We'll install TensorFlow without GPU support because `tensorflow-gpu` depends on CUDA and a recent NVIDIA GPU is required to use the GPU acceleration provided by the CUDA package. If you own a recent NVIDIA GPU, you can install the `tensorflow-gpu` package, but you have to take care to install the version of CUDA required by the TensorFlow package you are installing (TensorFlow 2.0 and TensorFlow 1.15 require CUDA 10). Moreover, you have to ensure that both the `tensorflow-gpu` packages installed in the `virtualenvs` depend on the same CUDA version (CUDA 10); otherwise, one installation will work and the other won't. However, if you stick with versions 2.0 and 1.15 of TensorFlow, both are compiled with CUDA 10 support, hence, installing them in their GPU version and having CUDA 10 installed on your system should work perfectly.

TensorFlow 1.x environment

Create a folder, tf1, step inside it, and run the following commands to create an environment, activate it, and install TensorFlow using pip:

```
# create the virtualenv in the current folder (tf1)
pipenv --python 3.7
# run a new shell that uses the just created virtualenv
pipenv shell
# install, in the current virtualenv, tensorflow
pip install tensorflow==1.15
#or for GPU support: pip install tensorflow-gpu==1.15
```

Using Python 3.7 is not strictly mandatory; TensorFlow comes with support for Python 3.5, 3.6, and 3.7. Hence, if you are using a distribution/operating system that ships an older Python version, such as Python 3.5, you just have to change the Python version in the pipenv command.

So far, so good. Right now, you are in an environment that uses Python 3.7 and has tensorflow==1.15 installed. In order to create a new environment for TensorFlow 2.0, we have to first exit from the pipenv shell created for us, which we're currently using. As a general rule, to switch from one virtualenv to another, we activate it using pipenv shell and deactivate it, exiting the session from the shell, by typing exit.

Thus, before creating the second virtual environment, just close the currently running shell by typing exit.

TensorFlow 2.0 environment

In the same manner as with the TensorFlow 1.x environment, create a folder, tf2, step inside it, and run the following commands:

```
# create the virtualenv in the current folder (tf2)
pipenv --python 3.7
# run a new shell that uses the just created virtualenv
pipenv shell
# install, in the current virtualenv, tensorflow
pip install tensorflow==2.0
#or for GPU support: pip install tensorflow-gpu==2.0
```

In the rest of the book, whether the TensorFlow 1.x or 2.0 environment should be used is indicated by the (tf1) or (tf2) symbol before the code.

We can now start digging inside the TensorFlow structure, analyzing, and describing something that was explicit in TensorFlow 1.x and hidden in TensorFlow 2.0 (but still present!): the data flow graph. Since the analysis that follows looks at the details of how a graph is built and how various low-level operations can be used to build graphs, almost every code snippet uses the TensorFlow 1.x environment. If you are interested in version 2.0 only because you already know and use TensorFlow 1.x, you can skip this section; although, reading it is also recommended for the experienced user.

It is possible to use only the tensorflow 2.0 environment and replace every call to the tensorflow package, tf, using the compatibility module present in TensorFlow 2; therefore, to have a single (tf2) environment, you must replace every tf. with tf.compat.v1. and disable eager execution by adding the tf.compat.v1.disable_eager_execution() line just after importing the TensorFlow package.

Now that we have our environment setup complete, let's move on to dataflow graphs and learn how to start working on some practical code.

Dataflow graphs

In order to be a highly efficient, flexible, and production-ready library, TensorFlow uses dataflow graphs to represent computation in terms of the relationships between individual operations. Dataflow is a programming model widely used in parallel computing and, in a dataflow graph, the nodes represent units of computation while the edges represent the data consumed or produced by a computation unit.

As seen in the previous chapter, Chapter 2, *Neural Networks and Deep Learning,* representing computation using graphs comes with the advantage of being able to run the forward and backward passes required to train a parametric machine learning model via gradient descent, applying the chain rule to compute the gradient as a local process to every node; however, this is not the only advantage of using graphs.

Reducing the abstraction level and thinking about the implementation details of representing computation using graphs brings the following advantages:

- **Parallelism**: Using nodes to represent operations and edges that represent their dependencies, TensorFlow is able to identify operations that can be executed in parallel.
- **Computation optimization**: Being a graph, a well-known data structure, it is possible to analyze it with the aim of optimizing execution speed. For example, it is possible to detect unused nodes in the graph and remove them, hence optimizing it for size; it is also possible to detect redundant operations or sub-optimal graphs and replace them with the best alternatives.
- **Portability**: A graph is a language-neutral and platform-neutral representation of computation. TensorFlow uses **Protocol Buffers** (**Protobuf**), which is a simple language-neutral, platform-neutral, and extensible mechanism for serializing structured data to store graphs. This, in practice, means that a model defined in Python using TensorFlow can be saved in its language-neutral representation (Protobuf) and then used inside another program written in another language.
- **Distributed execution**: Every graph's node can be placed on an independent device and on a different machine. TensorFlow will take care of the communication between the nodes and ensure that the execution of a graph is correct. Moreover, TensorFlow itself is able to partition a graph across multiple devices, knowing that certain operations perform better on certain devices.

Let's describe our first dataflow graph to compute a product and a sum between matrices and a vector; save the graphical representation and use TensorBoard to visualize it: (tf1)

```
import tensorflow as tf

# Build the graph
A = tf.constant([[1, 2], [3, 4]], dtype=tf.float32)
x = tf.constant([[0, 10], [0, 0.5]])
b = tf.constant([[1, -1]], dtype=tf.float32)
y = tf.add(tf.matmul(A, x), b, name="result") #y = Ax + b

writer = tf.summary.FileWriter("log/matmul", tf.get_default_graph())
writer.close()
```

In these few lines, there are a lot of peculiarities of TensorFlow and its way of building a computational graph. This graph represents the matrix product between the constant tensor identified by the A Python variable and the constant tensor identified by the x Python variable and the sum of the resulting matrix with the tensor identified by the b Python variable.

The result of the computation is represented by the y Python variable, also known as the output of the `tf.add` node named `result` in the graph.

 Please note the separation between the concept of a Python variable and a node in the graph: we're using Python only to describe the graph; the name of the Python variable means nothing in the graph definition.

Moreover, we created `tf.summary.SummaryWriter` to save a graphical representation of the graph we've built. The `writer` object has been created, specifying the path in which to store the representation (`log/matmul`) and a `tf.Graph` object obtained using the `tf.get_default_graph` function call that returns the default graph since at least one graph is always present in any TensorFlow application.

You can now visualize the graph using TensorBoard, the data visualization tool that comes free with TensorFlow. TensorBoard works by reading the log files placed in the specified --`logdir` and creates a web server so we're able to visualize our graph by using a browser.

To execute TensorBoard and visualize the graph, just type the command that follows and open a web browser at the address indicated by TensorBoard itself:

```
tensorboard --logdir log/matmul
```

The following screenshot shows the built graph, as seen in TensorBoard, and the detail of the node **result**. The screenshot allows an understanding of how TensorFlow represents the nodes and which features every node has:

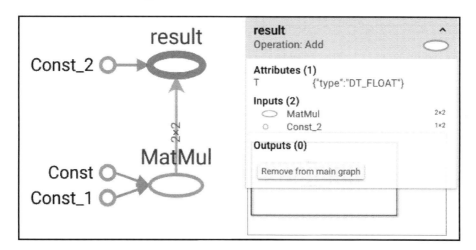

The computational graph that describes the operation y = Ax +b. The result node is highlighted in red and its details are shown in the right-hand column.

Please note that **we are just describing the graph**—the calls to the TensorFlow API are just adding operations (nodes) and connections (edges) among them; there is **no computation** performed in this phase. In TensorFlow 1.x, the following approach needs to be followed—static graph definition and execution, while this is no longer mandatory in 2.0.

Since the computational graph is the fundamental building block of the framework (in every version), it is mandatory to understand it in depth, since even after transitioning to 2.0, having an understanding of what's going on under the hood makes the difference (and it helps a lot with debugging!).

The main structure – tf.Graph

As stated in the previous section, there's no relation between the Python variables' name and the names of the nodes. Always keep in mind that TensorFlow is a C++ library and we're using Python to build a graph in an easy way. Python simplifies the graph description phase since it even creates a graph without the need to explicitly define it; in fact, there are two different ways to define a graph:

- **Implicit**: Just define a graph using the `tf.*` methods. If a graph is not explicitly defined, TensorFlow always defines a default `tf.Graph`, accessible by calling `tf.get_default_graph`. The implicit definition limits the expressive power of a TensorFlow application since it is constrained to using a single graph.
- **Explicit**: It is possible to explicitly define a computational graph and thus have more than one graph per application. This option has more expressive power, but is usually not needed since applications that need more than one graph are not common.

In order to explicitly define a graph, TensorFlow allows the creation of `tf.Graph` objects that, through the `as_default` method, create a context manager; every operation defined inside the context is placed inside the associated graph. In practice, a `tf.Graph` object defines a namespace for the `tf.Operation` objects it contains.

The second peculiarity of the `tf.Graph` structure is its **graph collections**. Every `tf.Graph` uses the collection mechanism to store metadata associated with the graph structure. A collection is uniquely identified by a key and its content is a list of objects/operations. The user does not usually need to worry about the existence of a collection since they are used by TensorFlow itself to correctly define a graph.

For example, when defining a parametric machine learning model, the graph must know which `tf.Variable` objects are the variables to update during the learning phase and which other variables are not part of the model but are something else (such as moving the mean/variance computed during the training process—these are variables but not trainable). In this case, when, as we will see in the following section, a `tf.Variable` is created, it is added by default to two collections: the global variable and trainable variable collections.

Graph definition – from tf.Operation to tf.Tensor

A dataflow graph is the representation of a computation where the nodes represent units of computation, and the edges represent the data consumed or produced by the computation.

In the context of `tf.Graph`, every API call defines `tf.Operation` (node) that can have multiple inputs and outputs `tf.Tensor` (edges). For instance, referring to our main example, when calling `tf.constant([[1, 2], [3, 4]], dtype=tf.float32)`, a new node (`tf.Operation`) named `Const` is added to the default `tf.Graph` inherited from the context. This node returns a `tf.Tensor` (edge) named `Const:0`.

Since each node in a graph is unique, if there is already a node named *Const* in the graph (that is the default name given to all the constants), TensorFlow will make it unique by appending the suffix '_1', '_2', and so on to the name. If a name is not provided, as in our example, TensorFlow gives a default name to each operation added and adds the suffix to make them unique in this case too.

The output `tf.Tensor` has the same name as the associated `tf.Operation`, with the addition of the *:ID* suffix. The ID is a progressive number that indicates how many outputs the operation produces. In the case of `tf.constant`, the output is just a single tensor, therefore *ID=0*; but there can be operations with more than one output, and in this case, the suffixes *:0, :1*, and so on are added to the `tf.Tensor` name generated by the operation.

It is also possible to add a name scope prefix to all operations created within a context—a context defined by the `tf.name_scope` call. The default name scope prefix is a / delimited list of names of all the active `tf.name_scope` context managers. In order to guarantee the uniqueness of the operations defined within the scopes and the uniqueness of the scopes themselves, the same suffix appending rule used for `tf.Operation` holds.

The following code snippet shows how our baseline example can be wrapped into a separate graph, how a second independent graph can be created in the same Python script, and how we can change the node names, adding a prefix, using `tf.name_scope`. First, we import the TensorFlow library:

(`tf1`)

```
import tensorflow as tf
```

Then, we define two `tf.Graph` objects (the scoping system allows you to use multiple graphs easily):

```
g1 = tf.Graph()
g2 = tf.Graph()

with g1.as_default():
    A = tf.constant([[1, 2], [3, 4]], dtype=tf.float32)
    x = tf.constant([[0, 10], [0, 0.5]])
    b = tf.constant([[1, -1]], dtype=tf.float32)
    y = tf.add(tf.matmul(A, x), b, name="result")

with g2.as_default():
    with tf.name_scope("scope_a"):
        x = tf.constant(1, name="x")
        print(x)
    with tf.name_scope("scope_b"):
        x = tf.constant(10, name="x")
        print(x)
    y = tf.constant(12)
    z = x * y
```

Then, we define two summary writers. We need to use two different `tf.summary.FileWriter` objects to log two separate graphs.

```
writer = tf.summary.FileWriter("log/two_graphs/g1", g1)
writer = tf.summary.FileWriter("log/two_graphs/g2", g2)
writer.close()
```

Run the example and use TensorBoard to visualize the two graphs, using the left-hand column on TensorBoard to switch between "runs."

Nodes with the same name, x in the example, can live together in the same graph, but they have to be under different scopes. In fact, being under different scopes makes the nodes completely independent and completely different objects. The node name, in fact, is not only the parameter name passed to the operation definition, but its full path, complete with all of the prefixes.

In fact, running the script, the output is as follows:

```
Tensor("scope_a/x:0", shape=(), dtype=int32)
Tensor("scope_b/x:0", shape=(), dtype=int32)
```

As we can see, the full names are different and we also have other information about the tensors produced. In general, every tensor has a name, a type, a rank, and a shape:

- The **name** uniquely identifies the tensor in the computational graphs. Using `tf.name_scope`, we can prefix tensor names, thus changing their full path. We can also specify the name using the `name` attribute of every `tf.*` API call.
- The **type** is the data type of the tensor; for example, `tf.float32`, `tf.int8`, and so on.
- The **rank**, in the TensorFlow world (this is different from the strictly mathematical definition), is just the number of dimensions of a tensor; for example, a scalar has rank 0, a vector has rank 1, a matrix has rank 2, and so on.
- The **shape** is the number of elements in each dimension; for example, a scalar has rank 0 and an empty shape of `()`, a vector has rank 1 and a shape of `(D0)`, a matrix has rank 2 and a shape of `(D0, D1)`, and so on.

Sometimes, it is possible to see a shape with a dimension of -1. This is a particular syntax that tells TensorFlow to infer from the other, well-defined, dimensions of the tensor which value should be placed in that position. Usually, a negative shape is used in the `tf.reshape` operation, which is able to change the shape of a tensor if the requested one is compatible with the number of elements of the tensor.

When defining a tensor, instead, it is possible to see one or more dimensions with the value of `None`. In this case, the full shape definition is delegated to the execution phase, since using `None` instructs TensorFlow to expect a value in that position known only at runtime.

Being a C++ library, TensorFlow is strictly statically typed. This means that the type of every operation/tensor must be known at graph definition time. Moreover, this also means that it is not possible to execute an operation among incompatible types.

Looking closely at the baseline example, it is possible to see that both matrix multiplication and addition operations are performed on tensors with the same type, `tf.float32`. The tensors identified by the Python variables A and b have been defined, making the type clear in the operation definition, while tensor x has the same `tf.float32` type; but in this case, it has been inferred by the Python bindings, which are able to look inside the constant value and infer the type to use when creating the operation.

Another peculiarity of Python bindings is their simplification in the definition of some common mathematical operations using operator overloading. The most common mathematical operations have their counterpart as `tf.Operation`; therefore, using operator overloading to simplify the graph definition is natural.

The following table shows the available operators overloaded in the TensorFlow Python API:

Python operator	Operation name
__neg__	unary –
__abs__	abs()
__invert__	unary ~
__add__	binary +
__sub__	binary –
__mul__	binary elementwise *
__floordiv__	binary //
__truediv__	binary /
__mod__	binary %
__pow__	binary **
__and__	binary &
__or__	binary |
__xor__	binary ^
__le__	binary <
__lt__	binary <=
__gt__	binary >
__ge__	binary <=
__matmul__	binary @

Operator overloading allows a faster graph definition and is completely equivalent to their `tf.*` API call (for example, using `__add__` is the same as using the `tf.add` function). There is only one case in which it is beneficial to use the TensorFlow API call instead of the associated operator overload: when a name for the operation is needed. Usually, when defining a graph, we're interested in giving meaningful names only to the input and output nodes, while any other node can just be automatically named by TensorFlow.

Using overloaded operators, we can't specify the node name and thus the output tensor's name. In fact, in the baseline example, we defined the addition operation using the `tf.add` method, because we wanted to give the output tensor a meaningful name (result). In practice, these two lines are equivalent:

```
# Original example, using only API calls
y = tf.add(tf.matmul(A, x), b, name="result")

# Using overloaded operators
y = A @ x + b
```

As mentioned at the beginning of this section, TensorFlow itself can place specific nodes on different devices better suited to the operation execution. The framework is so flexible that it allows the user to manually place operations on different local and remote devices just using the `tf.device` context manager.

Graph placement – tf.device

`tf.device` creates a context manager that matches a device. The function allows the user to request that all operations created within the context it creates are placed on the same device. The devices identified by `tf.device` are more than physical devices; in fact, it is capable of identifying devices such as remote servers, remote devices, remote workers, and different types of physical devices (GPUs, CPUs, and TPUs). It is required to follow a device specification to correctly instruct the framework to use the desired device. A device specification has the following form:

```
/job:<JOB_NAME>/task:<TASK_INDEX>/device:<DEVICE_TYPE>:<DEVICE_INDEX>
```

Broken down as follows:

- `<JOB_NAME>` is an alpha-numeric string that does not start with a number
- `<DEVICE_TYPE>` is a registered device type (such as GPU or CPU)

- `<TASK_INDEX>` is a non-negative integer representing the index of the task in the job named `<JOB_NAME>`
- `<DEVICE_NAME>` is a non-negative integer representing the index of the device; for example, `/GPU:0` is the first GPU

There is no need to specify every part of a device specification. For example, when running a single-machine configuration with a single GPU, you might use `tf.device` to pin some operations to the CPU and GPU.

We can thus extend our baseline example to place the operations on the device we choose. Thus, it is possible to place the matrix multiplication on the GPU, since it is hardware optimized for this kind of operation, while keeping all the other operations on the CPU. Please note that since this is only a graph description, there's no need to physically have a GPU or to use the `tensorflow-gpu` package. First, we import the TensorFlow library:

`(tf1)`

```
import tensorflow as tf
```

Now, use the context manager to place operations on different devices, first, on the first CPU of the local machine:

```
with tf.device("/CPU:0"):
    A = tf.constant([[1, 2], [3, 4]], dtype=tf.float32)
    x = tf.constant([[0, 10], [0, 0.5]])
    b = tf.constant([[1, -1]], dtype=tf.float32)
```

Then, on the first GPU of the local machine:

```
with tf.device("/GPU:0"):
    mul = A @ x
```

When the device is not forced by a scope, TensorFlow decides which device is better to place the operation on:

```
y = mul + b
```

Then, we define the summary writer:

```
writer = tf.summary.FileWriter("log/matmul_optimized",
tf.get_default_graph())
writer.close()
```

If we look at the generated graph, we'll see that it is identical to the one generated by the baseline example, with two main differences:

- Instead of having a meaningful name for the output tensor, we have just the default one
- Clicking on the matrix multiplication node, it is possible to see (in TensorBoard) that this operation must be executed in the first GPU of the local machine

The `matmul` node is placed on the first GPU of the local machine, while any other operation is executed in the CPU. TensorFlow takes care of communication among different devices in a transparent manner:

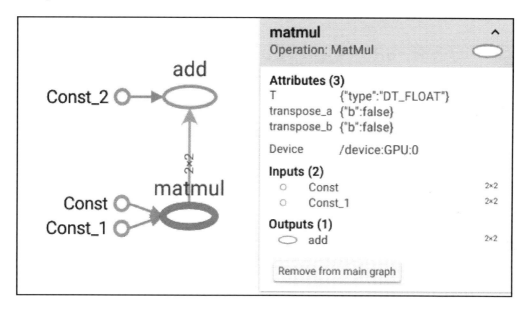

Please also note that even though we have defined constant operations that produce constant tensors, their values are not visible among the attributes of the node nor among the input/output properties.

When using the static-graph and session execution parading, the execution is completely separated from the graph definition. This is no longer true in eager execution, but since, in this chapter, the focus is on the TensorFlow architecture, it is worth also focusing on the execution part using `tf.Session`: in TensorFlow 2.0, the session is still present, but hidden, as we will see in the next chapter, `Chapter 4`, *TensorFlow 2.0 Architecture*.

Graph execution – tf.Session

`tf.Session` is a class that TensorFlow provides to represent a connection between the Python program and the C++ runtime.

The `tf.Session` object is the only object able to communicate directly with the hardware (through the C++ runtime), placing operations on the specified devices, using the local and distributed TensorFlow runtime, with the goal of concretely building the defined graph. The `tf.Session` object is highly optimized and, once correctly built, caches `tf.Graph` in order to speed up its execution.

Being the owner of physical resources, the `tf.Session` object must be used as a file descriptor to do the following:

- Acquire the resources by creating a `tf.Session` (the equivalent of the `open` operating system call)
- Use the resources (the equivalent of using the `read/write` operation on the file descriptor)
- Release the resources with `tf.Session.close` (the equivalent of the `close` call)

Typically, instead of manually defining a session and taking care of its creation and destruction, a session is used through a context manager that automatically closes the session at the block exit.

The constructor of `tf.Session` is fairly complex and highly customizable since it is used to configure and create the execution of the computational graph.

In the simplest and most common scenario, we just want to use the current local hardware to execute the previously described computational graph as follows:

(tf1)

```
# The context manager opens the session
with tf.Session() as sess:
    # Use the session to execute operations
    sess.run(...)
# Out of the context, the session is closed and the resources released
```

There are more complex scenarios in which we wouldn't want to use the local execution engine, but use a remote TensorFlow server that gives access to all the devices it controls. This is possible by specifying the `target` parameter of `tf.Session` just by using the URL (`grpc://`) of the server:

(tf1)

```
# the IP and port of the TensorFlow server
ip = "192.168.1.90"
port = 9877
with tf.Session(f"grpc://{ip}:{port}") as sess:
    sess.run(...)
```

By default, the `tf.Session` will capture and use the default `tf.Graph` object, but when working with multiple graphs, it is possible to specify which graph to use by using the `graph` parameter. It's easy to understand why working with multiple graphs is unusual, since even the `tf.Session` object is able to work with only a single graph at a time.

The third and last parameter of the `tf.Session` object is the hardware/network configuration specified through the `config` parameter. The configuration is specified through the `tf.ConfigProto` object, which is able to control the behavior of the session. The `tf.ConfigProto` object is fairly complex and rich with options, the most common and widely used being the following two (all the others are options used in distributed, complex environments):

- `allow_soft_placement`: If set to `True`, it enables a soft device placement. Not every operation can be placed indifferently on the CPU and GPU, because the GPU implementation of the operation may be missing, for example, and using this option allows TensorFlow to ignore the device specification made via `tf.device` and place the operation on the correct device when an unsupported device is specified at graph definition time.

- `gpu_options.allow_growth`: If set to `True`, it changes the TensorFlow GPU memory allocator; the default allocator allocates all the available GPU memory as soon as the `tf.Session` is created, while the allocator used when `allow_growth` is `True` gradually increases the amount of memory allocated. The default allocator works in this way because, in production environments, the physical resources are completely dedicated to the `tf.Session` execution, while, in a standard research environment, the resources are usually shared (the GPU is a resource that can be used by other processes while the TensorFlow `tf.Session` is in execution).

The baseline example can now be extended to not only define a graph, but to proceed on to an effective construction and the execution of it:

```
import tensorflow as tf
import numpy as np

A = tf.constant([[1, 2], [3, 4]], dtype=tf.float32)
x = tf.constant([[0, 10], [0, 0.5]])
b = tf.constant([[1, -1]], dtype=tf.float32)
y = tf.add(tf.matmul(A, x), b, name="result")

writer = tf.summary.FileWriter("log/matmul", tf.get_default_graph())
writer.close()

with tf.Session() as sess:
    A_value, x_value, b_value = sess.run([A, x, b])
    y_value = sess.run(y)

    # Overwrite
    y_new = sess.run(y, feed_dict={b: np.zeros((1, 2))})

print(f"A: {A_value}\nx: {x_value}\nb: {b_value}\n\ny: {y_value}")
print(f"y_new: {y_new}")
```

The first `sess.run` call evaluates the three `tf.Tensor` objects, `A`, `x`, `b`, and returns their values as `numpy` arrays.

The second call, `sess.run(y)`, works in the following way:

1. `y` is an output node of an operation: backtrack to its inputs
2. Recursively backtrack through every node until all the nodes without a parent are found
3. Evaluate the input; in this case, the `A`, `x`, `b` tensors
4. Follow the dependency graph: the multiplication operation must be executed before the addition of its result with `b`
5. Execute the matrix multiplication
6. Execute the addition

The addition is the entry point of the graph resolution (Python variable `y`) and the computation ends.

The first print call, therefore, produces the following output:

```
A:  [[1.  2.]
     [3.  4.]]
x:  [[ 0.  10. ]
     [ 0.  0.5]]
b:  [[ 1.  -1.]]
y:  [[ 1.  10.]
     [ 1.  31.]]
```

The third `sess.run` call shows how it is possible to inject into the computational graph values from the outside, as `numpy` arrays, overwriting a node. The `feed_dict` parameter allows you to do this: usually, inputs are passed to the graph using the `feed_dict` parameter and through the overwriting of the `tf.placeholder` operation created exactly for this purpose.

`tf.placeholder` is just a placeholder created with the aim of throwing an error when values from the outside are not injected inside the graph. However, the `feed_dict` parameter is more than just a way to feed the placeholders. In fact, the preceding example shows how it can be used to overwrite any node. The result produced by the overwriting of the node identified by the Python variable, `b`, with a `numpy` array that must be compatible, in terms of both type and shape, with the overwritten variable, is as follows:

```
y_new:  [[ 0.  11.]
         [ 0.  32.]]
```

The baseline example has been updated in order to show the following:

- How to build a graph
- How to save a graphical representation of the graph
- How to create a session and execute the defined graph

So far, we have used graphs with constant values and used the `feed_dict` parameter of the `sess.run` call to overwrite a node parameter. However, since TensorFlow is designed to solve complex problems, the concept of `tf.Variable` has been introduced: every parametric machine learning model can be defined and trained with TensorFlow.

Variables in static graphs

A variable is an object that maintains a state in the graph across multiple calls to `sess.run`. A variable is added to `tf.Graph` by constructing an instance of the `tf.Variable` class.

A variable is completely defined by the pair (type, shape), and variables created by calling `tf.Variable` can be used as input for other nodes in the graph; in fact, the `tf.Tensor` and `tf.Variable` objects can be used in the same manner when building a graph.

Variables have more attributes with respect to tensors: a variable object must be initialized and thus have its initializer; a variable is, by default, added to the global variables and trainable variable graph collections. If a variable is set as non-trainable, it can be used by the graph to store the state, but the optimizers will ignore it when performing the learning process.

There are two ways of declaring a variable in a graph: `tf.Variable` and `tf.get_variable`. Using `tf.Variable` is easier but less powerful—the second way is more complex to use, but has more expressive power.

tf.Variable

Creating a variable by calling `tf.Variable` will always create a new variable and it always requires an initial value to be specified. In the following lines, the creation of a variable named `W` with shape `(5, 5, size_in, size_out)` and a variable, `B`, with shape `(size_out)` is shown:

```
w = tf.Variable(tf.truncated_normal([5, 5, size_in, size_out], stddev=0.1),
name="W")
b = tf.Variable(tf.constant(0.1, shape=[size_out]), name="B")
```

The `w` initial value is generated by the `tf.truncated_normal` operation, which samples from a normal distribution with 0 mean and a standard deviation of 0.1 the `5 x 5 x size_in x size_out` (total number) values required to initialize the tensor, while `b` is initialized using the constant value of 0.1 generated by the `tf.constant` operation.

Since each call to `tf.Variable` creates a new variable in the graph, it is the perfect candidate for the creation of layers: every layer (for example, a convolutional layer/a fully connected layer) definition requires the creation of a new variable. For instance, the following lines of code show the definition of two functions that can be used to define a convolutional neural network and/or a fully connected neural network:

(tf1)

The first function creates a 2D convolutional layer (with a 5 x 5 kernel) followed by a max-pool operation to halve the output's spatial extent:

```
def conv2D(input, size_in, size_out, name="conv"):
"""Define a 2D convolutional layer + max pooling.
Args:
    input: Input tensor: 4D.
    size_in: it could be inferred by the input (input.shape[-1])
    size_out: the number of convolutional kernel to learn
    name: the name of the operation, using name_scope.
Returns:
    The result of the convolution as specified + a max pool operation
    that halves the spatial resolution.
"""
    with tf.name_scope(name):
        w = tf.Variable(tf.truncated_normal([5, 5, size_in, size_out],
stddev=0.1), name="W")
        b = tf.Variable(tf.constant(0.1, shape=[size_out]), name="B")
        conv = tf.nn.conv2d(input, w, strides=[1, 1, 1, 1], padding="SAME")
        act = tf.nn.relu(conv + b)
        tf.summary.histogram("w", w)
        tf.summary.histogram("b", b)
        return tf.nn.max_pool(act, ksize=[1, 2, 2, 1], strides=[1, 2, 2,
1], padding="SAME")
```

The second function defines a fully connected layer:

(tf1)

```
def fc(input, size_in, size_out, name="fc"):
"""Define a fully connected layer.
Args:
    input: Input tensor: 2D.
    size_in: it could be inferred by the input (input.shape[-1])
    size_out: the number of output neurons kernel to learn
    name: the name of the operation, using name_scope.
Returns:
    The linear neurons output.
"""
```

Both functions also use the `tf.summary` module to log the histograms of the weight, bias, and activation values, which can change during training.

The call to a `tf.summary` method automatically adds the summaries to a global collection that is used by `tf.Saver` and `tf.SummaryWriter` objects to log every summary value in the TensorBoard log directory:

(tf1)

```
with tf.name_scope(name):
    w = tf.Variable(tf.truncated_normal([size_in, size_out], stddev=0.1),
name="W")
    b = tf.Variable(tf.constant(0.1, shape=[size_out]), name="B")
    act = tf.matmul(input, w) + b
    tf.summary.histogram("w", w)
    tf.summary.histogram("b", b)
    return act
```

A layer definition made in this way is perfect for the most common scenarios in which a user wants to define a deep learning model composed by a stack of several layers and train it given a single input that flows from the first to the last layer.

What if, instead, the training phase is not standard and there is the need to share the variable's values among different inputs?

We need to use the TensorFlow feature called **variable sharing,** which is not possible using a layer definition made with `tf.Variable`, so we have to instead use the most powerful method, `tf.get_variable`.

tf.get_variable

Like `tf.Variable`, `tf.get_variable` also allows the definition and creation of new variables. The main difference is that its behavior changes if the variable has already been defined.

`tf.get_variable` is always used together with `tf.variable_scope` since it enables the variable sharing capabilities of `tf.get_variable` through its `reuse` parameter. The following example clarifies the concept:

(tf1)

```
with tf.variable_scope("scope"):
    a = tf.get_variable("v", [1]) # a.name == "scope/v:0"
with tf.variable_scope("scope"):
    b = tf.get_variable("v", [1]) # ValueError: Variable scope/v:0 already
```

```
exists
with tf.variable_scope("scope", reuse=True):
    c = tf.get_variable("v", [1]) # c.name == "scope/v:0"
```

In the preceding example, the Python variables a and c point to the same graph variable, named scope/v:0. Hence, a layer that uses tf.get_variable to define variables can be used in conjunction with tf.variable_scope to define or reuse the layer's variables. This is extremely useful and powerful when training generative models using adversarial training, as we will see in Chapter 9, *Generative Adversarial Networks*.

Different from tf.Variable, in this case, we can't pass an initial value in a raw way (passing the value directly as input to the call method); we always have to explicitly use an initializer. The previously defined layer can be written using tf.get_variable (and this is the recommended way to define variables) as follows:

(tf1)

```
def conv2D(input, size_in, size_out):
    w = tf.get_variable(
        'W', [5, 5, size_in, size_out],
        initializer=tf.truncated_normal_initializer(stddev=0.1))
    b = tf.get_variable(
        'B', [size_out], initializer=tf.constant_initializer(0.1))
    conv = tf.nn.conv2d(input, w, strides=[1, 1, 1, 1], padding="SAME")
    act = tf.nn.relu(conv + b)
    tf.summary.histogram("w", w)
    tf.summary.histogram("b", b)
    return tf.nn.max_pool(
        act, ksize=[1, 2, 2, 1], strides=[1, 2, 2, 1], padding="SAME")

def fc(input, size_in, size_out):
    w = tf.get_variable(
        'W', [size_in, size_out],
        initializer=tf.truncated_normal_initializer(stddev=0.1))
    b = tf.get_variable(
        'b', [size_out], initializer=tf.constant_initializer(0.1))
    act = tf.matmul(input, w) + b
    tf.summary.histogram("w", w)
    tf.summary.histogram("b", b)
    return act
```

Invoking `conv2D` or `fc` defines the variables needed to define a layer in the current scope; hence, to define two convolutional layers without having naming conflicts, `tf.variable_scope` must be used:

```
input = tf.placeholder(tf.float32, (None, 28,28,1))
with tf.variable_scope("first)":
    conv1 = conv2d(input, input.shape[-1].value, 10)
with tf.variable_scope("second"): #no conflict, variables under the second/
scope
    conv2 = conv2d(conv1, conv1.shape[-1].value, 1)
# and so on...
```

Manually defining layers is a good exercise, and knowing that TensorFlow has all the primitives required to define every ML layer is something every ML practitioner should know. However, manually defining every single layer is tedious and repetitive (we need fully connected, convolutional, dropout, and batch normalization layers in almost every project), and, for this reason, TensorFlow already comes with a module named `tf.layers`, which contains all the most common and widely used layers, defined using `tf.get_variable` under the hood, and therefore, layers can be used in conjunction with `tf.variable_scope` to share their variables.

Model definition and training

Disclaimer: the layer module has been completely removed in TensorFlow 2.0, and the layer definition using `tf.keras.layers` is the new standard; however, an overview of `tf.layers` is still worth reading because it shows how reasoning layer by layer to define deep models is the natural way to proceed and it also gives us an idea of the reasons behind the migration from `tf.layers` to `tf.keras.layers`.

Defining models with tf.layers

As shown in the previous section, TensorFlow provides all the primitive features to define a neural network layer: the user should take care when defining the variables, the operation nodes, the activation functions, and the logging, and define a proper interface to handle all cases (adding, or not, the bias term, adding regularization to the layer parameters, and so on).

The tf.layers module in TensorFlow 1.x and the tf.keras.layers module in
TensorFlow 2.0 provide an excellent API to define machine learning models in a convenient
and powerful way. Every layer in tf.layers, defines variables using tf.get_variable,
and therefore, each layer defined in this way can use the variable-sharing features provided
by tf.variable_scope.

The previously manually defined 2D convolution and fully connected layers are clearly
present and well-defined in tf.layers and using them to define a LeNet-like CNN is
easy, as shown. First, we define a convolutional neural network for classification:

(tf1)

```
def define_cnn(x, n_classes, reuse, is_training):
    """Defines a convolutional neural network for classification.
    Args:
        x: a batch of images: 4D tensor.
        n_classes: the number of classes, hence, the number of output
neurons.
        reuse: the `tf.variable_scope` reuse parameter.
        is_training: boolean variable that indicates if the model is in
training.
    Returns:
        The output layer.
    """
    with tf.variable_scope('cnn', reuse=reuse):
        # Convolution Layer with 32 learneable filters 5x5 each
        # followed by max-pool operation that halves the spatial extent.
        conv1 = tf.layers.conv2d(x, 32, 5, activation=tf.nn.relu)
        conv1 = tf.layers.max_pooling2d(conv1, 2, 2)

        # Convolution Layer with 64 learneable filters 3x3 each.
        # As above, max pooling to halve.
        conv2 = tf.layers.conv2d(conv1, 64, 3, activation=tf.nn.relu)
        conv2 = tf.layers.max_pooling2d(conv2, 2, 2)
```

Then, we flatten the data to a 1D vector so that we can use a fully connected layer. Please note how the new shape is computed and the negative dimension in the batch size position:

```
        shape = (-1,conv2.shape[1].value * conv2.shape[2].value *
conv2.shape[3].value)
        fc1 = tf.reshape(conv2, shape)

        # Fully connected layer
        fc1 = tf.layers.dense(fc1, 1024)
        # Apply (inverted) dropout when in training phase.
        fc1 = tf.layers.dropout(fc1, rate=0.5, training=is_training)

        # Prediction: linear neurons
        out = tf.layers.dense(fc1, n_classes)

    return out

input = tf.placeholder(tf.float32, (None, 28, 28, 1))
logits = define_cnn(input, 10, reuse=False, is_training=True)
```

Being high-level wrappers on primitive TensorFlow operations, there is no need to detail what every layer does in this book since it is pretty clear from the layer names themselves and from the documentation. The reader is invited to become familiar with the official TensorFlow documentation, and, in particular, to try to define their own classification model using layers: `https://www.tensorflow.org/versions/r1.15/api_docs/python/tf/layers`.

Using the baseline example and replacing the graph with this CNN definition, using TensorFlow, it is possible to see how every layer has its own scope, how the layers are connected among them, and, as shown in the second diagram, by double-clicking on a layer, it is possible to see its contents to understand how it is implemented without having to look at the code.

The following diagram shows the architecture of the defined LeNet-like CNN. The whole architecture is placed under the *cnn* scope; the input node is a placeholder. It is possible to visualize how the layers are connected and how TensorFlow added the _1 suffix to blocks with the same name to avoid conflicts:

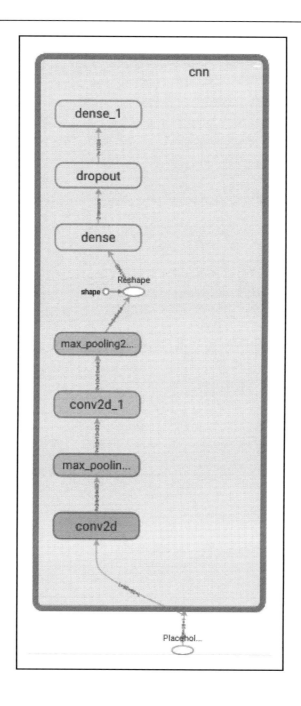

Double-clicking on the `conv2d` block allows you to analyze how the various components defined by the layers are connected to each other. Please note how, different from our layer implementation, the TensorFlow developers used an operation named `BiasAdd` to add the bias and not the raw `Add` operation. The behavior is the same, but the semantics are clearer:

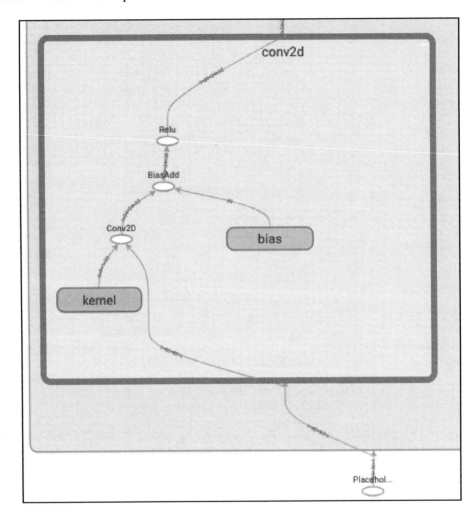

As an exercise, you can try to extend the baseline by defining a CNN like the one just presented to visualize and understand the layer structure.

We always have to keep in mind that TensorFlow 1.x follows the graph definition and session execution approach. This means that even the training phase should be described within the same `tf.Graph` object before being executed.

Automatic differentiation – losses and optimizers

TensorFlow uses automatic differentiation—a differentiator is an object that contains all the rules required to build a new graph that takes the derivative of each node it traverses. The `tf.train` module in TensorFlow 1.x contains the most widely used type of differentiator, called optimizers here. In the module, among the other optimizers, it is possible to find the ADAM optimizer as `tf.train.AdamOptimizer` and the standard gradient descent optimizer as `tf.train.GradientDescentOptimizer`. Each optimizer is an object that implements a common interface. The interface standardizes how to use an optimizer to train a model. Performing a mini-batch gradient descent step is just a matter of executing a train operation in a Python loop; that is, an operation returned by the `.minimize` method of every optimizer.

As you will know from the theory presented in the previous chapter, *Chapter 2, Neural Networks and Deep Learning,* to train a classifier using cross-entropy loss, it is necessary to one-hot encode the labels. TensorFlow has a module, `tf.losses`, that contains the most commonly used loss functions that are also capable of performing the one-hot encoding of labels by themselves. Moreover, every loss function expects the `logits` tensor as input; that is, the linear output of the model without the application of the softmax/sigmoid activation function. The name of the `logits` tensor is a TensorFlow design choice: it is called in this way even if no sigmoidal transformation has been applied to it (a better choice would be naming this parameter `unscaled_logits`).

The reason for this choice is to let the user focus on the network design without having to worry about the numerical instability problems that could arise when computing certain loss functions; in fact, every loss defined in the `tf.losses` module is numerically stable.

In order to have a complete understanding of the topic and to show that an optimizer just builds a graph connected to the previous one (it only adds nodes in practice), it is possible to mix the baseline example that logs the graph together with the example that defines the network with its loss function and an optimizer.

Thus, the previous example can be modified as follows. To define the input placeholder for the labels, we can define the loss function (`tf.losses.sparse_softmax_cross_entropy`) and instantiate the ADAM optimizer to minimize it:

```
# Input placeholders: input is the cnn input, labels is the loss input.
input = tf.placeholder(tf.float32, (None, 28, 28, 1))
labels = tf.placeholder(tf.int32, (None,))

logits = define_cnn(input, 10, reuse=False, is_training=True)
# Numerically stable loss
```

```
loss = tf.losses.sparse_softmax_cross_entropy(labels, logits)
# Instantiate the Optimizer and get the operation to use to minimize the
loss
train_op = tf.train.AdamOptimizer().minimize(loss)

# As in the baseline example, log the graph
writer = tf.summary.FileWriter("log/graph_loss", tf.get_default_graph())
writer.close()
```

TensorBoard allows us to visualize the graph built as shown:

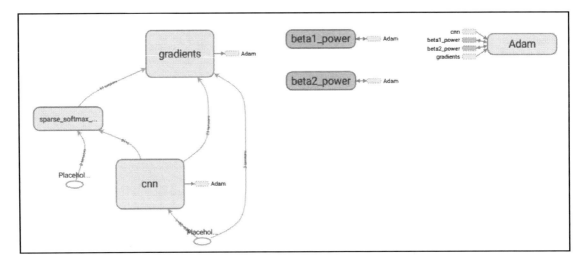

The preceding diagram shows the structure of the graph when a loss function is defined, and the `.minimize` method is invoked.

The ADAM optimizer is a separate block that only has inputs—the model (*cnn*), the gradients, and the nontrainable *beta1* and *beta2* parameters used by ADAM (and specified in its constructor, left at their default values in this case). The gradients, as you will know from the theory, are computed with respect to the model parameters to minimize the loss function: the graph on the left perfectly describes this construction. The gradient block created by the minimize method invocation is a named scope, and as such, it can be analyzed by double-clicking on it just like any other block in TensorBoard.

The following graph shows the gradient block expanded: it contains a mirrored structure of the graph used for the forward model. Every block the optimizer uses to optimize the parameters is an input of the gradient block. The gradients are the input of the optimizer (ADAM):

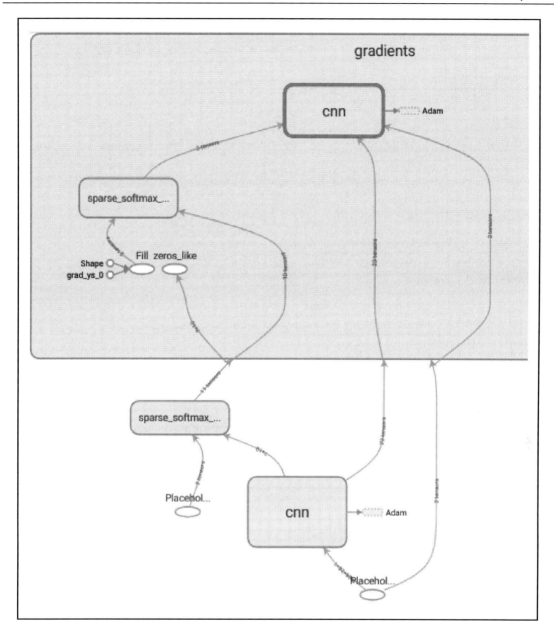

Following on from the theory, the differentiator (optimizer) created a new graph that mirrors the original graph; this second graph, inside the gradient block, performs the gradient calculation. The optimizer uses the gradients produced to apply the variables update rule it defines and implements the learning process.

A brief recap on what we have seen so far for the static-graph and session execution is as follows:

1. Define the model inputs using placeholders or other optimized methods, as shown in later chapters
2. Define the model as a function of the input
3. Define the loss function as a function of the model output
4. Define the optimizer and invoke the `.minimize` method to define the gradient computation graph

These four steps allow us to define a simple training loop and train our model. However, we're skipping some important parts:

- Model performance measurement on training and validation sets
- Saving the model parameters
- Model selection

Moreover, since the input is defined using placeholders, we have to take care of everything related to the input: splitting the dataset, creating the mini-batches, keeping track of the training epochs, and so on.

TensorFlow 2.0 with `tfds` (TensorFlow Datasets) simplified and standardized the input pipeline definition, as we will see in later chapters; however, having a clear idea about what happens under the hood is always an advantage, therefore, it's a good exercise for the reader to continue with the following low-level use of placeholders in order to have a better understanding of the problems `tfds` solves.

So far, you should have a clear understanding of the operations that must be executed in a computational graph, and you should have understood that Python is used only to build a graph and to do non-learning related operations (hence, it's not Python that performs the variable update, but it is the execution within a session of a Python variable that represents the training operation that triggers all the required operations to make the model learn).

In the next section, the previous CNN example is extended, adding all the functionality on the Python-side that is required to perform model selection (saving the model, measuring performance, making the training loop, and feeding the input placeholders).

Interacting with the graph using Python

Python is the language of choice to train a TensorFlow model; however, after defining a computational graph in Python, there are no constraints regarding using it with another language to execute the learning operations defined.

 Always keep in mind that we use Python to define a graph and this definition can be exported in a portable and language-agnostic representation (Protobuf)—this representation can then be used in any other language to create a concrete graph and using it within a session.

The TensorFlow Python API is complete and easy to use. Therefore, we can extend the previous example to measure the accuracy (defining the accuracy measurement operation in the graph) and use this metric to perform model selection.

Selecting the best model means storing the model parameters at the end of each epoch and moving the parameters that produced the highest metric value in a different folder. To do this, we have to define the input pipeline in Python and use the Python interpreter to interact with the graph.

Feeding placeholders

As mentioned in the previous section, placeholders are the easiest to use but are also the least performant and most error-prone way to build a data input pipeline. In later chapters, a better, highly efficient solution will be presented. This highly efficient solution has the complete input pipeline completely defined inside the graph. However, the placeholder solution is not only the easiest but also the only one that can be used in certain scenarios (for example, when training reinforcement learning agents, input via a placeholder is the preferred solution).

In Chapter 1, *What is Machine Learning?*, the Fashion-MNIST dataset was described, and we're now going to use it as the input dataset for our model—the previously defined CNN will be used to classify the fashion items.

Fortunately, we don't have to worry about the dataset download and processing part, since TensorFlow, in its keras module, already has a function that downloads and processes the dataset for us to have the training images and the test images together with their labels in the expected form (28 x 28 images):

(tf1)

```
from tensorflow.keras.datasets import fashion_mnist
```

```
(train_x, train_y), (test_x, test_y) = fashion_mnist.load_data()
# Scale input in [-1, 1] range
train_x = train_x / 255. * 2 - 1
test_x = test_x / 255. * 2 - 1
# Add the last 1 dimension, so to have images 28x28x1
train_x = np.expand_dims(train_x, -1)
test_x = np.expand_dims(test_x, -1)
```

train_x and test_x contain the whole dataset—training a model using a single batch containing the complete dataset is not tractable on a standard computer; therefore, using Python, we have to take care when splitting the dataset and building mini-batches to make the training process affordable.

Let's say we want to train the model for 10 epochs using batches of 32 elements each; it is easy to compute the number of batches needed to train the model for an epoch and then run a training loop that iterates over the batches:

(tf1)

```
epochs = 10
batch_size = 32
nr_batches_train = int(train_x.shape[0] / batch_size)
print(f"Batch size: {batch_size}")
print(f"Number of batches per epoch: {nr_batches_train}")
```

Of course, since we need to perform model selection, we need to first define an operation that computes the accuracy as a function of the model and the input and then use the tf.summary.SummaryWriter object to write the train and validation accuracy on the same graph.

Writing summaries

The baseline example already uses a tf.summary.SummaryWriter object to write the graph in the log directory and make it appear in the graph section of TensorBoard. However, SummaryWriter can be used to write not only the graph but also a histogram, scalar values, distributions, log images, and many other data types.

The tf.summary package is filled with easy-to-use methods to log any data. For instance, we are interested in logging the loss value; the loss value is a scalar and, therefore, tf.summary.scalar is the method to use. The package is well-documented, and you should take the time to explore it: https://www.tensorflow.org/versions/r1.15/api_docs/python/tf.

To extend the previous example, we can define the accuracy operation as a function of the input placeholders. In this way, we can run the same operation, changing the input when needed. For instance, we could be interested in measuring both the training and validation accuracy at the end of each training epoch.

The same reasoning applies to the loss value: defining the loss as a function of the model and the model as a function of a placeholder, we are able to measure how the loss changes on the training and validation input just by changing the input:

(tf1)

```
# Define the accuracy operation over a batch
predictions = tf.argmax(logits, 1)
# correct predictions: [BATCH_SIZE] tensor
correct_predictions = tf.equal(labels, predictions)
accuracy = tf.reduce_mean(
    tf.cast(correct_predictions, tf.float32), name="accuracy")

# Define the scalar summarie operation that once executed produce
# an input for the tf.train.SummaryWriter.

accuracy_summary = tf.summary.scalar("accuracy", accuracy)
loss_summary = tf.summary.scalar("loss", loss)
```

A single `tf.train.FileWriter` object is associated with a unique path on the disk, called **run**. A run represents a different configuration of the current experiment. For example, the default run is usually the training phase. At this phase, hence at this run, the metrics attached (loss, accuracy, logs of images, and so on) are measured during the training phase, on the training set.

A different run can be created by creating a new `tf.train.FileWriter` with a different path associated with it, but with the same root of the other (training) `FileWriter`. In this way, using TensorBoard, we can visualize different curves on the same graph; for example, visualizing the validation accuracy and the training accuracy on the same plot. This feature is of extreme importance when analyzing the behavior of an experiment and when you are interested in comparing different experiments at a glance.

Hence, since we want to visualize the training and the validation curves on the same plot, we can create two different writers:

```
writer = tf.summary.FileWriter("log/graph_loss", tf.get_default_graph())
validation_summary_writer = tf.summary.FileWriter(
    "log/graph_loss/validation")
```

The first one is the train phase writer; the second, the validation phase one.

Now, potentially, we could measure the validation accuracy and the training accuracy, just by running the `accuracy` tensor, changing the input placeholder values accordingly; this means that we are already able to perform model selection: the model with the highest validation accuracy is the one to select.

To save the model parameters, a `tf.Saver` object is required.

Saving model parameters and model selection

Saving model parameters is important since it's the only way to continue to train a model after an interruption, and the only way to checkpoint a model status for any reason—training finished, the model reached the best validation performance.

`tf.Saver` is the object the TensorFlow Python API provides to save the current model variables. Please note that the `tf.Saver` object saves the variables only and not the graph structure!

To save both the graph structure and variables, a `SavedModel` object is required; however, since the `SavedModel` object is more connected with putting a trained model into production, its definition and usage are demanded to the paragraph dedicated to the production.

The `tf.Saver` object saves the list of the trainable variables plus any other nontrainable variables specified in its constructor. Once created, the object provides the `save` method, which accepts the path used to store the variables. A single `Saver` object can be used to create several checkpoints and thus save the model that reached the top performance on the validation metric in a different path, in order to perform model selection.

Moreover, the `Saver` object offers the `restore` method, which can be used to populate the variables of the previously defined graph, before starting to train them, to restart an interrupted training phase. Eventually, it is possible to specify the list of the variables to restore from the checkpoint in the restore call, making it possible to use pre-trained layers and fine-tune them. The `tf.Saver` is the main object involved when doing transfer learning and fine-tuning a model.

The previous example can thus be extended to perform logging of the measured training/validation accuracy in TensorBoard (in the code, the accuracy is measured on a batch of 128 elements at the end of each epoch), the training/validation loss, and to perform model selection using the measured validation accuracy and a new saver.

You are invited to analyze and run the complete example to completely understand how every presented object works in detail. For any additional tests, always keep the TensorFlow API reference and documentation open and try everything:

```
(tf1)

    def train():
        input = tf.placeholder(tf.float32, (None, 28, 28, 1))
        labels = tf.placeholder(tf.int64, (None,))
        logits = define_cnn(input, 10, reuse=False, is_training=True)
        loss = tf.losses.sparse_softmax_cross_entropy(labels, logits)
        global_step = tf.train.get_or_create_global_step()
        train_op = tf.train.AdamOptimizer().minimize(loss, global_step)

        writer = tf.summary.FileWriter("log/graph_loss",
    tf.get_default_graph())
        validation_summary_writer = tf.summary.FileWriter(
            "log/graph_loss/validation")

        init_op = tf.global_variables_initializer()

        predictions = tf.argmax(logits, 1)
        # correct predictions: [BATCH_SIZE] tensor
        correct_predictions = tf.equal(labels, predictions)
        accuracy = tf.reduce_mean(
            tf.cast(correct_predictions, tf.float32), name="accuracy")

        accuracy_summary = tf.summary.scalar("accuracy", accuracy)
        loss_summary = tf.summary.scalar("loss", loss)
        # Input preprocessing a Python stuff
        (train_x, train_y), (test_x, test_y) = fashion_mnist.load_data()
        # Scale input in [-1, 1] range
        train_x = train_x / 255. * 2 - 1
        train_x = np.expand_dims(train_x, -1)
        test_x = test_x / 255. * 2 - 1
        test_x = np.expand_dims(test_x, -1)

        epochs = 10
        batch_size = 32
        nr_batches_train = int(train_x.shape[0] / batch_size)
        print(f"Batch size: {batch_size}")
        print(f"Number of batches per epoch: {nr_batches_train}")

        validation_accuracy = 0
        saver = tf.train.Saver()
        with tf.Session() as sess:
            sess.run(init_op)
```

```
        for epoch in range(epochs):
            for t in range(nr_batches_train):
                start_from = t * batch_size
                to = (t + 1) * batch_size

                loss_value, _, step = sess.run(
                    [loss, train_op, global_step],
                    feed_dict={
                        input: train_x[start_from:to],
                        labels: train_y[start_from:to]
                    })
                if t % 10 == 0:
                    print(f"{step}: {loss_value}")
            print(
                f"Epoch {epoch} terminated: measuring metrics and logging
    summaries"
            )

            saver.save(sess, "log/graph_loss/model")
            start_from = 0
            to = 128
            train_accuracy_summary, train_loss_summary = sess.run(
                [accuracy_summary, loss_summary],
                feed_dict={
                    input: train_x[start_from:to],
                    labels: train_y[start_from:to]
                })

            validation_accuracy_summary, validation_accuracy_value,
    validation_loss_summary = sess.run(
                [accuracy_summary, accuracy, loss_summary],
                feed_dict={
                    input: test_x[start_from:to],
                    labels: test_y[start_from:to]
                })

            # save values in TensorBoard
            writer.add_summary(train_accuracy_summary, step)
            writer.add_summary(train_loss_summary, step)

    validation_summary_writer.add_summary(validation_accuracy_summary,
                                            step)
            validation_summary_writer.add_summary(validation_loss_summary,
    step)

            validation_summary_writer.flush()
            writer.flush()
```

```
# model selection
if validation_accuracy_value > validation_accuracy:
    validation_accuracy = validation_accuracy_value
    saver.save(sess, "log/graph_loss/best_model/best")

writer.close()
```

The result, as seen in TensorBoard, is shown in the following two screenshots. The first one shows that, by using two different writers, it is possible to write two different curves on the same plot; while the second one shows the graph tab:

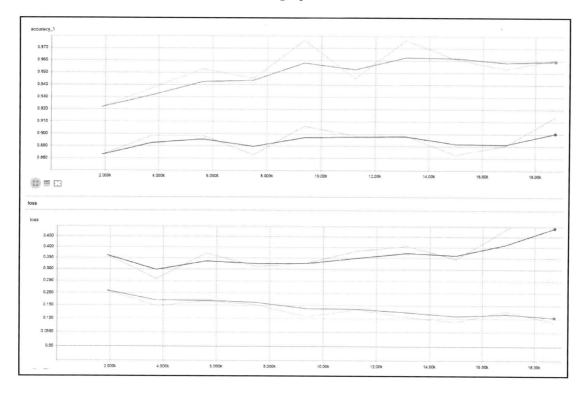

Using two SummaryWriter, it's possible to draw different curves on the same plot. The graph on top is the validation graph; the one on the bottom is the loss graph. Orange is the color of the training run, while blue is validation.

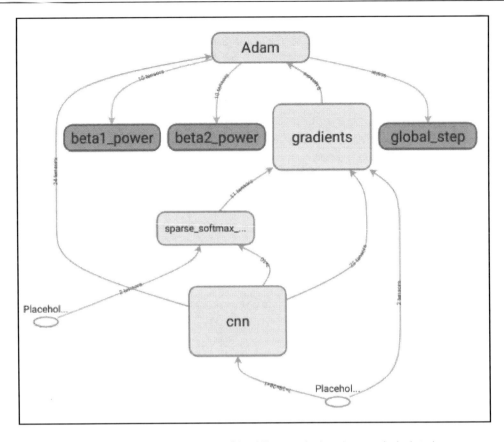

The resulting graph—please note how proper use of the variable scopes makes the graph easy to read and understand

It is worth noting that, even if trained for only a few epochs, the model defined already reaches notable performance, although it should be clear from the accuracy plot that it suffers from overfitting.

Summary

In this chapter, we analyzed how TensorFlow works under the hood—the separation between the graph definition phase and its execution within a session, how to use the Python API to interact with a graph, and how to define a model and measure the metrics during training.

It's worth noting that this chapter analyzed how TensorFlow works in its static graph version, which is no longer the default in TensorFlow 2.0; however, the graph is still present and even when used in eager mode, every API call produces operations that can be executed inside a graph to speed up execution. As will be shown in the next chapter, TensorFlow 2.0 still allows models to be defined in static graph mode, especially when defining models using the Estimator API.

Having knowledge of graph representation is of fundamental importance, and having at least an intuitive idea about the advantages that representing computation using dataflow graphs brings should make it clear why TensorFlow scales so well, even in huge, complex environments such as Google data centers.

The exercise section is incredibly important—it asks you to solve problems not introduced in the previous sections because this is the only way to become familiar with the TensorFlow documentation and code base. Keep track of the time it takes you to solve every exercise and try to figure out the solution by yourself with only the help of the TensorFlow documentation and some Stack Overflow questions!

In the next chapter, `Chapter 4`, *TensorFlow 2.0 Architecture,* you'll deep dive into the TensorFlow 2.0 world: eager mode; automatic graph conversion; a better, cleaner code base; and a Keras-based approach.

Exercises

1. Why is it possible to assess that the model suffers from overfitting only by looking at the graph?
2. Extend the baseline example to place the matrix multiplication operation on a remote device at IP 192.168.1.12; visualize the result on TensorBoard.
3. Is it necessary to have a remote device to place an operation on?
4. Extend the CNN architecture defined in the `define_cnn` method: add a batch normalization layer (from `tf.layers`) between the output of the convolutional layer and its activation function.
5. Try to train the model with the extended CNN architecture: the batch normalization layer adds two update operations that must be executed before running the training operation. Become familiar with the `tf.control_dependencies` method to force the execution of the operations contained inside the collection `tf.GraphKeys.UPDATE_OPS`, to be executed before the train operation (look at the documentation of `tf.control_dependencies` and `tf.get_collection`!).

6. Log the training and validation images in TensorBoard.
7. Has the model selection in the last example been performed correctly ? Probably not. Extend the Python script to measure the accuracy on the complete dataset and not just a batch.
8. Replace the accuracy measurement performed manually with the accuracy operation provided in the `tf.metrics` package.
9. Process the fashion-MNIST dataset and make it a binary dataset: all the items with a label different from 0 are now labeled as 1. The dataset is unbalanced now. Which metric should you use to measure the model performance and perform model selection? Give reasons for your answer (see `Chapter 1`, *What is Machine Learning?*) and implement the metric manually.
10. Replace the manually implemented metric using the same metric defined in the `tf.metrics` package.

TensorFlow 2.0 Architecture

In `Chapter 3`, *TensorFlow Graph Architecture*, we introduced the TensorFlow graph definition and execution paradigm that, although powerful and has high expressive power, has some disadvantages, such as the following:

- A steep learning curve
- Hard to debug
- Counter-intuitive semantics when it comes to certain operations
- Python is only used to build the graph

Learning how to work with computational graphs can be tough—defining the computation instead of executing the operations as the Python interpreter encounters them is a different way of thinking compared to what most programs do, especially the ones that only work with imperative languages.

However, it is still recommended that you have a deep understanding of DataFlow graphs and how TensorFlow 1.x forced its users to think since it will help you understand many parts of the TensorFlow 2.0 architecture.

Debugging a DataFlow graph is not easy—TensorBoard helps in visualizing the graph, but it is not a debugging tool. Visualizing the graph only ascertains whether the graph has been built as defined in Python, but the peculiarities such as the parallel execution of the non-dependant operations (remember the exercise at the end of the previous chapter regarding `tf.control_dependencies`?) are hard to find and are not explicitly shown in the graph visualization.

Python, the de facto data science and machine learning language, is only used to define the graph; the other Python libraries that could help solve the problem can't be used during the graph's definition since it is not possible to mix graph definition and session execution. Mixing graph definition, execution, and the usage of other libraries on graph generated data is difficult and makes the design of the Python application really ugly since it is nearly impossible to not rely on global variables, collections, and objects that are common to many different files. Organizing the code using classes and functions is not natural when using this graph definition and execution paradigm.

The release of TensorFlow 2.0 introduced several changes to the framework: from defaulting to eager execution to a complete cleanup of the APIs. The whole TensorFlow package, in fact, was full of duplicated and deprecated APIs that, in TensorFlow 2.0, have been finally removed. Moreover, by deciding to follow the Keras API specification, the TensorFlow developers decided to remove several modules that do not follow it: the most important removal was `tf.layers` (which we used in `Chapter 3`, *TensorFlow Graph Architecture*) in favor of `tf.keras.layers`.

Another widely used module, `tf.contrib`, has been completely removed. The `tf.contrib` module contained the community-added layers/software that used TensorFlow. From a software engineering point of view, having a module that contains several completely unrelated and huge projects in one package is a terrible idea. For this reason, they removed it from the main package and decided to move maintained and huge modules into separate repositories, while removing unused and unmaintained modules.

By defaulting on eager execution and removing (hiding) the graph definition and execution paradigm, TensorFlow 2.0 allows for better software design, thereby lowering the steepness of the learning curve and simplifying the debug phase. Of course, coming from a static graph definition and execution paradigm, you need to have a different way of thinking—this struggle is worth it since the advantages the version 2.0 brings in the long term will highly repay this initial struggle.

In this chapter, we will cover the following topics:

- Relearning the TensorFlow framework
- The Keras framework and its models
- Eager execution and new features
- Codebase migration

Relearning the framework

As we introduced in `Chapter 3`, *TensorFlow Graph Architecture*, TensorFlow works by building a computational graph first and then executing it. In TensorFlow 2.0, this graph definition is hidden and simplified; the execution and the definition can be mixed, and the flow of execution is always the one that's found in the source code—there's no need to worry about the order of execution in 2.0.

Prior to the 2.0 release, developers had to design the graph and the source by following this pattern:

- How can I define the graph? Is my graph composed of multiple layers that are logically separated? If so, I have to define every logical block inside a different `tf.variable_scope`.
- During the training or inference phase, do I have to use a part of the graph more than once in the same execution step? If so, I have to define this part by wrapping it inside a `tf.variable_scope` and ensuring that the `reuse` parameter is correctly used. We do this the first time to define the block; any other time, we reuse it.
- Is the graph definition completed? If so, I have to initialize all the global and local variables, thereby defining the `tf.global_variables_initializer()` operation and executing it as soon as possible.
- Finally, you have to create the session, load the graph, and run the `sess.run` calls on the node you want to execute.

After TensorFlow 2.0 was released, this reasoning completely changed, becoming more intuitive and natural for developers who are not used to working with DataFlow graphs. In fact, in TensorFlow 2.0, the following changes occurred:

- There are no more global variables. In 1.x, the graph is global; it doesn't matter if a variable has been defined inside a Python function—it is visible and separate from every other part of the graph.
- No more `tf.variable_scope`. A context manager can't change the behavior of a function by setting a `boolean` flag (`reuse`). In TensorFlow 2.0, variable sharing is made by **the model itself**. Every model is a Python object, every object has its own set of variables, and to share the variables, you just have to use the **same model** with different input.

- No more `tf.get_variable`. As we saw in Chapter 3, *TensorFlow Graph Architecture*, `tf.get_variable` allows you to declare variables that can be shared by using `tf.variable_scope`. Since every variable now matches 1:1 with a Python variable, the possibility of declaring global variables has been removed.
- No more `tf.layers`. Every layer that's declared inside the `tf.layers` module uses `tf.get_variable` to define its own variables. Use `tf.keras.layers` instead.
- No more global collections. Every variable was added to a collection of global variables that were accessible via `tf.trainable_variables()`—this was contradictory to every good software design principle. Now, the only way to access the variables of an object is by accessing its `trainable_variables` attribute, which returns the list of the trainable variables of that specific object.
- There's no need to manually call an operation that initializes all the variables.
- API cleanup and the removal of `tf.contrib` is now used in favor of the creation of several small and well-organized projects.

All of these changes have been made to simplify how TensorFlow is used, to organize the codebase better, to increase the expressive power of the framework, and to standardize its structure.

Eager execution, together with the adherence of TensorFlow to the Keras API, are the most important changes that came with TensorFlow's 2.0 release.

The Keras framework and its models

In contrast to what people who already familiar with Keras usually think, Keras is not a high-level wrapper around a machine learning framework (TensorFlow, CNTK, or Theano); instead, it is an API specification that's used for defining and training machine learning models.

TensorFlow implements the specification in its `tf.keras` module. In particular, TensorFlow 2.0 itself is an implementation of the specification and as such, many first-level submodules are nothing but aliases of the `tf.keras` submodules; for example, `tf.metrics` = `tf.keras.metrics` and `tf.optimizers` = `tf.keras.optimizers`.

TensorFlow 2.0 has, by far, the most complete implementation of the specification, making it the framework of choice for the vast majority of machine learning researchers. Any Keras API implementation allows you to build and train deep learning models. It is used for prototyping quick solutions that follow the natural human way of thinking due to its layer organization, as well as for advanced research due to its modularity and extendibility and for its ease of being deployed to production. The main advantages of the Keras implementation that are available in TensorFlow are as follows:

- **Ease of use**: The Keras interface is standardized. Every model definition must follow a common interface; every model is composed of layers, and each of them must implement a well-defined interface.
  Being standardized in every part—from the model definition to the training loop—makes learning to use a framework that implements the specification easy and extremely useful: any other framework that implements the Keras specification looks similar. This is a great advantage since it allows researchers to read code written in other frameworks without the struggle of learning about the details of the framework that was used.

- **Modular and extendible**: The Keras specification describes a set of building blocks that can be used to compose any kind of machine learning model. The TensorFlow implementation allows you to write custom building blocks, such as new layers, loss functions, and optimizers, and compose them to develop new ideas.

- **Built-in**: Since TensorFlow 2.0's release, there has been no need to download a separate Python package in order to use Keras. The `tf.keras` module is already built into the `tensorflow` package, and it has some TensorFlow-specific enhancements.
  Eager execution is a first-class citizen, just like the high-performance input pipeline module known as `tf.data`. Exporting a model that's been created using Keras is even easier than exporting a model defined in plain TensorFlow. Being exported in a language-agnostic format means that its compatibility with any production environment has already been configured, and so it is guaranteed to work with TensorFlow.

Keras, together with eager execution, are the perfect tools to prototype new ideas faster and design maintainable and well-organized software. In fact, you no longer need to think about graphs, global collections, and how to define the models in order to share their parameters across different runs; what's really important in TensorFlow 2.0 is to think in terms of Python objects, all of which carry their own variables.

TensorFlow 2.0 lets you design the whole machine learning pipeline while just thinking about objects and classes, and not about graphs and session execution.

Keras was already present in TensorFlow 1.x, but without eager execution enabled by default, which allowed you to define, train, and evaluate models through *assembling layers.* In the next few sections, we will demonstrate three ways to build a model and train it using a standard training loop

In the *Eager execution and new features* section, you will be shown how to create a custom training loop. The rule of thumb is to use Keras to build the models and use a standard training loop if the task to solve is quite standard, and then write a custom training loop when Keras does not provide a simple and ready-to-use training loop.

The Sequential API

The most common type of model is a stack of layers. The `tf.keras.Sequential` model allows you to define a Keras model by stacking `tf.keras.layers`.

The CNN that we defined in Chapter 3, *TensorFlow Graph Architecture,* can be recreated using a Keras sequential model in fewer lines and in an elegant way. Since we are training a classifier, we can use the Keras model's `compile` and `fit` methods to build the training loop and execute it, respectively. At the end of the training loop, we can also evaluate the performance of the model on the test set using the `evaluate` method—Keras will take care of all the boilerplate code:

```
(tf2)

    import tensorflow as tf
    from tensorflow.keras.datasets import fashion_mnist

    n_classes = 10
    model = tf.keras.Sequential([
     tf.keras.layers.Conv2D(
     32, (5, 5), activation=tf.nn.relu, input_shape=(28, 28, 1)),
     tf.keras.layers.MaxPool2D((2, 2), (2, 2)),
     tf.keras.layers.Conv2D(64, (3, 3), activation=tf.nn.relu),
     tf.keras.layers.MaxPool2D((2, 2), (2, 2)),
     tf.keras.layers.Flatten(),
     tf.keras.layers.Dense(1024, activation=tf.nn.relu),
     tf.keras.layers.Dropout(0.5),
     tf.keras.layers.Dense(n_classes)
    ])

    model.summary()

    (train_x, train_y), (test_x, test_y) = fashion_mnist.load_data()
    # Scale input in [-1, 1] range
```

```
train_x = train_x / 255. * 2 - 1
test_x = test_x / 255. * 2 - 1
train_x = tf.expand_dims(train_x, -1).numpy()
test_x = tf.expand_dims(test_x, -1).numpy()

model.compile(
  optimizer=tf.keras.optimizers.Adam(1e-5),
  loss='sparse_categorical_crossentropy',
  metrics=['accuracy'])

model.fit(train_x, train_y, epochs=10)
model.evaluate(test_x, test_y)
```

Some things to take note of regarding the preceding code are as follows:

- `tf.keras.Sequential` builds a `tf.keras.Model` object by stacking Keras layers. Every layer expects input and produces an output, except for the first one. The first layer uses the additional `input_shape` parameter, which is required to correctly build the model and print the summary before feeding in a real input. Keras allows you to specify the input shape of the first layer or leave it undefined. In the case of the former, every following layer knows its input shape and forward propagates its output shape to the next layer, making the input and output shape of every layer in the model known once the `tf.keras.Model` object has been created. In the case of the latter, the shapes are undefined and will be computed once the input has been fed to the model, making it impossible to generate the *summary*.

- `model.summary()` prints a complete description of the model, which is really useful if you want to check whether the model has been correctly defined and thereby check whether there are possible typos in the model definition, which layer weighs the most (in terms of the number of parameters), and how many parameters the whole model has. The CNN summary is presented in the following code. As we can see, the vast majority of parameters are in the fully connected layer:

```
Model: "sequential"
_____
Layer    (type)        Output Shape           Param #
=================================================================
conv2d (Conv2D) (None, 24, 24, 32) 832
_____
max_pooling2d (MaxPooling2D) (None, 12, 12, 32) 0
_____
conv2d_1 (Conv2D) (None, 10, 10, 64) 18496
_____
max_pooling2d_1 (MaxPooling2D) (None, 5, 5, 64) 0
```

```
flatten (Flatten) (None, 1600) 0
```

```
dense (Dense) (None, 1024) 1639424
```

```
dropout (Dropout) (None, 1024) 0
```

```
dense_1 (Dense) (None, 10) 10250
=================================================
Total params: 1,669,002
Trainable params: 1,669,002
Non-trainable params: 0
```

- The dataset preprocessing step was made without the use of NumPy but, instead, using **eager execution**. `tf.expand_dims(data, -1).numpy()` show how TensorFlow can be used as a replacement for NumPy (having a 1:1 API compatibility). By using `tf.expand_dims` instead of `np.expand_dims`, we obtained the same result (adding one dimension at the end of the input tensor), but created a `tf.Tensor` object instead of a `np.array` object. The `compile` method, however, requiresNumPy arrays as input, and so we need to use the `numpy()` method. Every `tf.Tensor` object has to get the corresponding NumPy value contained in the Tensor object.
- In the case of a standard classification task, Keras allows you to build the training loop in a single line using the `compile` method. To configure a training loop, the method only requires three arguments: the optimizer, the loss, and the metrics to monitor. In the preceding example, we can see that it is possible to use both strings and Keras objects as parameters to correctly build the training loop.
- `model.fit` is the method that you call after the training loop has been built in order to effectively start the training phase on the data that's passed for the desired number of epochs while measuring the metrics specified in the compile phase. The batch size can be configured by passing the `batch_size` parameter. In this case, we are using the default value of 32.
- At the end of the training loop, the model's performance can be measured on some unseen data. In this case, it's testing the test set of the fashion-MNIST dataset.

Keras takes care of giving the user feedback while the model is being training, logging a progress bar for each epoch and the live value of loss and metrics in the standard output:

```
Epoch 1/10
60000/60000 [================] - 126s 2ms/sample - loss: 1.9142 - accuracy:
0.4545
```

```
Epoch 2/10
60000/60000 [================] - 125s 2ms/sample - loss: 1.3089 - accuracy:
0.6333
Epoch 3/10
60000/60000 [================] - 129s 2ms/sample - loss: 1.1676 - accuracy:
0.6824
[ ... ]
Epoch 10/10
60000/60000 [================] - 130s 2ms/sample - loss: 0.8645 - accuracy:
0.7618

10000/10000 [================] - 6s 644us/sample - loss: 0.7498 - accuracy:
0.7896
```

The last line in the preceding code is the result of the `evaluate` call.

The Functional API

The Sequential API is the simplest and most common way of defining models. However, it cannot be used to define arbitrary models. The Functional API allows you to define complex topologies without the constraints of the sequential layers.

The Functional API allows you to define multi-input, multi-output models, easily sharing layers, defines residual connections, and in general define models with arbitrary complex topologies.

Once built, a Keras layer is a callable object that accepts an input tensor and produces an output tensor. It knows that it is possible to compose the layers by treating them as functions and building a `tf.keras.Model` object just by passing the input and output layers.

The following code shows how we can define a Keras model using the functional interface: the model is a fully connected neural network that accepts a 100-dimensional input and produces a single number as output (as we will see in `Chapter 9`, *Generative Adversarial Networks*, this will be our Generator architecture):

```
(tf2)

import tensorflow as tf

input_shape = (100,)
inputs = tf.keras.layers.Input(input_shape)
net = tf.keras.layers.Dense(units=64, activation=tf.nn.elu,
name="fc1")(inputs)
net = tf.keras.layers.Dense(units=64, activation=tf.nn.elu,
```

```
        name="fc2")(net)
    net = tf.keras.layers.Dense(units=1, name="G")(net)
    model = tf.keras.Model(inputs=inputs, outputs=net)
```

Being a Keras model, `model` can be compiled and trained exactly like any other Keras model that's defined using the Sequential API.

The subclassing method

The Sequential and Functional APIs cover almost any possible scenario. However, Keras offers another way of defining models that is object-oriented, more flexible, but error-prone and harder to debug. In practice, it is possible to subclass any `tf.keras.Model` by defining the layers in __init__ and the forward passing in the `call` method:

(tf2)

```
    import tensorflow as tf

    class Generator(tf.keras.Model):

        def __init__(self):
            super(Generator, self).__init__()
            self.dense_1 = tf.keras.layers.Dense(
                units=64, activation=tf.nn.elu, name="fc1")
            self.dense_2 = f.keras.layers.Dense(
                units=64, activation=tf.nn.elu, name="fc2")
            self.output = f.keras.layers.Dense(units=1, name="G")

        def call(self, inputs):
            # Build the model in functional style here
            # and return the output tensor
            net = self.dense_1(inputs)
            net = self.dense_2(net)
            net = self.output(net)
            return net
```

The subclassing method is not recommended since it separates the layer definition from its usage, making it easy to make mistakes while refactoring the code. However, defining the forward pass using this kind of model definition is sometimes the only way to proceed, especially when working with recurrent neural networks.

Subclassing from a `tf.keras.Model` the `Generator` object is a `tf.keras.Model` itself, and as such, it can be trained using the `compile` and `fit` commands, as shown earlier.

Keras can be used to train and evaluate models, but TensorFlow 2.0, with its eager execution, allows us to write our own custom training loop so that we have complete control of the training process and can debug easily.

Eager execution and new features

The following is stated in the eager execution official documentation (`https://www.tensorflow.org/guide/eager`):

> *TensorFlow's eager execution is an imperative programming environment that evaluates operations immediately, without building graphs: operations return concrete values instead of constructing a computational graph to run later. This makes it easy to get started with TensorFlow and debug models, and it reduces boilerplate as well. To follow along with this guide, run the following code samples in an interactive Python interpreter.*
>
> *Eager execution is a flexible machine learning platform for research and experimentation, providing the following:*
>
> - *An intuitive interface: Structure your code naturally and use Python data structures. Quickly iterate on small models and small data.*
> - *Easier debugging: Call ops directly to inspect running models and test changes. Use standard Python debugging tools for immediate error reporting.*
> - *Natural control flow: Use Python control flow instead of graph control flow, simplifying the specification of dynamic models.*

As shown in *The Sequential API* section, eager execution allows you to (among other features) use TensorFlow as a standard Python library that is executed immediately by the Python interpreter.

As we explained in `Chapter 3`, *TensorFlow Graph Architecture*, the graph definition and session execution paradigm is no longer the default. Don't worry! Everything you learned in the previous chapter is of extreme importance if you wish to master TensorFlow 2.0, and it will help you understand why certain parts of the framework work in this way, especially when you're using AutoGraph and the Estimator API, which we will talk about next.

Let's see how the baseline example from the previous chapter works when eager execution is enabled.

Baseline example

Let's recall the baseline example from the previous chapter:

(tf1)

```
import tensorflow as tf

A = tf.constant([[1, 2], [3, 4]], dtype=tf.float32)
x = tf.constant([[0, 10], [0, 0.5]])
b = tf.constant([[1, -1]], dtype=tf.float32)
y = tf.add(tf.matmul(A, x), b, name="result") #y = Ax + b

with tf.Session() as sess:
    print(sess.run(y))
```

The session's execution produces the NumPy array:

```
[[ 1. 10.]
 [ 1. 31.]]
```

Converting the baseline example into TensorFlow 2.0 is straightforward:

- Don't worry about the graph
- Don't worry about the session execution
- Just write what you want to be executed whenever you want it to be executed:

    (tf2)

```
import tensorflow as tf

A = tf.constant([[1, 2], [3, 4]], dtype=tf.float32)
x = tf.constant([[0, 10], [0, 0.5]])
b = tf.constant([[1, -1]], dtype=tf.float32)
y = tf.add(tf.matmul(A, x), b, name="result")
print(y)
```

The preceding code produces a different output with respect to the 1.x version:

```
tf.Tensor(
[[ 1. 10.]
 [ 1. 31.]], shape=(2, 2), dtype=float32)
```

The numerical value is, of course, the same, but the object that's returned is no longer a NumPy array—instead, it's a tf.Tensor object.

In TensorFlow 1.x, a `tf.Tensor` object was only a symbolic representation of the output of a `tf.Operation`; in 2.0, this is no longer the case.

Since the operations are executed as soon as the Python interpreter evaluates them, every `tf.Tensor` object is not only a symbolic representation of the output of a `tf.Operation`, but also a concrete Python object that contains the result of the operation.

Please note that a `tf.Tensor` object is still a symbolic representation of the output of a `tf.Operation`. This allows it to support and use 1.x features in order to manipulate `tf.Tensor` objects, thereby building graphs of `tf.Operation` that produce `tf.Tensor`.

The graph is still present and the `tf.Tensor` objects are returned as a result of every TensorFlow method.

The `y` Python variable, being a `tf.Tensor` object, can be used as input for any other TensorFlow operation. If, instead, we are interested in extracting the value `tf.Tensor` holds so that we have the identical result of the `sess.run` call of the 1.x version, we can just invoke the `tf.Tensor.numpy` method:

```
print(y.numpy())
```

TensorFlow 2.0, with its focus on eager execution, allows the user to design better-engineered software. In its 1.x version, TensorFlow had the omnipresent concepts of global variables, collections, and sessions.

Variables and collections could be accessed from everywhere in the source code since a default graph was always present.

The session is required in order to organize the complete project structure since it knows that only a single session can be present. Every time a node had to be evaluated, the session object had to be instantiated and being accessibe in the current scope.

TensorFlow 2.0 changed all of these aspects, increasing the overall quality of code that can be written using it. In practice, before 2.0, using TensorFlow to design a complex software system was tough, and many users just gave up and defined huge single file projects that had everything inside them. Now, it is possible to design software in a way better and cleaner way by following all the software engineering good practices.

Functions, not sessions

The tf.Session object has been removed from the TensorFlow API. By focusing on eager execution, you no longer need the concept of a session because the execution of the operation is immediate—we don't build a computational graph before running the computation.

This opens up a new scenario, in which the source code can be organized better. In TensorFlow 1.x, it was tough to design software by following object-oriented programming principles or even create modular code that used Python functions. However, in TensorFlow 2.0, this is natural and is highly recommended.

As shown in the previous example, the baseline example can be easily converted into its eager execution counterpart. This source code can be improved by following some Python best practices:

```
(tf2)

    import tensorflow as tf

    def multiply(x, y):
        """Matrix multiplication.
        Note: it requires the input shape of both input to match.
        Args:
            x: tf.Tensor a matrix
            y: tf.Tensor a matrix
        Returns:
            The matrix multiplcation x @ y
        """

        assert x.shape == y.shape
        return tf.matmul(x, y)

    def add(x, y):
        """Add two tensors.
        Args:
            x: the left hand operand.
            y: the right hand operand. It should be compatible with x.
        Returns:
            x + y
        """
        return x + y

    def main():
        """Main program."""
        A = tf.constant([[1, 2], [3, 4]], dtype=tf.float32)
```

```
        x = tf.constant([[0, 10], [0, 0.5]])
        b = tf.constant([[1, -1]], dtype=tf.float32)

        z = multiply(A, x)
        y = add(z, b)
        print(y)

    if __name__ == "__main__":
        main()
```

The two operations that could be executed singularly by calling `sess.run` (the matrix multiplication and the sum) have been moved to independent functions. Of course, the baseline example is simple, but just think about the training step of a machine learning model—it is easy to define a function that accepts the model and the input, and then executes a training step.

Let's go through some of the advantages of this:

- Better software organization.
- Almost complete control over the execution flow of the program.
- No need to carry a `tf.Session` object around the source code.
- No need to use `tf.placeholder`. To feed the graph, you only need to pass the data to the function.
- We can document the code! In 1.x, in order to understand what was happening in a certain part of the program, we had to read the complete source code, understand its organization, understand which operations were executed when a node was evaluated in a `tf.Session`, and only then did we have an idea of what was going on.
  Using functions we can write self-contained and well-documented code that does exactly what the documentation states.

The second and most important advantage that eager execution brings is that global graphs are no longer needed and, by extension, neither are its global collections and variables.

No more globals

Global variables are a bad software engineering practice—everyone agrees on that.

In TensorFlow 1.x, there is a strong separation between the concept of Python variables and graph variables. A Python variable is a variable with a certain name and type that follows the Python language rules: it can be deleted using `del` and it is visible only in its scope and scopes that are at a lower level in the hierarchy.

The graph variable, on the other hand, is a graph that's declared in the computational graph and lives outside the Python language rules. We can declare a Graph variable by assigning it to a Python variable, but this bond is not tight: the Python variable gets destroyed as soon as it goes out of scope, while the graph variable is still present: it is a global and persistent object.

In order to understand the great advantages this change brings, we will take a look at what happens to the baseline operation definitions when the Python variables are garbage-collected:

(tf1)

```python
import tensorflow as tf

def count_op():
    """Print the operations define in the default graph
    and returns their number.
    Returns:
        number of operations in the graph
    """
    ops = tf.get_default_graph().get_operations()
    print([op.name for op in ops])
    return len(ops)


A = tf.constant([[1, 2], [3, 4]], dtype=tf.float32, name="A")
x = tf.constant([[0, 10], [0, 0.5]], name="x")
b = tf.constant([[1, -1]], dtype=tf.float32, name="b")

assert count_op() == 3
del A
del x
del b
assert count_op() == 0 # FAIL!
```

The program fails on the second assertion and the output of `count_op` is the same in the invocation of `[A, x, b]`.

Deleting Python variables is completely useless since all the operations defined in the graph are still there and we can access their output tensor, thus restoring the Python variables if needed or creating new Python variables that point to the graph nodes. We can do this by using the following code:

```python
A = tf.get_default_graph().get_tensor_by_name("A:0")
x = tf.get_default_graph().get_tensor_by_name("x:0")
b = tf.get_default_graph().get_tensor_by_name("b:0")
```

Why is this behavior bad? Consider the following:

- The operations, once defined in the graph, are always there.
- If any operation that's defined in the graph has a side effect (see the following example regarding variable initialization), deleting the corresponding Python variable is useless and the side effects will remain.
- In general, even if we declared the A, x, b variables inside a separate function that has its own Python scope, we can access them from every function by getting the tensor by name, which breaks every sort of encapsulation process out there.

The following example shows some of the side effects of not having global graph variables connected to Python variables:

(tf1)

```python
import tensorflow as tf

def get_y():
    A = tf.constant([[1, 2], [3, 4]], dtype=tf.float32, name="A")
    x = tf.constant([[0, 10], [0, 0.5]], name="x")
    b = tf.constant([[1, -1]], dtype=tf.float32, name="b")
    # I don't know what z is: if is a constant or a variable
    z = tf.get_default_graph().get_tensor_by_name("z:0")
    y = A @ x + b - z
    return y

test = tf.Variable(10., name="z")
del test
test = tf.constant(10, name="z")
del test

y = get_y()

with tf.Session() as sess:
    print(sess.run(y))
```

This code fails to run and highlights several downsides of the global variables approach, alongside the downsides of the naming system used by Tensorfow 1.x:

- `sess.run(y)` triggers the execution of an operation that depends on the `z:0` tensor.
- When fetching a tensor using its name, we don't know whether the operation that generates it is an operation without side effects or not. In our case, the operation is a `tf.Variable` definition, which requires the variable's initialization to be executed before the `z:0` tensor can be evaluated; that's why the code fails to run.
- The Python variable name means nothing to TensorFlow 1.x: `test` contains a graph variable named `z` first, and then `test` is destroyed and replaced with the graph constant we require, that is, `z`.
- Unfortunately, the call to `get_y` found a tensor named `z:0`, which refers to the `tf.Variable` operation (that has side effects) and not the constant node, `z`. Why? Even though we deleted the `test` variable in the graph variable, `z` is still defined. Therefore, when calling `tf.constant`, we have a name that conflicts with the graph that TensorFlow solves for us. It does this by adding the `_1` suffix to the output tensor.

All of these problems are gone in TensorFlow 2.0—we just have to write Python code that we are used to. There's no need to worry about graphs, global scopes, naming conflicts, placeholders, graph dependencies, and side effects. Even the control flow is Python-like, as we will see in the next section.

Control flow

Executing sequential operations in TensorFlow 1.x was not an easy task if the operations had no explicit order of execution constraints. Let's say we want to use TensorFlow to do the following:

1. Declare and initialize two variables: y and y.
2. Increment the value of y by 1.
3. Compute x*y.
4. Repeat this five times.

The first, non-working attempt, in TensorFlow 1.x is to just declare the code by following the preceding steps:

(tf1)

```
import tensorflow as tf

x = tf.Variable(1, dtype=tf.int32)
y = tf.Variable(2, dtype=tf.int32)

assign_op = tf.assign_add(y, 1)
out = x * y
init = tf.global_variables_initializer()

with tf.Session() as sess:
    sess.run(init)
    for _ in range(5):
        print(sess.run(out))
```

Those of you who completed the exercises that were provided in the previous chapter will have already noticed the problem in this code.

The output node, out, has no explicit dependency on the assign_op node, and so it never evaluates when out is executed, making the output just a sequence of 2. In TensorFlow 1.x, we have to explicitly force the order of execution using tf.control_dependencies, conditioning the assignment operation so that it's executed before the evaluation of out:

```
with tf.control_dependencies([assign_op]):
    out = x * y
```

Now, the output is the sequence of 3, 4, 5, 6, 7, which is what we wanted.

More complex examples, such as declaring and executing loops directly inside the graph where conditional execution (using tf.cond) could occur, are possible, but the point is the same—in TensorFlow 1.x, we have to worry about the side effects of our operations, we have to think about the graph's structure when writing Python code, and we can't even use the Python interpreter that we're used to. The conditions have to be expressed using tf.cond instead of a Python if statement and the loops have to be defined using tf.while_loop instead of using the Python for and while statements.

TensorFlow 2.x, with its eager execution, makes it possible to use the Python interpreter to control the flow of execution:

(tf2)

```
import tensorflow as tf
```

```
x = tf.Variable(1, dtype=tf.int32)
y = tf.Variable(2, dtype=tf.int32)

for _ in range(5):
    y.assign_add(1)
    out = x * y
    print(out)
```

The previous example, which was developed using eager execution, is simpler to develop, debug, and understand—it's just standard Python, after all!

By simplifying the control flow, eager execution was possible, and is one of the main features that was introduced in TensorFlow 2.0—now, even users without any previous experience of DataFlow graphs or descriptive programming languages can start writing TensorFlow code. Eager execution reduces the overall framework's complexity and lowers the entry barrier.

Users coming from TensorFlow 1.x may start wondering how can we train machine learning models since, in order to compute gradients using automatic differentiation, we need to have a graph of the executed operations.

TensorFlow 2.0 introduced the concept of GradienTape to efficiently combat this problem.

GradientTape

The `tf.GradientTape()` invocation creates a context that records the operations for automatic differentiation. Every operation that's executed within the context manager is recorded on tape if at least one of their inputs is watchable and is being watched.

An input is watchable when the following occurs:

- It's a trainable variable that's been created by using `tf.Variable`
- It's being explicitly watched by the tape, which is done by calling the `watch` method on the `tf.Tensor` object

The tape records every operation that's executed within the context in order to build a graph of the forward pass that was executed; then, the tape can be unrolled in order to compute the gradients using reverse-mode automatic differentiation. It does this by calling the `gradient` method:

```
x = tf.constant(4.0)
with tf.GradientTape() as tape:
    tape.watch(x)
```

```
      y = tf.pow(x, 2)
 # Will compute 8 = 2*x, x = 8
 dy_dx = tape.gradient(y, x)
```

In the preceding example, we explicitly asked `tape` to watch a constant value that, by its nature, is not watchable (since it is not a `tf.Variable` object).

A `tf.GradientTape` object such as `tape` releases the resources that it's holding as soon as the `tf.GradientTape.gradient()` method is called. This is desirable for the most common scenarios, but there are cases in which we need to invoke `tf.GradientTape.gradient()` more than once. To do that, we need to create a persistent gradient tape that allows multiple calls to the gradient method without it releasing the resources. In this case, it is up to the developer to take care of releasing the resources when no more are needed. They do this by dropping the reference to the tape using Python's `del` instruction:

```
x = tf.Variable(4.0)
y = tf.Variable(2.0)
with tf.GradientTape(persistent=True) as tape:
    z = x + y
    w = tf.pow(x, 2)
dz_dy = tape.gradient(z, y)
dz_dx = tape.gradient(z, x)
dw_dx = tape.gradient(w, x)
print(dz_dy, dz_dx, dw_dx) # 1, 1, 8
# Release the resources
del tape
```

It is also possible to nest more than one `tf.GradientTape` object in higher-order derivatives (this should be easy for you to do now, so I'm leaving this as an exercise).

TensorFlow 2.0 offers a new and easy way to build models using Keras and a highly customizable and efficient way to compute gradients using the concept of tape.

The Keras models that we mentioned in the previous sections already come with methods to train and evaluate them; however, Keras can't cover every possible training and evaluation scenario. Therefore, TensorFlow 1.x can be used to build custom training loops so that you can train and evaluate the models and have complete control over what's going on. This gives you the freedom to experiment with controlling every part of the training. For instance, as shown in Chapter 9, *Generative Adversarial Networks*, the best way to define the adversarial training process is by defining a custom training loop.

Custom training loop

The `tf.keras.Model` object, through its `compile` and `fit` methods, allows you to train a great number of machine learning models, from classifiers to generative models. The Keras way of training can speed up the definition of the training phase of the most common models, but the customization of the training loop remains limited.

There are models, training strategies, and problems that require a different kind of model training. For instance, let's say we need to face the gradient explosion problem. It could happen that, during the training of a model using gradient descent, the loss function starts diverging until it becomes `NaN` because of the size of the gradient update, which becomes higher and higher until it overflows.

A common strategy that you can use to face this problem is clipping the gradient or capping the threshold: the gradient update can't have a magnitude greater than the threshold value. This prevents the network from diverging and usually helps us find a better local minima during the minimization process. There are several gradient clipping strategies, but the most common is L2 norm gradient clipping.

In this strategy, the gradient vector is normalized in order to make the L2 norm less than or equal to a threshold value. In practice, we want to update the gradient update rule in this way:

```
gradients = gradients * threshold / l2(gradients)
```

TensorFlow has an API for this task: `tf.clip_by_norm`. We only need to access the gradients that have been computed, apply the update rule, and feed it to the chosen optimizer.

In order to create a custom training loop using `tf.GradientTape` to compute the gradients and post-process them, the image classifier training script that we developed at the end of the previous chapter needs to be migrated to its TensorFlow 2.0 version.

Please take the time to read the source code carefully: have a look at the new modular organization and compare the previous 1.x code with this new code.

There are several differences between these APIs:

- The optimizers are now Keras optimizers.
- The losses are now Keras losses.
- The accuracy is easily computed using the Keras metrics package.

- There is always a TensorFlow 2.0 version of any TensorFlow 1.x symbol.
- There are no more global collections. The tape needs a list of the variables it needs to use to compute the gradient and the `tf.keras.Model` object has to carry its own set of `trainable_variables`.

While in version 1.x there was method invocation, in 2.0, there is a Keras method that returns a callable object. The constructor of almost every Keras object is used to configure it, and they use the `call` method to use it.

First, we import the `tensorflow` library and then define the `make_model` function:

```
import tensorflow as tf
from tensorflow.keras.datasets import fashion_mnist

def make_model(n_classes):
 return tf.keras.Sequential([
   tf.keras.layers.Conv2D(
     32, (5, 5), activation=tf.nn.relu, input_shape=(28, 28, 1)),
   tf.keras.layers.MaxPool2D((2, 2), (2, 2)),
   tf.keras.layers.Conv2D(64, (3, 3), activation=tf.nn.relu),
   tf.keras.layers.MaxPool2D((2, 2), (2, 2)),
   tf.keras.layers.Flatten(),
   tf.keras.layers.Dense(1024, activation=tf.nn.relu),
   tf.keras.layers.Dropout(0.5),
   tf.keras.layers.Dense(n_classes)
 ])
```

Then, we define the `load_data` function:

```
def load_data():
    (train_x, train_y), (test_x, test_y) = fashion_mnist.load_data()
    # Scale input in [-1, 1] range
    train_x = tf.expand_dims(train_x, -1)
    train_x = (tf.image.convert_image_dtype(train_x, tf.float32) - 0.5) * 2
    train_y = tf.expand_dims(train_y, -1)

    test_x = test_x / 255. * 2 - 1
    test_x = (tf.image.convert_image_dtype(test_x, tf.float32) - 0.5) * 2
    test_y = tf.expand_dims(test_y, -1)

    return (train_x, train_y), (test_x, test_y)
```

Afterward, we define the `train()` functions that instantiate the model, the input data, and the training parameters:

```
def train():
    # Define the model
    n_classes = 10
    model = make_model(n_classes)

    # Input data
    (train_x, train_y), (test_x, test_y) = load_data()

    # Training parameters
    loss = tf.losses.SparseCategoricalCrossentropy(from_logits=True)
    step = tf.Variable(1, name="global_step")
    optimizer = tf.optimizers.Adam(1e-3)
    accuracy = tf.metrics.Accuracy()
```

To conclude, we need to define the `train_step` function inside the `train` function and use it inside the training loop:

```
    # Train step function
    def train_step(inputs, labels):
        with tf.GradientTape() as tape:
            logits = model(inputs)
            loss_value = loss(labels, logits)

        gradients = tape.gradient(loss_value, model.trainable_variables)
        # TODO: apply gradient clipping here
        optimizer.apply_gradients(zip(gradients,
 model.trainable_variables))
        step.assign_add(1)

        accuracy_value = accuracy(labels, tf.argmax(logits, -1))
        return loss_value, accuracy_value

    epochs = 10
    batch_size = 32
    nr_batches_train = int(train_x.shape[0] / batch_size)
    print(f"Batch size: {batch_size}")
    print(f"Number of batches per epoch: {nr_batches_train}")

    for epoch in range(epochs):
        for t in range(nr_batches_train):
            start_from = t * batch_size
            to = (t + 1) * batch_size
            features, labels = train_x[start_from:to],
 train_y[start_from:to]
            loss_value, accuracy_value = train_step(features, labels)
```

```
        if t % 10 == 0:
            print(
                f"{step.numpy()}: {loss_value} - accuracy:
{accuracy_value}"
            )
        print(f"Epoch {epoch} terminated")

if __name__ == "__main__":
    train()
```

The previous example does not include model saving, model selection, and TensorBoard logging. Moreover, the gradient clipping part has been left as an exercise for you (see the TODO section of the preceding code).

 At the end of this chapter, all of the missing functionalities will be included; in the meantime, take your time to read through the new version carefully and compare it with the 1.x version.

The next section will focus on how to save the model parameters, restart the training process, and make model selection.

Saving and restoring the model's status

TensorFlow 2.0 introduced the concept of a checkpointable object: every object that inherits from tf.train.Checkpointable is automatically serializable, which means that it is possible to save it in a checkpoint. Compared to the 1.x version, where only the variables were checkpointable, in 2.0, whole Keras layers/models inherit from tf.train.Checkpointable. Due to this, it is possible to save whole layers/models instead of worrying about their variables; as usual, Keras introduced an additional abstraction layer that simplifies the usage of the framework. There are two ways of saving a model:

- Using a checkpoint
- Using a SavedModel

As we explained in Chapter 3, *TensorFlow Graph Architecture*, checkpoints do not contain any description of the model itself: they are just an easy way to store the model parameters and let the developer restore them correctly by defining the model that maps the checkpoint saved variables with Python tf.Variable objects or, at a higher level, with tf.train.Checkpointable objects.

The SavedModel format, on the other hand, is the serialized description of the computation, in addition to the parameter's value. We can summarize these two objects as follows:

- **Checkpoint**: An easy way to store variables on disk
- **SavedModel**: Model structure and checkpoint

SavedModels are language-agnostic representations (Protobuf serialized graphs) that are suitable for deployment in other languages. The last chapter of this book, `Chapter 10`, *Bringing a Model to Production,* is dedicated to the SavedModel since it is the correct way to bring a model to production.

While training a model, we have the model definition available in Python. Due to this, we are interested in saving the model status, which we can do as follows:

- Restart the training process in the case of failures, without wasting all the previous computation.
- Save the model parameters at the end of the training loop so that we can test the trained model on the test set.
- Save the model parameters in different locations so that we can save the status of the models that reached the best validation performance (model selection).

To save and restore the model parameters in TensorFlow 2.0, we can use two objects:

- `tf.train.Checkpoint` is the object-based serializer/deserializer.
- `tf.train.CheckpointManager` is an object that can use a `tf.train.Checkpoint` instance to save and manage checkpoints.

Compared to TensorFlow 1.x's `tf.train.Saver` method, the `Checkpoint.save` and `Checkpoint.restore` methods write and read object-based checkpoints; the former was only able to write and read `variable.name`-based checkpoints.

Saving objects instead of variables is more robust when it comes to making changes in the Python program and it works correctly with the eager execution paradigm. In TensorFlow 1.x, saving only the `variable.name` was enough since the graph wouldn't change once defined and executed. In 2.0, where the graph is hidden and the control flow can make the objects and their variables appear/disappear, saving objects is the only way to preserve their status.

Using `tf.train.Checkpoint` is amazingly easy—do you want to store a checkpointable object? Just pass it to its constructor or create a new attribute for the object during its lifetime.

Once you've defined the checkpoint object, use it to build a `tf.train.CheckpointManager` object, where you can specify where to save the model parameters and how many checkpoints to keep.

Because of this, the save and restore capabilities of the previous model's training are as easy as adding the following lines, right after the model and optimizer definition:

(tf2)

```
ckpt = tf.train.Checkpoint(step=step, optimizer=optimizer, model=model)
manager = tf.train.CheckpointManager(ckpt, './checkpoints', max_to_keep=3)
ckpt.restore(manager.latest_checkpoint)
if manager.latest_checkpoint:
    print(f"Restored from {manager.latest_checkpoint}")
else:
    print("Initializing from scratch.")
```

Trainable and not-trainable variables are automatically added for the checkpoint variables to monitor, allowing you to restore the model and restart the training loop without introducing unwanted fluctuations in the loss functions. In fact, the optimizer object, which usually carries its own set of non-trainable variables (moving means and variances), is a checkpointable object that is added to the checkpoint, allowing you to restart the training loop in the same exact status as when it was interrupted.

When a condition is met (`i % 10 == 0`, or when the validation metric is improved), is it possible to use the `manager.save` method invocation to checkpoint the model's status:

(tf2)

```
save_path = manager.save()
print(f"Checkpoint saved: {save_path}")
```

The manager can save the model parameters in the directory that's specified during its construction; therefore, to perform model selection, you need to create a second manager object that is invoked when the model selection condition is met. This is left as an exercise for you.

Summaries and metrics

TensorBoard is still the default and recommended data logging and visualization tool for TensorFlow. The `tf.summary` package contains all the required methods to save scalar values, images, plot histograms, distributions, and more.

Together with the `tf.metrics` package, it is possible to log aggregated data. Metrics are usually measured on mini-batches and not on the whole training/validation/test set: aggregating data while looping on the complete dataset split allows us to measure the metrics correctly.

The objects in the `tf.metrics` package are stateful, which means they are able to accumulate/aggregate values and return a cumulative result when calling `.result()`.

In the same way as TensorFlow 1.x, to save a summary to disk, you need a File/Summary writer object. You can create one by doing the following:

`(tf2)`

```
summary_writer = tf.summary.create_file_writer(path)
```

This new object doesn't work like it does in 1.x—its usage is now simplified and more powerful. Instead of using a session and executing the `sess.run(summary)` line to get the line to write inside the summary, the new `tf.summary.*` objects are able to detect the context they are used within and log the correct summary inside the writer once the summary line has been computed.

In fact, the summary writer object defines a context manager by calling `.as_default()`; every `tf.summary.*` method that's invoked within this context will add its result to the default summary writer.

Combining `tf.summary` with `tf.metrics` allows us to measure and log the training/validation/test metrics correctly and in an easier way with respect to TensorFlow 1.x. In fact, if we decide to log every 10 training steps for the computed metric, we have to visualize the mean value that's computed over those 10 training steps and not just the last one.

Thus, at the end of every training step, we have to invoke the metric object's `.update_state` method to aggregate and save the computed value inside the object status and then invoke the `.result()` method.

The `.result()` method takes care of correctly computing the metric over the aggregated values. Once computed, we can reset the internal states of the metric by calling `reset_states()`. Of course, the same reasoning holds for every value that's computed during the training phase because the loss is quite common:

```
mean_loss = tf.metrics.Mean(name='loss')
```

This defines the metric's `Mean`, which is the mean of the input that's passed during the training phase. In this case, this is the loss value, but the same metric can be used to compute the mean of every scalar value.

The `tf.summary` package also contains methods that you can use to log images (`tf.summary.image`), therefore extending the previous example to log both scalar metrics and batches of images on TensorBoard in an extremely easy. The following code shows how the previous example can be extended to log the training loss, accuracy, and three training images—please take the time to analyze the structure, see how metrics and logging are performed, and try to understand how the code structure can be improved by defining more functions in order to make it more modular and easy to maintain:

```python
def train():
    # Define the model
    n_classes = 10
    model = make_model(n_classes)

    # Input data
    (train_x, train_y), (test_x, test_y) = load_data()

    # Training parameters
    loss = tf.losses.SparseCategoricalCrossentropy(from_logits=True)
    step = tf.Variable(1, name="global_step")
    optimizer = tf.optimizers.Adam(1e-3)

    ckpt = tf.train.Checkpoint(step=step, optimizer=optimizer, model=model)
    manager = tf.train.CheckpointManager(ckpt, './tf_ckpts', max_to_keep=3)
    ckpt.restore(manager.latest_checkpoint)
    if manager.latest_checkpoint:
        print(f"Restored from {manager.latest_checkpoint}")
    else:
        print("Initializing from scratch.")

    accuracy = tf.metrics.Accuracy()
    mean_loss = tf.metrics.Mean(name='loss')
```

Here, we define the `train_step` function:

```python
    # Train step function
    def train_step(inputs, labels):
        with tf.GradientTape() as tape:
            logits = model(inputs)
            loss_value = loss(labels, logits)

        gradients = tape.gradient(loss_value, model.trainable_variables)
        # TODO: apply gradient clipping here
        optimizer.apply_gradients(zip(gradients,
```

```
model.trainable_variables))
        step.assign_add(1)

        accuracy.update_state(labels, tf.argmax(logits, -1))
        return loss_value, accuracy.result()

    epochs = 10
    batch_size = 32
    nr_batches_train = int(train_x.shape[0] / batch_size)
    print(f"Batch size: {batch_size}")
    print(f"Number of batches per epoch: {nr_batches_train}")
    train_summary_writer = tf.summary.create_file_writer('./log/train')
    with train_summary_writer.as_default():
        for epoch in range(epochs):
            for t in range(nr_batches_train):
                start_from = t * batch_size
                to = (t + 1) * batch_size

                features, labels = train_x[start_from:to],
train_y[start_from:to]

                loss_value, accuracy_value = train_step(features, labels)
                mean_loss.update_state(loss_value)

                if t % 10 == 0:
                    print(f"{step.numpy()}: {loss_value} - accuracy:
{accuracy_value}")
                    save_path = manager.save()
                    print(f"Checkpoint saved: {save_path}")
                    tf.summary.image(
                        'train_set', features, max_outputs=3,
step=step.numpy())
                    tf.summary.scalar(
                        'accuracy', accuracy_value, step=step.numpy())
                    tf.summary.scalar(
                        'loss', mean_loss.result(), step=step.numpy())
                    accuracy.reset_states()
                    mean_loss.reset_states()
            print(f"Epoch {epoch} terminated")
            # Measuring accuracy on the whole training set at the end of
the epoch
            for t in range(nr_batches_train):
                start_from = t * batch_size
                to = (t + 1) * batch_size
                features, labels = train_x[start_from:to],
train_y[start_from:to]
                logits = model(features)
                accuracy.update_state(labels, tf.argmax(logits, -1))
```

```
print(f"Training accuracy: {accuracy.result()}")
accuracy.reset_states()
```

On TensorBoard, at the end of the first epoch, is it possible to see the loss value measured every 10 steps:

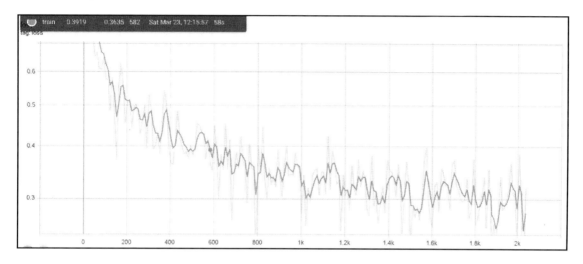

The loss value, measured every 10 steps, as visualized in TensorBoard

We can also see the training accuracy, measured at the same time as the loss:

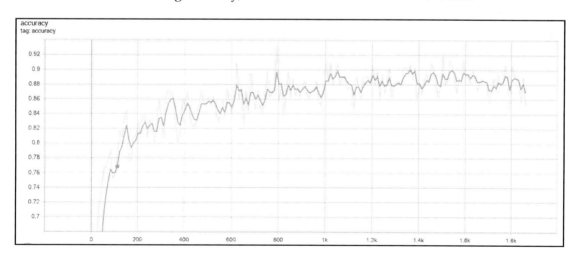

The training accuracy, as visualized in TensorBoard

Moreover, we can also see the images sampled for the training set:

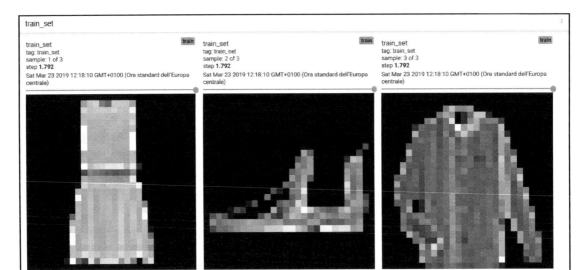

Three image samples from the training set—a dress, a sandal, and a pullover from the fashion-MNIST dataset

Eager execution allows you to create and execute models on the fly, without explicitly creating a graph. However, working in eager mode does not mean that a graph can't be built from TensorFlow code. In fact, as we saw in the previous section, by using `tf.GradientTape`, is it possible to register what happens during a training step, build a computational graph by tracing the operations that are executed, and use this graph to automatically compute the gradient using automatic differentiation.

Tracing what happens during a function's execution allows us to analyze what operations are executed at runtime. Knowing the operations, their input relations, and their output relation makes it possible to build graphs.

This is of extreme importance since it can be exploited to execute a function once, trace its behavior, convert its body into its graph representation, and fall back to the more efficient graph definition and session execution, which has a huge performance boost. It does all of this automatically: this is the concept of AutoGraph.

AutoGraph

Automatically converting Python code into its graphical representation is done with the use of **AutoGraph**. In TensorFlow 2.0, AutoGraph is automatically applied to a function when it is decorated with @tf.function. This decorator creates callable graphs from Python functions.

A function, once decorated correctly, is processed by tf.function and the tf.autograph module in order to convert it into its graphical representation. The following diagram shows a schematic representation of what happens when a decorated function is called:

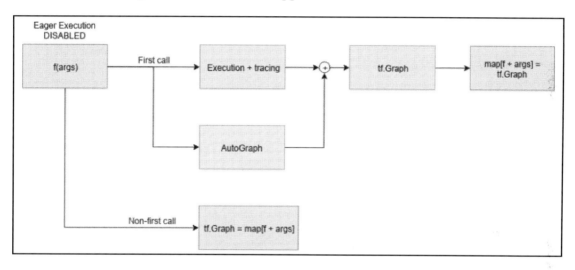

Schematic representation of what happens when a function, f, decorated with @tf.function, which is called on the first call and on any other subsequent call

On the first call of the annotated function, the following occurs:

1. The function is executed and traced. Eager execution is disabled in this context, and so every tf.* method defines a tf.Operation node that produces a tf.Tensor output, exactly like it does in TensorFlow 1.x.

2. The tf.autograph module is used to detect Python constructs that can be converted into their graph equivalent. The graph representation is built from the function trace and AutoGraph information. This is done in order to preserve the execution order that's defined in Python.

3. The tf.Graph object has now been built.

4. Based on the function name and the input parameters, a unique ID is created and associated with the graph. The graph is then cached into a map so that it can be reused when a second invocation occurs and the ID matches.

Converting a function into its graph representation usually requires us to think; in TensorFlow 1.x, not every function that works in eager mode can be converted painlessly into its graph version.

For instance, a variable in eager mode is a Python object that follows the Python rules regarding its scope. In graph mode, as we found out in the previous chapter, a variable is a persistent object that will continue to exist, even if its associated Python variable goes out of scope and is garbage-collected.

Therefore, special attention has to be placed on software design: if a function has to be graph-accelerated and it creates a status (using `tf.Variable` and similar objects), it is up to the developer to take care of avoiding having to recreate the variable every time the function is called.

For this reason, `tf.function` parses the function body multiple times while looking for the `tf.Variable` definition. If, at the second invocation, it finds out that a variable object is being recreated, it raises an exception:

```
ValueError: tf.function-decorated function tried to create variables on
non-first call.
```

In practice, if we have defined a function that performs a simple operation that uses a `tf.Variable` inside it, we have to ensure that the object is only created once.

The following function works correctly in eager mode, but it fails to execute if it is decorated with `@tf.function` and is raising the preceding exception:

```
(tf2)

    def f():
        a = tf.constant([[10,10],[11.,1.]])
        x = tf.constant([[1.,0.],[0.,1.]])
        b = tf.Variable(12.)
        y = tf.matmul(a, x) + b
        return y
```

Handling functions that create a state means that we have to rethink our usage of graph-mode. A state is a persistent object, such as a variable, and the variable can't be redeclared more than once. Due to this, the function definition can be changed in two ways:

- By passing the variable as an input parameter
- By breaking the function scope and inheriting a variable from the external scope

The first option requires changing the function definition that's making it:

(tf2)

```
@tf.function
def f(b):
    a = tf.constant([[10,10],[11.,1.]])
    x = tf.constant([[1.,0.],[0.,1.]])
    y = tf.matmul(a, x) + b
    return y

var = tf.Variable(12.)
f(var)
f(15)
f(tf.constant(1))
```

f now accepts a Python input variable, b. This variable can be a tf.Variable, a tf.Tensor, and also a NumPy object or a Python type. Every time the input type changes, a new graph is created in order to make an accelerated version of the function that works for any required input type (this is required because of how a TensorFlow graph is statically typed).

The second option, on the other hand, requires breaking down the function scope, making the variable available outside the scope of the function itself. In this case, there are two paths we can follow:

- **Not recommended**: Use global variables
- **Recommended**: Use Keras-like objects

The first path, which is **not recommended**, consists of declaring the variable outside the function body and using it inside, ensuring that it will only be declared once:

(tf2)

```
b = None

@tf.function
def f():
    a = tf.constant([[10, 10], [11., 1.]])
    x = tf.constant([[1., 0.], [0., 1.]])
    global b
    if b is None:
        b = tf.Variable(12.)
    y = tf.matmul(a, x) + b
    return y

f()
```

The second path, which is **recommended**, is to use an object-oriented approach and declare the variable as a private attribute of a class. Then, you need to make the objects that were instantiated callable by putting the function body inside the __call__ method:

(tf2)

```
class F():
    def __init__(self):
        self._b = None

    @tf.function
    def __call__(self):
        a = tf.constant([[10, 10], [11., 1.]])
        x = tf.constant([[1., 0.], [0., 1.]])
        if self._b is None:
            self._b = tf.Variable(12.)
        y = tf.matmul(a, x) + self._b
        return y

f = F()
f()
```

AutoGraph and the graph acceleration process work best when it comes to optimizing the training process.

In fact, the most computationally-intensive part of the training is the forward pass, followed by gradient computation and parameter updates. In the previous example, following the new structure that the absence of tf.Session allows us to follow, we separate the training step from the training loop. The training step is a function without a state that uses variables inherited from the outer scope. Therefore, it can be converted into its graph representation and accelerated just by decorating it with the @tf.function decorator:

(tf2)

```
@tf.function
def train_step(inputs, labels):
# function body
```

You are invited to measure the speedup that was introduced by the graph conversion of the train_step function.

The speedup is not guaranteed since eager execution is already fast and there are simple scenarios in which eager execution is as fast as its graphical counterpart. However, the performance boost is visible when the models become more complex and deeper.

AutoGraph automatically converts Python constructs into their `tf.*` equivalent, but since converting source code that preserves semantics is not an easy task, there are scenarios in which it is better to help AutoGraph perform source code transformation.

In fact, there are constructs that work in eager execution that are already drop-in replacements for Python constructs. In particular, `tf.range` replaces `range`, `tf.print` replaces `print`, and `tf.assert` replaces `assert`.

For instance, AutoGraph is not able to automatically convert `print` into `tf.print` in order to preserve its semantic. Therefore, if we want a graph-accelerated function to print something when executed in graph mode, we have to write the function using `tf.print` instead of `print`.

You are invited to define simple functions that use `tf.range` instead of `range` and `print` instead of `tf.print`, and then visualize how the source code is converted using the `tf.autograph` module.

For instance, take a look at the following code:

(tf2)

```
import tensorflow as tf

@tf.function
def f():
    x = 0
    for i in range(10):
        print(i)
        x += i
    return x


f()
print(tf.autograph.to_code(f.python_function))
```

This produces 0, 1, 2, ..., 10 when f is called—does this happens every time f is invoked, or only the first time?

You are invited to carefully read through the following AutoGraph-generated function (this is machine-generated, and so it is hard to read) in order to understand why f behaves in this way:

```
def tf__f():
  try:
    with ag__.function_scope('f'):
      do_return = False
```

```
                retval_ = None
                x = 0

                def loop_body(loop_vars, x_1):
                  with ag__.function_scope('loop_body'):
                    i = loop_vars
                    with ag__.utils.control_dependency_on_returns(ag__.print_(i)):
                      x, i_1 = ag__.utils.alias_tensors(x_1, i)
                      x += i_1
                      return x,
                x, = ag__.for_stmt(ag__.range_(10), None, loop_body, (x,))
                do_return = True
                retval_ = x
                return retval_
        except:
          ag__.rewrite_graph_construction_error(ag_source_map__)
```

Migrating an old codebase from Tensorfow 1.x to 2.0 can be a time-consuming process. This is why the TensorFlow authors created a conversion tool that allows us to automatically migrate the source code (it even works on Python notebooks!).

Codebase migration

As we have already seen, TensorFlow 2.0 brings a lot of breaking changes, which means that we have to relearn how to use the framework. TensorFlow 1.x is the most widely used machine learning framework and so there is a lot of existing code that needs to be upgraded.

The TensorFlow engineers developed a conversion tool that can help in the conversion process: unfortunately, it relies on the tf.compat.v1 module, and it does not remove the graph nor the session execution. Instead, it just rewrites the code, prefixing it using tf.compat.v1, and applies some source code transformations to fix some easy API changes.

However, it is a good starting point to migrate a whole codebase. In fact, the suggested migration process is as follows:

1. Run the migration script.
2. Manually remove every tf.contrib symbol, looking for the new location of the project that was used in the contrib namespace.

3. Manually switch the models to their Keras equivalent. Remove the sessions.
4. Define the training loop in eager execution mode.
5. Accelerate the computationally-intensive parts using `tf.function`.

The migration tool, `tf_upgrade_v2`, is installed automatically when TensorFlow 2.0 is installed via `pip`. The upgrade script works on single Python files, notebooks, or complete project directories.

To migrate a single Python file (or notebook), use the following code:

```
tf_upgrade_v2 --infile file.py --outfile file-migrated.py
```

To run it on a directory tree, use the following code:

```
tf_upgrade_v2 --intree project --outtree project-migrated
```

In both cases, the script will print errors if it cannot find a fix for the input code.

Moreover, it always reports a list of detailed changes in the `report.txt` file, which can help us understand why certain changes have been applied by the tool; for example:

```
Added keyword 'input' to reordered function 'tf.argmax'
Renamed keyword argument from 'dimension' to 'axis'

    Old: tf.argmax([[1, 2, 2]], dimension=0))
                              ~~~~~~~~~~
    New: tf.argmax(input=[[1, 2, 2]], axis=0))
```

Migrating the codebase, even using the conversion tool, is a time-consuming process since most of the work is manual. Converting a codebase into TensorFlow 2.0 is worth it since it brings many advantages, such as the following:

- Easy debugging.
- Increased code quality using an object-oriented approach.
- Fewer lines of code to maintain.
- Easy to document.
- Future-proof—TensorFlow 2.0 follows the Keras standard and the standard will last the test of time.

Summary

In this chapter, all the major changes that were introduced in TensorFlow 2.0 have been presented, including the standardization of the framework on the Keras API specification, the way models are defined using Keras, and how to train them using a custom training loop. We even looked at graph acceleration, which was introduced by AutoGraph, and `tf.function`.

AutoGraph, in particular, still requires us to know how the TensorFlow graph architecture works since the Python function that's defined and used in eager mode needs to be re-engineered if there is the need to graph-accelerate them.

The new API is more modular, object-oriented, and standardized; these groundbreaking changes have been made to make the usage of the framework easier and more natural, although the subtleties from the graph architecture are still present and always will be.

Those of you who have years of experience working with TensorFlow 1.0 may find it really difficult to change your way of thinking to the new object-based and no more graph- and session-based approach; however, it is a struggle that's worth it since the overall quality of the written software increases.

In the next chapter, we will learn about efficient data input pipelines and the Estimator API.

Exercises

Please go through the following exercises and answer all questions carefully. This is the only way (by making exercises, via trial and error, and with a lot of struggle) you will be able to master the framework and become an expert:

1. Define a classifier using the Sequential, Functional, and Subclassing APIs so that you can classify the fashion-MNIST dataset.
2. Train the model using the Keras model's built-in methods and measure the prediction accuracy.
3. Write a class that accepts a Keras model in its constructor and that it trains and evaluates.
   The API should work as follows:

   ```
   # Define your model
   trainer = Trainer(model)
   # Get features and labels as numpy arrays (explore the dataset
   available in the keras module)
   trainer.train(features, labels)
   ```

```
# measure the accuracy
trainer.evaluate(test_features, test_labels)
```

4. Accelerate the training method using the `@tf.function` annotation. Create a private method called `_train_step` to accelerate only the most computationally-intensive part of the training loop.
   Run the training and measure the performance boost in milliseconds.

5. Define a Keras model with multiple (2) inputs and multiple (2) outputs. The model must accept a grayscale 28 x 28 x 1 image as input, as well as a second grayscale image that's 28 x 28 x 1 in size. The first layer should be a concatenation on the depth of these two images (28 x 28 x 1).
   The architecture should be an autoencoder-like structure of convolutions that will reduce the input to a vector of 1 x 1 x 128 first, and then in its decoding part will upsample (using the `tf.keras.layer.UpSampling2D` layer) the layers until it gets back to 28 x 28 x D, where D is the depth of your choice.
   Then, two unary convolutional layers should be added on top of this last layer, each of them producing a 28 x 28 x 1 image.

6. Define a training loop using the fashion-MNIST dataset that generates (`image`, `condition`) pairs, where `condition` is a 28 x 28 x 1 image completely white if the label associated with `image` is 6; otherwise, it needs to be a black image.
   Before feeding the network, scale the input images in the `[-1, 1]` range.
   Train the network using the sum of two losses. The first loss is the L2 between the first input and the first output of the network. The second loss is the L1 between the `condition` and the second output.
   Measure the L1 reconstruction error on the first pair during the training. Stop the training when the value is less than 0.5.

7. Use the TensorFlow conversion tool to convert all the scripts in order to solve the exercises that were presented in *Chapter 3, TensorFlow Graph Architecture*.

8. Analyze the result of the conversion: does it uses Keras? If not, manually migrate the models by getting rid of every `tf.compat.v1` reference. Is this always possible?

9. Pick a training loop you wrote for one of the preceding exercises: the gradients can be manipulated before applying the updates. Constraints should be the norm of the gradients and in the range of [-1, 1] before the updates are applied. Use the TensorFlow primitives to do that: it should be compatible with `@tf.function`.

10. Does the following function produce any output if it's decorated with `@tf.function`? Describe what happens under the hood:

```
def output():
    for i in range(10):
        tf.print(i)
```

11. Does the following function produce any output if it's decorated with `@tf.function`? Describe what happens under the hood:

```
def output():
    for i in tf.range(10):
        print(i)
```

12. Does the following function produce any output if it's decorated with `@tf.function`? Describe what happens under the hood:

```
def output():
    for i in tf.range(10):
        tf.print(f"{i}", i)
        print(f"{i}", i)
```

13. Given $f(x,y) = \dfrac{x^2}{2y} + 6xy - \sqrt{xy}$, compute the first and second-order partial derivatives using `tf.GradientTape` in $x = 2$ and $y = 1$.

14. Remove the side effects from the example that fails to execute in the *No more globals* section and use the constant instead of the variable.

15. Extend the custom training loop defined in the *Custom training loop* section in order to measure the accuracy of the whole training set, of the whole validation set, and at the end of each training epoch. Then, perform model selection using two `tf.train.CheckpointManager` objects.

    If the validation accuracy stops increasing (with a variation of +/-0.2 at most) for 5 epochs, stop the training.

16. In the following training functions, has the `step` variable been converted into a `tf.Variable` object? If not, what are the cons of this?

```
@tf.function
def train(model, optimizer):
  train_ds = mnist_dataset()
  step = 0
  loss = 0.0
  accuracy = 0.0
  for x, y in train_ds:
    step += 1
    loss = train_one_step(model, optimizer, x, y)
    if tf.equal(step % 10, 0):
      tf.print('Step', step, ': loss', loss, '; accuracy',
compute_accuracy.result())
  return step, loss, accuracy
```

Keep working on all of these exercises throughout this book.

5
Efficient Data Input Pipelines and Estimator API

In this chapter, we will look at two of the most common modules of the TensorFlow API: `tf.data` and `tf.estimator`.

The TensorFlow 1.x design was so good that almost nothing changed in TensorFlow 2.0; in fact, `tf.data` and `tf.estimator` were the first two high-level modules introduced during the life cycle of TensorFlow 1.x.

The `tf.data` module is a high-level API that allows you to define high-efficiency input pipelines without worrying about threads, queues, synchronization, and distributed filesystems. The API was designed with simplicity in mind to overcome the usability issues of the previous low-level API.

The `tf.estimator` API was designed to simplify and standardize machine learning programming, allowing to train, evaluate, run inference, and export for serving a parametric model, letting the user focus on the model and input definition only.

The `tf.data` and `tf.estimator` APIs are fully compatible, and it is highly encouraged to use them together. Moreover, as we will see in the next sections, every Keras model, the whole eager execution, and even AutoGraph are fully compatible with the `tf.data.Dataset` object. This compatibility speeds up the training and evaluation phases by defining and using high-efficiency data input pipelines in a few lines.

In this chapter, we will cover the following topics:

- Efficient data input pipelines
- The `tf.estimator` API

Efficient data input pipelines

Data is the most critical part of every machine learning pipeline; the model learns from it, and its quantity and quality are game-changers of every machine learning application.

Feeding data to a Keras model has so far seemed natural: we can fetch the dataset as a NumPy array, create the batches, and feed the batches to the model to train it using mini-batch gradient descent.

However, the way of feeding the input shown so far is, in fact, hugely inefficient and error-prone, for the following reasons:

- The complete dataset can weight several thousands of GBs: no single standard computer or even a deep learning workstation has the memory required to load huge datasets in memory.
- Manually creating the input batches means taking care of the slicing indexes manually; errors can happen.
- Doing data augmentation, applying random perturbations to each input sample, slows down the model training phase since the augmentation process needs to complete before feeding the data to the model. Parallelizing these operations means you worry about synchronization problems among threads and many other common issues related to parallel computing. Moreover, the boilerplate code increases.
- Feeding a model whose parameters are on a GPU/TPU from the main Python process that resides on the CPU involves loading/unloading data, and this is a process that can make the computation suboptimal: the hardware utilization can be below 100% and is a complete waste.

The TensorFlow implementation of the Keras API specification, `tf.keras`, has native support for feeding models via the `tf.data` API, as it is possible and suggested to use them while using, eager execution, AutoGraph, and estimator API.

Defining an input pipeline is a common practice that can be framed as an ETL (Extract Transform and Load) process.

Input pipeline structure

Defining a training input pipeline is a standard process; the steps to follow can be framed as an **Extract Transform and Load** (ETL) process: that is, the procedure of copying the data from a data source to a destination system that will use it.

The ETL process consists of the following three steps that the `tf.data.Dataset` object allows us to implement easily:

1. **Extract**: Read the data from the data source. It can be either local (persistent storage, already loaded in memory) or remote (cloud storage, remote filesystem).
2. **Transform**: Apply transformations to the data to clean, augment (random crop image, flip, color distortion, add noise), make it interpretable by the model. Conclude the transformation by shuffling and batching the data.
3. **Load**: Load the transformed data into the device that better fits the training needs (GPUs or TPUs) and execute the training.

These ETL steps can be performed not only during the training phases but also during the inference.

If the target device for the training/inference is not the CPU but a different device, the `tf.data` API effectively utilizes the CPU, reserving the target device for the inference/training of the model; in fact, target devices such as GPUs or TPUs make it possible to train parametric models faster, while the CPU is heavily utilized for the sequential processing of the input data.

This process, however, is prone to becoming the bottleneck of the whole training process since target devices could consume the data at a faster rate than the CPU produces it.

The `tf.data` API, through its `tf.data.Dataset` class, allows us to easily define data input pipelines that transparently solve all the previous issues while adding powerful high-level features that make using them a pleasure. Special attention has to be given to performance optimization since it is still up to the developer to define the ETL process correctly to have 100% usage of the target devices, manually removing any bottleneck.

The tf.data.Dataset object

A `tf.data.Dataset` object represents an input pipeline as a collection of elements accompanied by an ordered set of transformations that act on those elements.

Each element contains one or more `tf.Tensor` objects. For example, for an image classification problem, the `tf.data.Dataset` elements might be single training examples with a pair of tensors representing the image and its associated label.

There are several ways of creating a dataset object, depending on the *data source*.

Depending on the data position and format, the `tf.data.Dataset` class offers many static methods to use to create a dataset easily:

- **Tensors in memory**: `tf.data.Dataset.from_tensors` or `tf.data.Dataset.from_tensor_slices`. In this case, the tensors can be NumPy arrays or `tf.Tensor` objects.
- **From a Python generator**: `tf.data.Dataset.from_generator`.
- **From a list of files that matches a pattern**: `tf.data.Dataset.list_files`.

Also, there are two specializations of the `tf.data.Dataset` object created for working with two commonly used file formats:

- `tf.data.TFRecordDataset` to work with the `TFRecord` files
- `tf.data.TextLineDataset` to work with text files, reading them line by line

A description of the `TFRecord` file format is presented in the optimization section that follows.

Once the dataset object has been constructed, it is possible to transform it into a new `tf.data.Dataset` object by chaining method calls. The `tf.data` API extensively uses method chaining to naturally express the set of transformations applied to the data as a sequence of actions.

In TensorFlow 1.x, it was required to create an iterator node since the input pipeline was a member of the computational graph, too. From version 2.0 onward, the `tf.data.Dataset` object is iterable, which means you can either enumerate its elements using a `for` loop or create a Python iterator using the `iter` keyword.

Please note that being iterable does not imply being a Python iterator. You can loop in a dataset by using a `for` loop, `for value in dataset`, but you can't extract elements by using `next(dataset)`.

Instead, it is possible to use `next(iterator)` after creating an iterator by using the Python `iter` keyword:
```
iterator = iter(dataset)
value = next(iterator).
```

A dataset object is a very flexible data structure that allows creating a dataset not only of numbers or a tuple of numbers but of every Python data structure. As shown in the next snippet, it is possible to mix Python dictionaries with TensorFlow generated values efficiently:

(tf2)

```
dataset = tf.data.Dataset.from_tensor_slices({
    "a": tf.random.uniform([4]),
    "b": tf.random.uniform([4, 100], maxval=100, dtype=tf.int32)
})
for value in dataset:
    # Do something with the dict value
    print(value["a"])
```

The set of transformations the tf.data.Dataset object offers through its methods supports datasets of any structure.

Let's say we want to define a dataset that produces an unlimited number of vectors, each one with 100 elements, of random values (we will do so in the chapter dedicated to the GANs, Chapter 9, *Generative Adversarial Networks*); using tf.data.Dataset.from_generator, it is possible to do so in a few lines:

(tf2)

```
def noise():
    while True:
        yield tf.random.uniform((100,))

dataset = tf.data.Dataset.from_generator(noise, (tf.float32))
```

The only peculiarity of the from_generator method is the need to pass the type of the parameters (tf.float32, in this case) as the second parameter; this is required since to build a graph we need to know the type of the parameters in advance.

Using method chaining, it is possible to create new dataset objects, transforming the one just built to get the data our machine learning model expects as input. For example, if we want to sum 10 to every component of the noise vector, shuffle the dataset content, and create batches of 32 vectors each, we can do so by calling just three methods:

(tf2)

```
buffer_size = 10
batch_size = 32
dataset = dataset.map(lambda x: x +
10).shuffle(buffer_size).batch(batch_size)
```

The `map` method is the most widely used method of the `tf.data.Dataset` object since it allows us to apply a function to every element of the input dataset, producing a new, transformed dataset.

The `shuffle` method is used in every training pipeline since this transformation randomly shuffles the input dataset using a fixed-sized buffer; this means that the shuffled data first fetches the `buffer_size` element from its input, then shuffles them and produces the output.

The `batch` method gathers the `batch_size` elements from its input and creates a batch as output. The only constraint of this transformation is that all elements of the batch must have the same shape.

To train a model, it has to be fed with all the elements of the training set for multiple epochs. The `tf.data.Dataset` class offers the `repeat(num_epochs)` method to do this.

Thus, the input data pipeline can be summarized as shown in the following diagram:

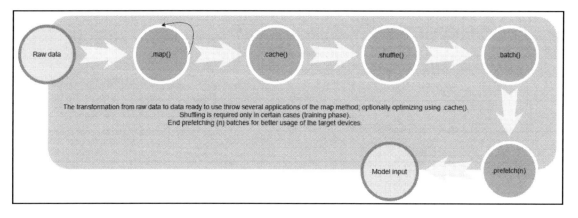

The diagram shows the typical data input pipeline: the transformation from raw data to data ready to be used by the model, just by chaining method calls. Prefetching and caching are optimization tips that are explained in the next section.

Please note that until not a single word has been said about the concept of thread, synchronization, or remote filesystems.

All this is hidden by the `tf.data` API:

- The input paths (for example, when using the `tf.data.Dataset.list_files` method) can be remote. TensorFlow internally uses the `tf.io.gfile` package, which is a file input/output wrapper without thread locking. This module makes it possible to read from a local filesystem or a remote filesystem in the same way. For instance, it is possible to read from a Google Cloud Storage bucket by using its address in the `gs://bucket/` format, without the need to worry about authentication, remote requests, and all the boilerplate required to work with a remote filesystem.
- Every transformation applied to the data is executed using all the CPU resources efficiently—a number of threads equal to the number of CPU cores are created together with the dataset object and are used to process the data sequentially and in parallel whenever parallel transformation is possible.
- The synchronization among these threads is all managed by the `tf.data` API.

All the transformations described by chaining method calls are executed by threads on the CPU that `tf.data.Dataset` instantiates to perform operations that can be executed in parallel automatically, which is a great performance boost.

Furthermore, `tf.data.Dataset` is high-level enough to make invisible all the threads execution and synchronization, but the automated solution can be suboptimal: the target device could be not completely used, and it is up to the user to remove the bottlenecks to reach the 100% usage of the target devices.

Performance optimizations

The `tf.data` API as shown so far describes a sequential data input pipeline that transforms the data from a raw to a useful format by applying transformations.

All these operations are executed on the CPU while the target device (CPUs, TPUs, or, in general, the consumer) waits for the data. If the target device consumes the data faster than it is produced, there will be moments of 0% utilization of the target devices.

In parallel programming, this problem has been solved by using prefetching.

Prefetching

When the consumer is working, the producer shouldn't be idle but must work in the background to produce the data the consumer will need in the next iteration.

The `tf.data` API offers the `prefetch(n)` method to apply a transformation that allows overlapping the work of the producer and the consumer. The best practice is adding `prefetch(n)` at the end of the input pipeline to overlap the transformation performed on the CPU with the computation done on the target.

Choosing `n` is easy: `n` is the number of elements consumed by a training step, and since the vast majority of models are trained using batches of data, one batch per training step, then `n=1`.

The process of reading from disks, especially if reading big files, reading from slow HDDs, or using remote filesystems can be time-consuming. Caching is often used to reduce this overhead.

Cache elements

The `cache` transformation can be used to cache the data in memory, completely removing the accesses to the data sources. This can bring huge benefits when using remote filesystems, or when the reading process is slow. Caching data after the first epoch is only possible if the data can fit into memory.

The `cache` method acts as a barrier in the transformation pipeline: everything executed before the `cache` method is executed only once, thus placing this transformation in the pipeline can bring immense benefits. In fact, it can be applied after a computationally intensive transformation or after any slow process to speed up everything that comes next.

Using TFRecords

Reading data is a time-intensive process. Often, data can't be read as it is stored on the disk linearly, but the files have to be processed and transformed to be correctly read.

The `TFRecord` format is a binary and language-agnostic format (defined using `protobuf`) for storing a sequence of binary records. TensorFlow allows reading and writing `TFRecord` files that are composed of a series of `tf.Example` messages.

A `tf.Example` is a flexible message type that represents a `{"key": value}` mapping where `key` is the feature name, and `value` is its binary representation.

For example, `tf.Example` could be the dictionary (in pseudocode):

```
{
    "height": image.height,
    "width": image.widht,
    "depth": image.depth,
    "label": label,
    "image": image.bytes()
}
```

Where a row of the dataset (image, label, together with additional information) is serialized as an example and stored inside a `TFRecord` file, in particular, the image is not stored using a compression format but directly using its binary representation. This allows reading the image linearly, as a sequence of bytes, without the need to apply any image decoding algorithm on it, saving time (but using disk space).

Before the introduction of `tfds` (TensorFlow Datasets), reading and writing `TFRecord` files was a repetitive and tedious process since we had to take care of how to serialize and deserialize the input features to be compatible with the `TFRecord` binary format. TensorFlow Datasets, that is, a high-level API built over the `TFRecord` file specification, standardized the process of high-efficiency dataset creation, forcing the creation of the `TFRecord` representation of any dataset. Furthermore, `tfds` already contains a lot of ready-to-use datasets correctly stored in the `TFRecord` format, and its official guide explains perfectly how to build a dataset, by describing its features, to create the `TFRecord` representation of the dataset ready to use.

Since the `TFRecord` description and usage goes beyond the scope of this book, in the next sections we will cover only the utilization of TensorFlow Datasets. For a complete guide on the creation of a TensorFlow Dataset Builder see `Chapter 8`, *Semantic Segmentation and Custom Dataset Builder*. If you are interested in the `TFRecord` representation please refer to the official documentation: `https://www.tensorflow.org/beta/tutorials/load_data/tf_records`.

Building your dataset

The following example shows how to build a `tf.data.Dataset` object using the Fashion-MNIST dataset. This is the first complete example of a dataset that uses all the best practices described previously; please take the time to understand why the method chaining is performed in this way and where the performance optimizations have been applied.

In the following code, we define the `train_dataset` function, which returns the `tf.data.Dataset` object ready to use:

(tf2)

```
import tensorflow as tf
from tensorflow.keras.datasets import fashion_mnist


def train_dataset(batch_size=32, num_epochs=1):
    (train_x, train_y), (test_x, test_y) = fashion_mnist.load_data()
    input_x, input_y = train_x, train_y

    def scale_fn(image, label):
        return (tf.image.convert_image_dtype(image, tf.float32) - 0.5) *
2.0, label

    dataset = tf.data.Dataset.from_tensor_slices(
        (tf.expand_dims(input_x, -1), tf.expand_dims(input_y, -1))
    ).map(scale_fn)

    dataset = dataset.cache().repeat(num_epochs)
    dataset = dataset.shuffle(batch_size)

    return dataset.batch(batch_size).prefetch(1)
```

A training dataset, however, should contain augmented data in order to address the overfitting problem. Applying data augmentation on image data is straightforward using the TensorFlow `tf.image` package.

Data augmentation

The ETL process defined so far only transforms the raw data, applying transformations that do not change the image content. Data augmentation, instead, requires to apply meaningful transformation the raw data with the aim of creating a bigger dataset and train, thus, a model more robust to these kinds of variations.

Working with images, it is possible to use the whole API offered by the `tf.image` package to augment the dataset. The augmentation step consists in the definition of a function and its application to the training set, using the dataset `map` method.

The set of valid transformations depends on the dataset—if we were using the MNIST dataset, for instance, flipping the input image upside down won't be a good idea (nobody wants to feed an image of the number 6 labeled as 9), but since we are using the fashion-MNIST dataset we can flip and rotate the input image as we like (a pair of trousers remains a pair of trousers, even if randomly flipped or rotated).

The `tf.image` package already contains functions with stochastic behavior, designed for data augmentation. These functions apply the transformation to the input image with a 50% chance; this is the desired behavior since we want to feed the model with both original and augmented images. Thus, a function that applies meaningful transformations to the input data can be defined as follows:

(tf2)

```
def augment(image):
    image = tf.image.random_flip_left_right(image)
    image = tf.image.random_flip_up_down(image)
    image = tf.image.random_brightness(image, max_delta=0.1)
    return image
```

Applying this augmentation function to the dataset, using the dataset `map` method, is left as an exercise for you.

Although it is easy, thanks to the `tf.data` API, building your own datasets to benchmark every new algorithm on a standard task (classification, object detection, or semantic segmentation) can be a repetitive and, therefore, error-prone process. The TensorFlow developers, together with the TensorFlow developer community, standardized the *extraction* and *transformation* process of the ETL pipeline, developing TensorFlow Datasets.

The data augmentation functions offered by TensorFlow sometimes are not enough, especially when working with small datasets that require a lot of argumentation to become useful. There are many data augmentation libraries written in Python that can be easily integrated into the dataset augmentation step. Two of the most common are the following:
- **imgaug**: https://github.com/aleju/imgaug
- **albumentations**: https://github.com/albu/albumentations
Using `tf.py_function` it is possible to execute Python code inside the `map` method, and thus use these libraries to generate a rich set of transformations (not offered by the `tf.image` package).

TensorFlow Datasets – tfds

TensorFlow Datasets is a collection of ready-to-use datasets that handle the downloading and preparation phases of the ETL process, constructing a `tf.data.Dataset` object.

The significant advantage this project has brought to machine learning practitioners is the extreme simplification of the data download and preparation of the most commonly used benchmark dataset.

TensorFlow Datasets (`tfds`) not only downloads and converts the dataset to a standard format but also locally converts the dataset to its `TFRecord` representation, making the reading from disk highly efficient and giving the user a `tf.data.Dataset` object that reads from `TFRecord` and is ready to use. The API comes with the concept of a builder. Every builder is an available dataset.

Different from the `tf.data` API, TensorFlow Datasets comes as a separate package that needs to be installed.

Installation

Being a Python package, installing it using `pip` is straightforward:

```
pip install tensorflow-datasets
```

That's it. The package is lightweight since all the datasets are downloaded only when needed.

Usage

The package comes with two main methods: `list_builders()` and `load()`:

- `list_builders()` returns the list of the available datasets.
- `load(name, split)` accepts the name of an available builder and the desired split. The split value depends on the builder since every builder carries its information.

Using `tfds` to load the train and test splits of MNIST, in the list of the available builders, is shown as follows:

(tf2)

```
import tensorflow_datasets as tfds

# See available datasets
print(tfds.list_builders())
# Construct 2 tf.data.Dataset objects
# The training dataset and the test dataset
ds_train, ds_test = tfds.load(name="mnist", split=["train", "test"])
```

In a single line of code, we downloaded, processed, and converted the dataset to TFRecord, and created two `tf.data.Dataset` objects to read them.

In this single line of code, we don't have any information about the dataset itself: no clue about the data type of the returned objects, the shape of the images and labels, and so on.

To gain a complete description of the whole dataset, it is possible to use the builder associated with the dataset and print the `info` property; this property contains all the information required to work with the dataset, from the academic citation to the data format:

(tf2)

```
builder = tfds.builder("mnist")
print(builder.info)
```

Executing it, we get the following:

```
tfds.core.DatasetInfo(
    name='mnist',
    version=1.0.0,
    description='The MNIST database of handwritten digits.',
    urls=['http://yann.lecun.com/exdb/mnist/'],
    features=FeaturesDict({
        'image': Image(shape=(28, 28, 1), dtype=tf.uint8),
        'label': ClassLabel(shape=(), dtype=tf.int64, num_classes=10)
    },
    total_num_examples=70000,
    splits={
        'test': <tfds.core.SplitInfo num_examples=10000>,
        'train': <tfds.core.SplitInfo num_examples=60000>
    },
    supervised_keys=('image', 'label'),
    citation='"""
```

```
          @article{lecun2010mnist,
             title={MNIST handwritten digit database},
             author={LeCun, Yann and Cortes, Corinna and Burges, CJ},
             journal={ATT Labs [Online]. Available: http://yann. lecun.
   com/exdb/mnist},
             volume={2},
             year={2010}
          }
      """,
   )
```

That's all we need.

Using `tfds` is highly encouraged; moreover, since the `tf.data.Dataset` objects are returned, there is no need to learn how to use another fancy API as the `tf.data` API is the standard, and we can use it everywhere in TensorFlow 2.0.

Keras integration

Dataset objects are natively supported by the TensorFlow implementation of the Keras `tf.keras` specification. This means that using NumPy arrays or using a `tf.data.Dataset` object is the same when it comes to training/evaluating a model. The classification model defined in Chapter 4, *TensorFlow 2.0 Architecture*, using the `tf.keras.Sequential` API, can be trained more quickly using the `tf.data.Dataset` object created by the `train_dataset` function previously defined.

In the following code, we just use the standard `.compile` and `.fit` method calls, to compile (define the training loop) and fit the dataset (that is a `tf.data.Dataset`):

```
(tf2)

   model.compile(
      optimizer=tf.keras.optimizers.Adam(1e-5),
      loss='sparse_categorical_crossentropy',
      metrics=['accuracy'])

   model.fit(train_dataset(num_epochs=10))
```

TensorFlow 2.0, being eager by default, natively allows iterating over a `tf.data.Dataset` object to build our own custom training loop.

Eager integration

The `tf.data.Dataset` object is iterable, which means one can either enumerate its elements using a for loop or create a Python iterator using the `iter` keyword. Please note that being iterable does not imply being a Python iterator as pointed out at the beginning of this chapter.

Iterating over a dataset object is extremely easy: we can use the standard Python `for` loop to extract a batch at each iteration.

Configuring the input pipeline by using a dataset object is a better solution than the one used so far.

The manual process of extracting elements from a dataset by computing the indices is error-prone and inefficient, while the `tf.data.Dataset` objects are highly-optimized. Moreover, the dataset objects are fully compatible with `tf.function`, and therefore the whole training loop can be graph-converted and accelerated.

Furthermore, the lines of code get reduced a lot, increasing the readability. The following code block represents the graph-accelerated (via `@tf.function`) custom training loop from the previous chapter, `Chapter 4`, *TensorFlow 2.0 Architecture*; the loop uses the `train_dataset` function defined previously:

```
(tf2)

    def train():
        # Define the model
        n_classes = 10
        model = make_model(n_classes)

        # Input data
        dataset = train_dataset(num_epochs=10)

        # Training parameters
        loss = tf.losses.SparseCategoricalCrossentropy(from_logits=True)
        step = tf.Variable(1, name="global_step")
        optimizer = tf.optimizers.Adam(1e-3)
        accuracy = tf.metrics.Accuracy()

        # Train step function
        @tf.function
        def train_step(inputs, labels):
            with tf.GradientTape() as tape:
                logits = model(inputs)
                loss_value = loss(labels, logits)
```

```
        gradients = tape.gradient(loss_value, model.trainable_variables)
        optimizer.apply_gradients(zip(gradients,
model.trainable_variables))
        step.assign_add(1)

        accuracy_value = accuracy(labels, tf.argmax(logits, -1))
        return loss_value, accuracy_value

    @tf.function
    def loop():
        for features, labels in dataset:
            loss_value, accuracy_value = train_step(features, labels)
            if tf.equal(tf.math.mod(step, 10), 0):
                tf.print(step, ": ", loss_value, " - accuracy: ",
                    accuracy_value)

    loop()
```

You are invited to read the source code carefully and compare it with the custom training loop from the previous chapter, Chapter 4, *TensorFlow 2.0 Architecture*.

Estimator API

In the previous section, we saw how the tf.data API simplifies and standardizes the input pipeline definition. Also, we saw that the tf.data API is completely integrated into the TensorFlow Keras implementation and the eager or graph-accelerated version of a custom training loop.

Just as for the input data pipelines, there are a lot of repetitive parts in the whole machine learning programming. In particular, after defining the first version of the machine learning model, the practitioner is interested in:

- Training
- Evaluating
- Predicting

After many iterations of these points, exporting the trained model for serving is the natural consequence.

Of course, defining a training loop, the evaluation process, and the predicting process are very similar for each machine learning process. For example, for a predictive model, we are interested in training the model for a certain number of epochs, measuring a metric on the training and validation set at the end of the process, and repeating this process, changing the hyperparameters until the results are satisfactory.

To simplify machine learning programming and help the developer to focus on the nonrepetitive parts of the process, TensorFlow introduced the concept of Estimator through the `tf.estimator` API.

The `tf.estimator` API is a high-level API that encapsulates the repetitive and standard processes of the machine learning pipeline. For more information on estimators, see the official documentation (`https://www.tensorflow.org/guide/estimators`). Here are the main advantages estimators bring:

- You can run Estimator-based models on a local host or a distributed multiserver environment without changing your model. Furthermore, you can run Estimator-based models on CPUs, GPUs, or TPUs without recoding your model.
- Estimators simplify sharing implementations between model developers.
- You can develop a state-of-the-art model with high-level, intuitive code. In short, it is generally much easier to create models with Estimators than with the low-level TensorFlow APIs.
- Estimators are themselves built on `tf.keras.layers`, which simplifies customization.
- Estimators build the graph for you.
- Estimators provide a safely distributed training loop that controls how and when to:
  - Build the graph
  - Initialize variables
  - Load data
  - Handle exceptions
  - Create checkpoint files and recover from failures

- Save summaries for TensorBoard

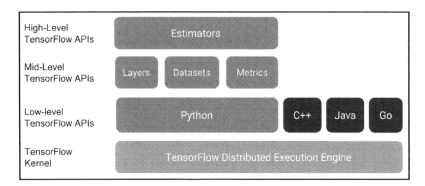

The Estimator API is built upon the TensorFlow mid-level layers; in particular, estimators themselves are built using the Keras layers in order to simplify the customization. Image credits: tensorflow.org

The standardization process of the machine learning pipeline passes through the definition of a class that describes it: `tf.estimator.Estimator`.

To use this class, you need to use a well-defined programming model that is enforced by the public methods of the `tf.estimator.Estimator` object, as shown in the following screenshot:

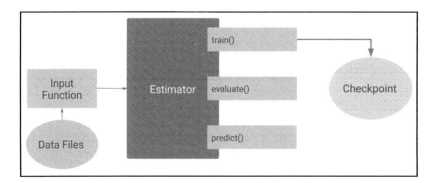

The estimator programming model is enforced by the Estimator object public methods; the API itself takes care of the checkpoint saving and reloading; the user must implement only the input function and the model itself; the standard processes of training, evaluate, and predict are implemented by the API. Image credits: tensorflow.org

It is possible to use the Estimator API in two different ways: building custom Estimators or using premade Estimators.

Premade and custom Estimators follow the same programming model; the only difference is that in custom Estimators the user must write a `model_fn` model function, while in the premade Estimator the model definition comes for free (at the cost of lower flexibility).

The programming model the Estimator API forces you to use consists of the implementation of two components:

- The implementation of the data input pipeline, implementing the `input_fn` function
- (optional) The implementation of the model, handling the training, evaluation, and predict cases, and implementing the `model_fn` function

Please note that the documentation talks about graphs. In fact, to guarantee high performance, the Estimator API is built upon the (hidden) graph representation. Even if TensorFlow 2.0 defaults on the eager execution paradigm, neither `model_fn` and `input_fn` are executed eagerly, the Estimator switches to graph mode before calling these functions, which is why the code has to be compatible with graph mode execution.

In practice, the Estimator API is a standardization of the good practice of separating the data from the model. This is well highlighted by the constructor of the `tf.estimator.Estimator` object, which is the subject of this chapter:

```
__init__(
    model_fn,
    model_dir=None,
    config=None,
    params=None,
    warm_start_from=None
)
```

It is worth noticing that there is no mention of `input_fn` in the constructor, and this makes sense since the input can change during the estimator's lifetime, whereas the model can't.

Let's see how the `input_fn` function should be implemented.

Data input pipeline

Firstly, let's look at the standard ETL process:

- **Extract**: Read the data from the data source. It can be either local (persistent storage, already loaded in memory) or remote (Cloud Storage, remote filesystem).

- **Transform**: Apply transformations to the data to clean, augment (random crop image, flip, color distortion, adding noise), and make the data interpretable by the model. Conclude the transformation by shuffling and batching the data.
- **Load**: Load the transformed data into the device that better fits the training needs (GPUs or TPUs) and execute the training.

The `tf.estimator.Estimator` API merges the first two phases in the implementation of the `input_fn` function passed to the `train` and `evaluate` methods.

The `input_fn` function is a Python function that returns a `tf.data.Dataset` object, which yields the `features` and `labels` objects consumed by the model, that's all.

As known from the theory presented in Chapter 1, *What is machine learning?*, the correct way of using a dataset is to split it into three non-overlapping parts: training, validation, and test set.

To correctly implement it, it is suggested to define an input function that accepts an input parameter able to change the returned `tf.data.Dataset` object, returning a new function to pass as input to the Estimator object. The estimator API comes with the concept of *mode*.

The model, and dataset too, can be in a different mode, depending on which phases of the pipeline we are at. The mode is implemented in the `enum` type `tf.estimator.ModeKeys`, which contains the three standard keys:

- `TRAIN`: Training mode
- `EVAL`: Evaluation mode
- `PREDICT`: Inference mode

It is thus possible to use a `tf.estimator.ModeKeys` input variable to change the returned dataset (the fact that this is not required by the Estimator API is something that comes in handy).

Suppose we are interested in defining the correct input pipeline for a classification model of the fashion-MNIST dataset, we just have to get the data, split the dataset (since the evaluation set is not provided, we halve the test set), and build the dataset object we need.

The input signature of the input function is completely up to the developer; this freedom allows us to define the dataset objects parametrically by passing every dataset parameter as function inputs:

```
(tf2)

    import tensorflow as tf
```

```
from tensorflow.keras.datasets import fashion_mnist


def get_input_fn(mode, batch_size=32, num_epochs=1):
    (train_x, train_y), (test_x, test_y) = fashion_mnist.load_data()
    half = test_x.shape[0] // 2
    if mode == tf.estimator.ModeKeys.TRAIN:
        input_x, input_y = train_x, train_y
        train = True
    elif mode == tf.estimator.ModeKeys.EVAL:
        input_x, input_y = test_x[:half], test_y[:half]
        train = False
    elif mode == tf.estimator.ModeKeys.PREDICT:
        input_x, input_y = test_x[half:-1], test_y[half:-1]
        train = False
    else:
        raise ValueError("tf.estimator.ModeKeys required!")

    def scale_fn(image, label):
        return (
            (tf.image.convert_image_dtype(image, tf.float32) - 0.5) * 2.0,
            tf.cast(label, tf.int32),
        )

    def input_fn():
        dataset = tf.data.Dataset.from_tensor_slices(
            (tf.expand_dims(input_x, -1), tf.expand_dims(input_y, -1))
        ).map(scale_fn)
        if train:
            dataset = dataset.shuffle(10).repeat(num_epochs)
        dataset = dataset.batch(batch_size).prefetch(1)
        return dataset

    return input_fn
```

After defining the input function, the programming model introduced by the Estimator API gives us two choices: create our own custom estimator by manually defining the model to train, or use the so-called canned or premade estimators.

Custom estimators

Premade and custom estimators share a common architecture: both aim to build a tf.estimator.EstimatorSpec object that fully defines the model to be run by tf.estimator.Estimator; the return value of any model_fn is, therefore, the Estimator specification.

The model_fn function follows this signature:

```
model_fn(
    features,
    labels,
    mode = None,
    params = None,
    config = None
)
```

The function parameters are:

- features is the first item returned from input_fn
- labels is the second item returned from input_fn
- mode is the tf.estimator.ModeKeys object that specifies the status of the model, if it is in the training, evaluation, or prediction phase
- params is a dictionary of hyperparameters that can be used to tune the model easily
- config is a tf.estimator.RunConfig object that allows you to configure parameters related to the runtime execution, such as the model parameters directory and the number of distributed nodes to use

Note that features, labels, and mode are the most important part of the model_fn definition, and that the signature of model_fn must use these parameter names; otherwise, a ValueError exception is raised.

The requirement of having a complete match with the input signature is proof that estimators must be used in standard scenarios when the whole machine learning pipeline can get a huge speedup from this standardization.

The goals of model_fn are twofold: it has to define the model using Keras, and define its behavior during the various mode. The way to specify the behavior is to return a correctly built tf.estimator.EstimatorSpec.

Since even writing the model function is straightforward using the Estimator API, a complete implementation of a classification problem solution using the Estimator API follows. The model definition is pure Keras, and the function used is the `make_model(num_classes)` previously defined.

You are invited to look carefully at how the behavior of the model changes when the `mode` parameter changes:

Important: The Estimator API, although present in TensorFlow 2.0, still works in graph mode. `model_fn`, thus, can use Keras to build the model, but the training and summary logging operation must be defined using the `tf.compat.v1` compatibility module.
Please refer to `Chapter 3`, *TensorFlow Graph Architecture*, for a better understanding of the graph definition.

```
(tf2)
    def model_fn(features, labels, mode):
        v1 = tf.compat.v1
        model = make_model(10)
        logits = model(features)

        if mode == tf.estimator.ModeKeys.PREDICT:
            # Extract the predictions
            predictions = v1.argmax(logits, -1)
            return tf.estimator.EstimatorSpec(mode, predictions=predictions)

        loss = v1.reduce_mean(
            v1.nn.sparse_softmax_cross_entropy_with_logits(
                logits=logits, labels=v1.squeeze(labels)
            )
        )

        global_step = v1.train.get_global_step()

        # Compute evaluation metrics.
        accuracy = v1.metrics.accuracy(
            labels=labels, predictions=v1.argmax(logits, -1), name="accuracy"
        )
        # The metrics dictionary is used by the estimator during the evaluation
        metrics = {"accuracy": accuracy}

        if mode == tf.estimator.ModeKeys.EVAL:
            return tf.estimator.EstimatorSpec(mode, loss=loss,
    eval_metric_ops=metrics)
        if mode == tf.estimator.ModeKeys.TRAIN:
            opt = v1.train.AdamOptimizer(1e-4)
```

```
        train_op = opt.minimize(
            loss, var_list=model.trainable_variables,
    global_step=global_step
            )

        return tf.estimator.EstimatorSpec(mode, loss=loss,
    train_op=train_op)

    raise NotImplementedError(f"Unknown mode {mode}")
```

The model_fn function works exactly like a standard graph model of TensorFlow 1.x; the whole model behavior (three possible scenarios) is encoded inside the function, inside the Estimator specification the function returns.

A few lines of code are required to train and evaluate the model performance at the end of every training epoch:

(tf2)

```
print("Every log is on TensorBoard, please run TensorBoard --logidr log")
estimator = tf.estimator.Estimator(model_fn, model_dir="log")
for epoch in range(50):
    print(f"Training for the {epoch}-th epoch")
    estimator.train(get_input_fn(tf.estimator.ModeKeys.TRAIN,
num_epochs=1))
    print("Evaluating...")
    estimator.evaluate(get_input_fn(tf.estimator.ModeKeys.EVAL))
```

The loop for 50 epochs shows that the estimator API takes care of restoring the model parameters and saving them at the end of each .train invocation, without any user intervention, all automatically.

By running TensorBoard --logdir log, it is possible to see the loss and accuracy trends. The orange is the training run while the blue is the validation run:

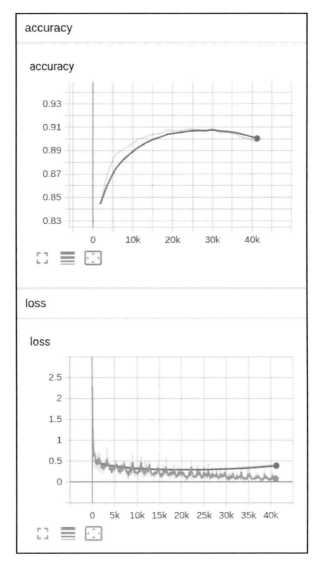

The validation accuracy and the training and validation loss values as shown in TensorBoard

Writing custom estimators requires you to think about the TensorFlow graph architecture and use them as in the 1.x version.

In TensorFlow 2.0, as in the 1.x version, it is possible to define computational graphs by using premade estimators that define the `model_fn` function automatically, without the need to think in the graph-way.

Premade estimators

TensorFlow 2.0 has two different kinds of premade Estimators: the one automatically created from the Keras model definition, and the canned-estimators built upon the TensorFlow 1.x API.

Using a Keras model

The recommended way of constructing an Estimator object in TensorFlow 2.0 is to use a Keras model itself.

The `tf.keras.estimator` package offers all the tools required to automatically convert a `tf.keras.Model` object to its Estimator counterpart. In fact, when a Keras model is compiled, the whole training and evaluation loops are defined; it naturally follows that the `compile` method almost defines an Estimator-like architecture that the `tf.keras.estimator` package is able to use.

Even when using Keras, you must always define the `tf.estimator.EstimatorSpec` objects that define the `input_fn` function to use during the training and evaluation phases.

There is no need to define a single `EstimatorSpec` object for both cases, but it is possible and recommended to use `tf.estimator.TrainSpec` and `tf.estimator.EvalSpec` to define the behavior of the model separately.

Therefore, given the usual `make_model(num_classes)` function, which creates a Keras model, it is really easy to define the specs and convert the model to an estimator:

```
(tf2)
    # Define train & eval specs
    train_spec =
    tf.estimator.TrainSpec(input_fn=get_input_fn(tf.estimator.ModeKeys.TRAIN,
    num_epochs=50))
    eval_spec =
    tf.estimator.EvalSpec(input_fn=get_input_fn(tf.estimator.ModeKeys.EVAL,
    num_epochs=1))

    # Get the Keras model
    model = make_model(10)
    # Compile it
    model.compile(optimizer='adam',
                  loss='sparse_categorical_crossentropy',
                  metrics=['accuracy'])
```

```
# Convert it to estimator
estimator = tf.keras.estimator.model_to_estimator(
    keras_model = model
)

# Train and evalution loop
tf.estimator.train_and_evaluate(estimator, train_spec, eval_spec)
```

Using a canned estimator

Model architectures are pretty much standard: convolutional neural networks are made of convolutional layers interleaved by pooling layers; fully connected neural networks are made by a stack of dense layers, each with a different number of hidden units, and so on.

The `tf.estimator` package comes with a huge list of premade models, ready to use. The full list is available in the documentation: `https://www.tensorflow.org/versions/r2.0/api_docs/python/tf/estimator`.

The process of the input function definition is pretty similar to what has been described so far; the main difference is that instead of feeding the model with the data as is, the canned Estimator requires an input description using feature columns.

Feature columns are intermediaries between the `tf.data.Dataset` object and the Estimator. In fact, they can be used to apply standard transformations to the input data, working exactly like an additional `.map` method added to the input pipeline.

Unfortunately, the `tf.estimator` API was added to TensorFlow 2.0 because of the popularity of the Estimator-based solution in 1.x, but this package lacks many features that a Keras-based or pure TensorFlow with eager execution plus AutoGraph offers. When TensorFlow 1.x was the standard, it was tough and time-consuming to experiment with many standard solutions and to manually define several standard computational graphs; that's why the Estimator package gained popularity quickly. Using TensorFlow 2.0 in eager mode and defining models using Keras, instead, allows you to prototype and experiment with many different solutions easily. Moreover, the `tf.data` API is so flexible that correctly defining the input pipeline is straightforward.

For this reason, canned Estimators are only cited in this book. This knowledge is not mandatory, and there is a high chance that in future versions of TensorFlow the, `tf.estimator` package will be removed or moved to a separate project.

Summary

In this chapter, two of the most widely used high-level APIs were presented. `tf.estimator` and `tf.data` APIs have maintained almost the same structure they had in TensorFlow 1.x since they were designed with simplicity in mind.

The `tf.data` API, through `tf.data.Dataset`, allows you to define a high-efficiency data input pipeline by chaining transformations in an ETL fashion, using the method chaining paradigm. `tf.data.Dataset` objects are integrated with every part of TensorFlow, from eager execution to AutoGraph, passing through the training methods of Keras models and the Estimator API. The ETL process is made easy and the complexity is hidden.

TensorFlow Datasets is the preferred way of creating a new `tf.data.Dataset` object, and is the perfect tool to use when a machine learning model has been developed, and it is time to measure the performance on every publicly available benchmark.

The Estimator API standardized machine learning programming but reduces flexibility while increasing productivity. In fact, it is the perfect tool to use to define the input pipeline once and to test with different standard models if a solution to the problem can be easily found.

The custom estimators, on the other hand, are the perfect tool to use when a non-standard architecture could solve the problem, but the training process is the standard one. Instead of wasting time rewriting the training loops, the metrics measurements, and all the standard machine learning training pipeline, you can focus only on the model definition. The `tf.estimator` and `tf.data` APIs are two powerful tools TensorFlow offers, and using them together speeds up the development a lot. The whole path from the development to the production is handled by these tools, making putting a model into production almost effortless.

This is the last chapter dedicated to the TensorFlow framework architecture. In the following chapters, we will look at several machine learning tasks, all of them with an end-to-end TensorFlow 2.0 solution. During the hands-on solution, we will use other features of TensorFlow 2.0, such as the integration of TensorFlow Hub with the Keras framework. The following chapters are a complete tutorial on how to use TensorFlow 2.0 to solve a certain machine learning task using neural networks.

Exercises

Once again, you are invited to answer all the following questions. You will struggle to find answers when the problems are hard, since this is the only way to master Estimator and Data APIs:

1. What is an ETL process?
2. How is an ETL process related to the `tf.data` API?
3. Why can't a `tf.data.Dataset` object can't be manipulated directly, but every non-static method returns a new dataset object that's the result of the transformation applied?
4. Which are the most common optimizations in the context of the `tf.data` API? Why is prefetching so important?
5. Given the two datasets of the next question, which one loops faster? Explain your response.
6. Given the following two datasets:

   ```
   data = tf.data.Dataset.range(100)
   data2 = tf.data.Dataset.from_generator(lambda: range(100),
   (tf.int32))

   def l1():
       for v in data:
           tf.print(v)
   def l2():
       for v in data2:
           tf.print(v)
   ```

   Can functions `l1` and `l2` be converted to their graph representations using `@tf.function`? Analyze the resulting code using the `tf.autograph` module to explain the answer.

7. When should the `tf.data.Dataset.cache` method be used?
8. Use the `tf.io.gfile` package to store an uncompressed copy of the fashion-MNIST dataset locally.
9. Create a `tf.data.Dataset` object reading the files created in the previous point; use the `tf.io.gfile` package.
10. Convert the complete example of the previous chapter to `tf.data`.
11. Convert the complete example of the previous chapter to `tf.Estimator`.

12. Use `tfds` to load the "`cat_vs_dog`" dataset. Look at its builder information: it's a single split dataset. Split it in three non-overlapping parts: the training set, the validation set, and the test set, using the `tf.data.Dataset.skip` and `tf.data.dataset.take` methods. Resize every image to `32x32x3`, and swap the labels.

13. Use the three datasets created previously to define `input_fn`, which chooses the correct split when the `mode` changes.

14. Define a custom `model_fn` function using a simple convolutional neural network to classify cats and dogs (with swapped labels). Log the results on TensorBoard and measure the accuracy, the loss value, and the distribution of the output neuron on the validation set.

15. Use a canned estimator to solve question 11. Is it possible to reproduce the same solution developed using a custom `model_fn` function with a premade Estimator?

16. From the accuracy and validation loss curves shown in the section dedicated to the custom Estimator, it is possible to see that the model is not behaving correctly; what is the name of this pathological condition and how can it be mitigated?

17. Try to reduce the pathological condition of the model (referred to in the previous question) by tweaking the `loss` and/or changing the model architecture. Your solution should reach at least a validation accuracy value of 0.96.

Section 3: The Application of Neural Networks

3

This section teaches you how to implement various neural network applications in a variety of domains and demonstrates how powerful neural networks are, especially when used with a good framework such as TensorFlow. At the end of this section, you will have theoretical, as well as practical, knowledge of different neural network architectures, and you will know how to implement them and how to put a model into production using the SavedModel format.

This section comprises the following chapters:

- Chapter 6, *Image Classification Using TensorFlow Hub*
- Chapter 7, *Introduction to Object Detection*
- Chapter 8, *Semantic Segmentation and Custom Dataset Builder*
- Chapter 9, *Generative Adversarial Networks*
- Chapter 10, *Bringing a Model to Production*

6
Image Classification Using TensorFlow Hub

We have discussed the image classification task in all of the previous chapters of this book. We have seen how it is possible to define a convolutional neural network by stacking several convolutional layers and how to train it using Keras. We also looked at eager execution and saw that using AutoGraph is straightforward.

So far, the convolutional architecture used has been a LeNet-like architecture, with an expected input size of 28 x 28, trained end to end every time to make the network learn how to extract the correct features to solve the fashion-MNIST classification task.

Building a classifier from scratch, defining the architecture layer by layer, is an excellent didactical exercise that allows you to experiment with how different layer configurations can change the network performance. However, in real-life scenarios, the amount of data available to train a classifier is often limited. Gathering clean and correctly labeled data is a time-consuming process, and collecting a dataset with thousands of samples is tough. Moreover, even when the dataset size is adequate (thus, we are in a big data regime), training a classifier on it is a slow process; the training process might require several hours of GPU time since architectures more complicated than our LeNet-like architecture are necessary to achieve satisfactory results. Different architectures have been developed over the years, all of them introducing some novelties that have allowed the correct classification of color images with a resolution higher than 28 x 28.

Academia and industry release new classification architectures to improve the state of the art year on year. Their performance for an image classification task is measured by looking at the top-1 accuracy reached by the architecture when trained and tested on massive datasets such as ImageNet.

ImageNet is a dataset of over 15 million high-resolution images with more than 22,000 categories, all of them manually labeled. The **ImageNet Large Scale Visual Recognition Challenge (ILSVRC)** is a yearly object detection and classification challenge that uses a subset of ImageNet of 1,000 images for 1,000 categories. The dataset used for the computation is made up of roughly 1.2 million training images, 50,000 validation images, and 100,000 testing images.

To achieve impressive results on an image classification task, researchers found that deep architectures were needed. This approach has a drawback—the deeper the network, the higher the number of parameters to train. But a higher number of parameters implies that a lot of computing power is needed (and computing power costs!). Since academia and industry have already developed and trained their models, why don't we take advantage of their work to speed up our development without reinventing the wheel every time?

In this chapter, we'll discuss transfer learning and fine-tuning, showing how they can speed up development. TensorFlow Hub is used as a tool to quickly get the models we need and speed up development.

By the end of this chapter, you will know how to transfer the knowledge embedded in a model to a new task, using TensorFlow Hub easily, thanks to its Keras integration.

In this chapter, we will cover the following topics:

- Getting the data
- Transfer learning
- Fine-tuning

Getting the data

The task we are going to solve in this chapter is a classification problem on a dataset of flowers, which is available in **tensorflow-datasets (tfds)**. The dataset's name is `tf_flowers` and it consists of images of five different flower species at different resolutions. Using `tfds`, gathering the data is straightforward, and we can get the dataset's information by looking at the `info` variable returned by the `tfds.load` invocation, as shown here:

```
(tf2)

    import tensorflow_datasets as tfds

    dataset, info = tfds.load("tf_flowers", with_info=True)
    print(info)
```

The preceding code produces the following dataset description:

```
tfds.core.DatasetInfo(
    name='tf_flowers',
    version=1.0.0,
    description='A large set of images of flowers',
urls=['http://download.tensorflow.org/example_images/flower_photos.tgz'],
    features=FeaturesDict({
        'image': Image(shape=(None, None, 3), dtype=tf.uint8),
        'label': ClassLabel(shape=(), dtype=tf.int64, num_classes=5)
    },
    total_num_examples=3670,
    splits={
        'train': <tfds.core.SplitInfo num_examples=3670>
    },
    supervised_keys=('image', 'label'),
    citation='"""
        @ONLINE {tfflowers,
        author = "The TensorFlow Team",
        title = "Flowers",
        month = "jan",
        year = "2019",
        url =
"http://download.tensorflow.org/example_images/flower_photos.tgz" }
        """',
    redistribution_info=,
)
```

There is a single split train with 3,670 labeled images. The image resolution is not fixed, as we can see from the None value in the height and width position of the Image shape feature. There are five classes, as expected. Looking at the download folder of the dataset (default to ~/tensorflow_datasets/downloads/extracted), we can find the dataset structure and look at the labels, which are as follows:

- Daisy
- Dandelion
- Roses
- Sunflowers
- Tulips

Every image of the dataset is licensed under a Creative Commons by attribution license. As we can see from the LICENSE.txt file, the dataset has been gathered by scraping Flickr. The following is an image sampled from the dataset:

Image labeled as sunflower. Filesunflowers/2694860538_b95d60122c_m.jpg - CC-BY by Ally Aubry (https://www.flickr.com/photos/ allyaubryphotography/2694860538/).

Very often, datasets are not made of pictures where only the labeled subject appears, and these kinds of datasets are perfect for developing algorithms that are robust at handling noise in the data.

The dataset is ready, although it is not correctly split following the guidelines. In fact, there is only a single split when, instead, three splits (train, validation, and test) are recommended. Let's create the three non-overlapping splits, by creating three separate tf.data.Dataset objects. We'll use the take and skip methods of the dataset object:

```
dataset = dataset["train"]
tot = 3670

train_set_size = tot // 2
validation_set_size = tot - train_set_size - train_set_size // 2
test_set_size = tot - train_set_size - validation_set_size


print("train set size: ", train_set_size)
print("validation set size: ", validation_set_size)
print("test set size: ", test_set_size)
```

```
train, test, validation = (
    dataset.take(train_set_size),
    dataset.skip(train_set_size).take(validation_set_size),
    dataset.skip(train_set_size + validation_set_size).take(test_set_size),
)
```

Alright. Now we have the required three splits, and we can start using them to train, evaluate, and test our classification model, which will be built by reusing a model that someone else trained on a different dataset.

Transfer learning

Only academia and some industries have the required budget and computing power to train an entire CNN from scratch, starting from random weights, on a massive dataset such as ImageNet.

Since this expensive and time-consuming work has already been done, it is a smart idea to reuse parts of the trained model to solve our classification problem.

In fact, it is possible to transfer what the network has learned from one dataset to a new one, thereby transferring the knowledge.

Transfer learning is the process of learning a new task by relying on a previously learned task: the learning process can be faster, more accurate, and require less training data.

The transfer learning idea is bright, and it can be successfully applied when using convolutional neural networks.

In fact, all convolutional architectures for classification have a fixed structure, and we can reuse parts of them as building blocks for our applications. The general structure is composed of three elements:

- **Input layer**: The architecture is designed to accept an image with a precise resolution. The input resolution influences all of the architecture; if the input layer resolution is high, the network will be deeper.
- **Feature extractor**: This is the set of convolution, pooling, normalizations, and every other layer that is in between the input layer and the first dense layer. The architecture learns to summarize all the information contained in the input image in a low-dimensional representation (in the diagram that follows, an image with a size of 227 x 227 x 3 is projected into a 9216-dimensional vector).

- **Classification layers**: These are a stack of fully connected layers—a fully-connected classifier built on top of the low-dimensional representation of the input extracted by the classifier:

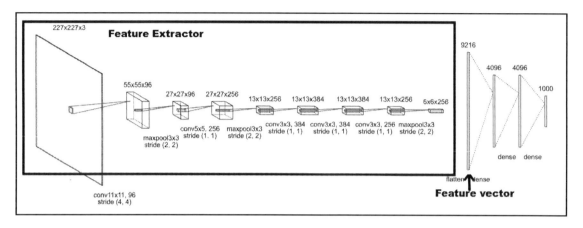

The AlexNet architecture; the first deep neural network used to win the ImageNet challenge. Like every other convolutional neural network for classification, its structure is fixed. The input layer consists of an expected input image with a resolution of 227 x 227 x 227. The feature extractor is a series of convolutional layers followed by max-pooling to reduce the resolution while going deeper; the last feature map 6 x 6 x 256, is reshaped in a 6 * 6 * 256 = 9216 feature vector. The classification layers are a traditional fully-connected architecture, which ends with 1,000 output neurons since the network was trained on 1,000 classes.

Transferring the knowledge of a trained model to a new one requires us to remove the task-specific part of the network (which is the classification layers) and keep the CNN fixed as the feature extractor.

This approach allows us to use the feature extractor of a pre-trained model as a building block for our new classification architecture. When doing transfer learning, the pre-trained model is kept constant, while only the new classification layers attached on top of the feature vector are trainable.

In this way, we can train a classifier by reusing the knowledge learned on a massive dataset and embedding it into the model. This leads to two significant advantages:

- It speeds up the training process since the number of trainable parameters is low
- It potentially mitigates the overfitting problem since the extracted features come from a different domain and the training process can't make them change

So far, so good. The transfer learning idea is bright, and it can help to deal with several real-life problems when datasets are small and resources are constrained. The only missing part, which also happens to be the most important one, is: where can we find pre-trained models?

For this reason, the TensorFlow team created TensorFlow Hub.

TensorFlow Hub

The description of TensorFlow Hub that can be found on the official documentation describes what TensorFlow Hub is and what it's about pretty well:

> *TensorFlow Hub is a library for the publication, discovery, and consumption of reusable parts of machine learning models. A module is a self-contained piece of a TensorFlow graph, along with its weights and assets, that can be reused across different tasks in a process known as transfer learning. Transfer learning can:*
>
> *- Train a model with a smaller dataset*
> *- Improve generalization, and*
> *- Speed up training*

Thus, TensorFlow Hub is a library we can browse while a looking for a pre-trained model that best fits our needs. TensorFlow Hub comes both as a website we can browse (https://tfhub.dev) and as a Python package.

Installing the Python package allows us to have perfect integration with the modules loaded on TensorFlow Hub and TensorFlow 2.0:

```
(tf2)
```

```
pip install tensorflow-hub>0.3
```

That is all we need to do to get access to a complete library of pre-trained models compatible and integrated with TensorFlow.

The TensorFlow 2.0 integration is terrific—we only need the URL of the module on TensorFlow Hub to create a Keras layer that contains the parts of the model we need!

Browsing the catalog on `https://tfhub.dev` is intuitive. The screenshot that follows shows how to use the search engine to find any module that contains the string `tf2` (this is a fast way to find an uploaded module that is TensorFlow 2.0 compatible and ready to use):

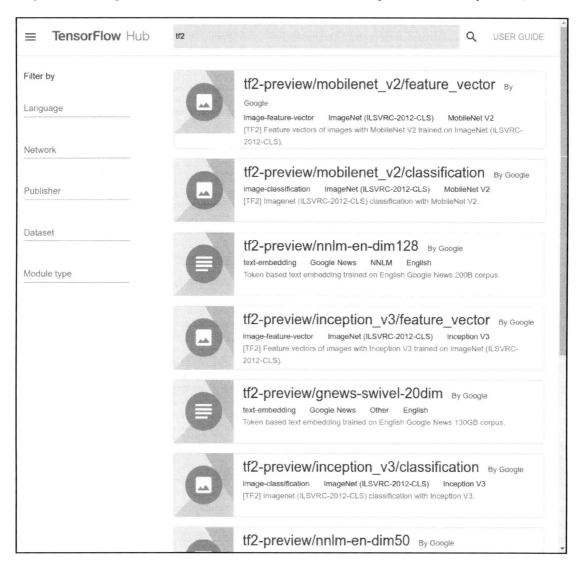

The TensorFlow Hub website (`https://tfhub.dev`): it is possible to search for modules by query string (in this case, tf2) and refine the results by using the filter column on the left.

There are models in both versions: feature vector-only and classification, which means a feature vector plus the trained classification head. The TensorFlow Hub catalog already contains everything we need for transfer learning. In the next section, we will see how easy it is to integrate the Inception v3 module from TensorFlow Hub into TensorFlow 2.0 source code, thanks to the Keras API.

Using Inception v3 as a feature extractor

The complete analysis of the Inception v3 architecture is beyond the scope of this book; however, it is worth noting some peculiarities of this architecture so as to use it correctly for transfer learning on a different dataset.

Inception v3 is a deep architecture with 42 layers, which won the **ImageNet Large Scale Visual Recognition Competition (ILSVRC)** in 2015. Its architecture is shown in the following screenshot:

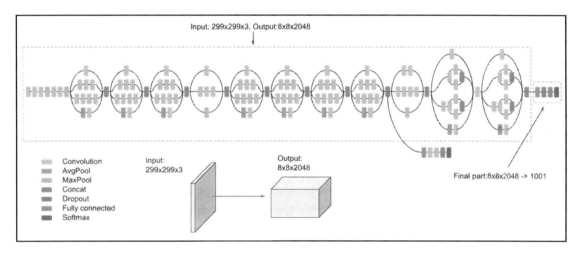

Inception v3 architecture. The model architecture is complicated and very deep. The network accepts a 299 x 299 x 3 image as input and produces an 8 x 8 x 2,048 feature map, which is the input of the final part; that is, a classifier trained on 1,000 +1 classes of ImageNet. Image source: https://cloud.google.com/tpu/docs/inception-v3-advanced.

The network expects an input image with a resolution of 299 x 299 x 3 and produces an 8 x 8 x 2,048 feature map. It has been trained on 1,000 classes of the ImageNet dataset, and the input images have been scaled in the [0,1] range.

All this information is available on the module page, reachable by clicking on the search result on the TensorFlow Hub website. Unlike the official architecture shown previously, on this page, we can find information about the extracted feature vector. The documentation says that it is a 2,048-feature vector, which means that the feature vector used is not the flattened feature map (that would have been an 8 * 8 * 2048 dimensional vector) but one of the fully-connected layers placed at the end of the network.

It is essential to know the expected input shape and the feature vector size to feed the network with correctly resized images and to attach the final layers, knowing how many connections there would be between the feature vector and the first fully-connected layer.

More importantly, it is necessary to know on which dataset the network was trained since transfer learning works well if the original dataset shares some features with the target (new) dataset. The following screenshot shows some samples gathered from the dataset used for the ILSVRC in 2015:

Samples gathered from the dataset used in the ILSVRC 2015 competition. High-resolution images, with complex scenes and rich details.

As you can see, the images are high-resolution images of various scenes and subjects, rich in detail. The variance of details and subjects is high. Therefore, we expect the feature extractor learned to extract a feature vector that is a good summary of images with these features. This means that if we feed the pre-trained network with an image that contains similar features to the one the network saw during the training, it will extract a meaningful representation as a feature vector. On the contrary, if we fed the network with an image that does not contain similar features (an image that, for instance, is not rich in detail like ImageNet, such as a simple image of a geometric shape), the feature extractor would be unlikely to extract a good representation.

The feature extractor of Inception v3 is certainly good enough to be used as a building block for our flowers classifier.

Adapting data to the model

The information found on the module page also tells us that it is necessary to add a pre-processing step to the dataset split built earlier: the tf_flower images are tf.uint8, which means they are in the [0,255] range, while Inception v3 has been trained on images in the [0,1] range, which are thus tf.float32:

(tf2)

```
def to_float_image(example):
    example["image"] = tf.image.convert_image_dtype(example["image"],
tf.float32)
    return example
```

Moreover, the Inception architecture requires a fixed input shape of 299 x 299 x 3. Therefore, we have to ensure that all our images are correctly resized to the expected input size:

(tf2)

```
def resize(example):
    example["image"] = tf.image.resize(example["image"], (299, 299))
    return example
```

All the required pre-processing operations have been defined, so we are ready to apply them to the train, validation, and test splits:

(tf2)

```
train = train.map(to_float_image).map(resize)
validation = validation.map(to_float_image).map(resize)
test = test.map(to_float_image).map(resize)
```

To summarize: the target dataset is ready; we know which model we want to use as a feature extractor; the module information page told us that some preprocessing steps were required to make the data compatible with the model.

Everything is set up to design the classification model that uses Inception v3 as the feature extractor. In the next section, the extreme ease of use of the tensorflow-hub module is shown, thanks to its Keras integration.

Building the model – hub.KerasLayer

The TensorFlow Hub Python package has already been installed, and this is all we need to do:

1. Download the model parameters and graph description
2. Restore the parameters in its graph
3. Create a Keras layer that wraps the graph and allows us to use it like any other Keras layer we are used to using

These three points are executed under the hook of the `KerasLayer tensorflow-hub` function:

```
import tensorflow_hub as hub

hub.KerasLayer(
    "https://tfhub.dev/google/tf2-preview/inception_v3/feature_vector/2",
    output_shape=[2048],
    trainable=False)
```

The `hub.KerasLayer` function creates `hub.keras_layer.KerasLayer`, which is a `tf.keras.layers.Layer` object. Therefore, it can be used in the same way as any other Keras layer—this is powerful!

This strict integration allows us to define a model that uses the Inception v3 as a feature extractor and it has two fully connected layers as classification layers in very few lines:

```
(tf2)
    num_classes = 5

    model = tf.keras.Sequential(
        [
            hub.KerasLayer(
    "https://tfhub.dev/google/tf2-preview/inception_v3/feature_vector/2",
                output_shape=[2048],
                trainable=False,
            ),
            tf.keras.layers.Dense(512),
            tf.keras.layers.ReLU(),
            tf.keras.layers.Dense(num_classes), # linear
        ]
    )
```

The model definition is straightforward, thanks to the Keras integration. Everything is set up to define the training loop, measure the performance, and see whether the transfer learning approach gives us the expected classification results.

Unfortunately, the process of downloading a pre-trained model from TensorFlow Hub is fast only on high-speed internet connections. A progress bar that shows the download progress is not enabled by default and, therefore, a lot of time could be required (depending on the internet speed) to build the model for the first time.

To enable a progress bar, using the `TFHUB_DOWNLOAD_PROGRESS` environment variable is required by `hub.KerasLayer`. Therefore, on top of the script, the following snippet can be added, which defines this environment variable and puts the value of 1 inside it; in this way, a handy progress bar will be shown on the first download:

```
import os
os.environ["TFHUB_DOWNLOAD_PROGRESS"] = "1"
```

Training and evaluating

Using a pre-trained feature extractor allows us to speed up the training while keeping the training loop, the losses, and optimizers unchanged, using the same structure of every standard classifier train.

Since the dataset labels are `tf.int64` scalars, the loss that is going to be used is the standard sparse categorical cross-entropy, setting the `from_logits` parameter to `True`. As seen in the previous chapter, Chapter 5, *Efficient Data Input Pipelines and Estimator API*, setting this parameter to `True` is a good practice since, in this way, it's the loss function itself that applies the softmax activation function, being sure to compute it in a numerically stable way, and thereby preventing the loss becoming `NaN`:

```
# Training utilities
loss = tf.losses.SparseCategoricalCrossentropy(from_logits=True)
step = tf.Variable(1, name="global_step", trainable=False)
optimizer = tf.optimizers.Adam(1e-3)

train_summary_writer =
tf.summary.create_file_writer("./log/transfer/train")
validation_summary_writer =
tf.summary.create_file_writer("./log/transfer/validation")

# Metrics
accuracy = tf.metrics.Accuracy()
mean_loss = tf.metrics.Mean(name="loss")
```

```
@tf.function
def train_step(inputs, labels):
    with tf.GradientTape() as tape:
        logits = model(inputs)
        loss_value = loss(labels, logits)

    gradients = tape.gradient(loss_value, model.trainable_variables)
    optimizer.apply_gradients(zip(gradients, model.trainable_variables))
    step.assign_add(1)

    accuracy.update_state(labels, tf.argmax(logits, -1))
    return loss_value


# Configure the training set to use batches and prefetch
train = train.batch(32).prefetch(1)
validation = validation.batch(32).prefetch(1)
test = test.batch(32).prefetch(1)

num_epochs = 10
for epoch in range(num_epochs):

    for example in train:
        image, label = example["image"], example["label"]
        loss_value = train_step(image, label)
        mean_loss.update_state(loss_value)

        if tf.equal(tf.math.mod(step, 10), 0):
            tf.print(
                step, " loss: ", mean_loss.result(), " acccuracy: ",
accuracy.result()
            )
            mean_loss.reset_states()
            accuracy.reset_states()

    # Epoch ended, measure performance on validation set
    tf.print("## VALIDATION - ", epoch)
    accuracy.reset_states()
    for example in validation:
        image, label = example["image"], example["label"]
        logits = model(image)
        accuracy.update_state(label, tf.argmax(logits, -1))
    tf.print("accuracy: ", accuracy.result())
    accuracy.reset_states()
```

The training loop produces the following output (cut to highlight only the essential parts):

```
10 loss: 1.15977693 acccuracy: 0.527777791
20 loss: 0.626715124 acccuracy: 0.75
30 loss: 0.538604617 acccuracy: 0.8125
40 loss: 0.450686693 acccuracy: 0.834375
50 loss: 0.56412369 acccuracy: 0.828125
## VALIDATION - 0
accuracy: 0.872410059

[...]

530 loss: 0.0310602095 acccuracy: 0.986607134
540 loss: 0.0334353112 acccuracy: 0.990625
550 loss: 0.029923955 acccuracy: 0.9875
560 loss: 0.0309863128 acccuracy: 1
570 loss: 0.0372043774 acccuracy: 0.984375
580 loss: 0.0412098244 acccuracy: 0.99375
## VALIDATION - 9
accuracy: 0.866957486
```

After a single training epoch, we got a validation accuracy of 0.87, while the training accuracy was even lower (0.83). But by the end of the tenth epoch, the validation accuracy had even decreased (0.86), while the model was overfitting the training data.

In the *Exercises* section, you will find several exercises that use the previous code as a starting point; the overfitting problem should be tackled from several points of view, finding the best way to deal with it.

Before starting the next main section, it's worth adding a simple performance measurement that measures how much time is needed to compute a single training epoch.

Training speed

Faster prototyping and training is one of the strengths of the transfer learning approach. One of the reasons behind the fact that transfer learning is often used in industry is the financial savings that it produces, reducing both the development and training time.

To measure the training time, the Python time package can be used. time.time() returns the current timestamp, allowing you to measure (in milliseconds) how much time is needed to perform a training epoch.

The training loop of the previous section can thus be extended by adding the time module import and the duration measurement:

```
(tf2)
```

```
from time import time

# [...]
for epoch in range(num_epochs):
    start = time()
    for example in train:
        image, label = example["image"], example["label"]
        loss_value = train_step(image, label)
        mean_loss.update_state(loss_value)

        if tf.equal(tf.math.mod(step, 10), 0):
            tf.print(
                step, " loss: ", mean_loss.result(), " acccuracy: ",
accuracy.result()
            )
            mean_loss.reset_states()
            accuracy.reset_states()
    end = time()
    print("Time per epoch: ", end-start)
# remeaning code
```

On average, running the training loop on a Colab notebook (https://colab.research. google.com) equipped with an Nvidia k40 GPU, we obtain an execution speed as follows:

```
Time per epoch: 16.206
```

As shown in the next section, transfer learning using a pre-trained model as a feature extractor gives a considerable speed boost.

Sometimes, using a pre-trained model as a feature extractor only is not the best way to transfer knowledge from one domain to another, often because the domains are too different and the features learned are useless for solving the new task.

In these cases, it is possible—and recommended—to not have a fixed-feature extractor part but let the optimization algorithm change it, training the whole model end to end.

Fine-tuning

Fine-tuning is a different approach to transfer learning. Both share the same goal of transferring the knowledge learned on a dataset on a specific task to a different dataset and a different task. Transfer learning, as shown in the previous section, reuses the pre-trained model without making any changes to its feature extraction part; in fact, it is considered a non-trainable part of the network.

Fine-tuning, instead, consists of fine-tuning the pre-trained network weights by continuing backpropagation.

When to fine-tune

Fine-tuning a network requires having the correct hardware; backpropagating the gradients through a deeper network requires you to load more information in memory. Very deep networks have been trained from scratch in data centers with thousands of GPUs. Therefore, prepare to lower your batch size to as low as 1, depending on how much available memory you have.

Hardware requirements aside, there are other different points to keep in mind when thinking about fine-tuning:

- **Dataset size**: Fine-tuning a network means using a network with a lot of trainable parameters, and, as we know from the previous chapters, a network with a lot of parameters is prone to overfitting.
  If the target dataset size is small, it is not a good idea to fine-tune the network. Using the network as a fixed-feature extractor will probably bring in better results.
- **Dataset similarity**: If the dataset size is large (where large means with a size comparable to the one the pre-trained model has been trained on) and it is similar to the original one, fine-tuning the model is probably a good idea. Slightly adjusting the network parameters will help the network to specialize in the extraction of features that are specific to this dataset, while correctly reusing the knowledge from the previous, similar dataset.
  If the dataset size is large and it is very different from the original, fine-tuning the network could help. In fact, the initial solution of the optimization problem is likely to be close to a good minimum when starting with a pre-trained model, even if the dataset has different features to learn (this is because the lower layers of the CNN usually learn low-level features that are common to every classification task).

If the new dataset satisfies the similarity and size constraints, fine-tuning the model is a good idea. One important parameter to look at closely is the learning rate. When fine-tuning a pre-trained model, we suppose the model parameters are good (and they are since they are the parameters of the model that achieved state-of-the-art results on a difficult challenge), and, for this reason, a small learning rate is suggested.

Using a high learning rate would change the network parameters too much, and we don't want to change them in this way. Instead, using a small learning rate, we slightly adjust the parameters to make them adapt to the new dataset, without distorting them too much, thus reusing the knowledge without destroying it.

Of course, if the fine-tuning approach is chosen, the hardware requirements have to be kept in mind: lowering the batch size is perhaps the only way to fine-tune very deep models when using a standard GPU to do the work.

TensorFlow Hub integration

Fine-tuning a model downloaded from TensorFlow Hub might sound difficult; we have to do the following:

- Download the model parameters and graph
- Restore the model parameters in the graph
- Restore all the operations that are executed only during the training (activating dropout layers and enabling the moving mean and variance computed by the batch normalization layers)
- Attach the new layers on top of the feature vector
- Train the model end to end

In practice, the integration of TensorFlow Hub and Keras models is so tight that we can achieve all this by setting the `trainable` Boolean flag to `True` when importing the model using `hub.KerasLayer`:

```
(tf2)
```

```
hub.KerasLayer(
    "https://tfhub.dev/google/tf2-preview/inception_v3/feature_vector/2",
    output_shape=[2048],
    trainable=True) # <- That's all!
```

Train and evaluate

What happens if we build the same model as in the previous chapter, Chapter 5, *Efficient Data Input Pipelines and Estimator API*, and we train it on the tf_flower dataset, fine-tuning the weights?

The model is thus the one that follows; please note how the learning rate of the optimizer has been reduced from 1e-3 to 1e-5:

(tf2)

```
optimizer = tf.optimizers.Adam(1e-5)
# [ ... ]
model = tf.keras.Sequential(
    [
        hub.KerasLayer(
"https://tfhub.dev/google/tf2-preview/inception_v3/feature_vector/2",
            output_shape=[2048],
            trainable=True, # <- enables fine tuning
        ),
        tf.keras.layers.Dense(512),
        tf.keras.layers.ReLU(),
        tf.keras.layers.Dense(num_classes), # linear
    ]
)

# [ ... ]
# Same training loop
```

In the following box, the first and last training epochs' output is shown:

```
10 loss: 1.59038031 acccuracy: 0.288194448
20 loss: 1.25725865 acccuracy: 0.55625
30 loss: 0.932323813 acccuracy: 0.721875
40 loss: 0.63251847 acccuracy: 0.81875
50 loss: 0.498087496 acccuracy: 0.84375
## VALIDATION - 0
accuracy: 0.872410059

[...]

530 loss: 0.000400377758 acccuracy: 1
540 loss: 0.000466914673 acccuracy: 1
550 loss: 0.000909397728 acccuracy: 1
560 loss: 0.000376881275 acccuracy: 1
570 loss: 0.000533850689 acccuracy: 1
580 loss: 0.000438459858 acccuracy: 1
```

```
## VALIDATION - 9
accuracy: 0.925845146
```

As expected, the test accuracy reached the constant value of 1; hence we overfitted the training set. This was something expected since the `tf_flower` dataset is smaller and simpler than ImageNet. However, to see the overfitting problem clearly, we had to wait longer since having more parameters to train makes the whole learning process extremely slow, especially compared to the previous train when the pre-trained model was not trainable.

Training speed

By adding the time measurements as we did in the previous section, it is possible to see how the fine-tuning process is extremely slow compared to transfer learning, using the model as a non-trainable feature extractor.

In fact, if, in the previous scenario, we reached an average training speed per epoch of about 16.2 seconds, now we have to wait, on average, 60.04 seconds, which is a 370% slowdown!

Moreover, it is interesting to see that at the end of the first epoch, we reached the same validation accuracy as was achieved in the previous training and that, despite overfitting the training data, the validation accuracy obtained at the end of the tenth epoch is greater than the previous one.

This simple experiment showed how using a pre-trained model as a feature extractor could lead to worse performance than fine-tuning it. This means that the features the network learned to extract on the ImageNet dataset are too different from the features that would be needed to classify the flowers, dataset correctly.

Choosing whether to use a pre-trained model as a fixed-feature extractor or to fine-tune it is a tough decision, involving a lot of trade-offs. Understanding whether the pre-trained model extracts features that are correct for the new task is complicated; merely looking at dataset size and similarity is a guideline, but in practice, this decision requires several tests.

Of course, it is better to use the pre-trained model as a feature extractor first, and, if the new model's performance is already satisfactory, there is no need to waste time trying to fine-tune it. If the results are not satisfying, it is worth trying a different pre-trained model and, as a last resort, trying the fine-tuning approach (because this requires more computational power, and it is expansive).

Summary

In this chapter, the concepts of transfer learning and fine-tuning were introduced. Training a very deep convolutional neural network from scratch, starting from random weights, requires the correct equipment, which is only found in academia and some big companies. Moreover, it can be a costly process since finding the architecture that achieves state-of-the-art results on a classification task requires multiple models to be designed and trained and for each of them to repeat the training process to search for the hyperparameter configuration that achieves the best results.

For this reason, transfer learning is the recommended practice to follow. It is especially useful when prototyping new solutions since it speeds up the training time and reduces the training costs.

TensorFlow Hub is the online library offered by the TensorFlow ecosystem. It contains an online catalog that anyone can browse to search for a pre-trained model ready to be used. The models come with all the required information to use them, from the input size to the feature vector size, through to the dataset that has been used to train the model and its data type. All this information can be used to design the correct data input pipeline that correctly feeds the network with the right data (shape and data type).

The Python package that comes with TensorFlow Hub is perfectly integrated with TensorFlow 2.0 and the Keras ecosystem, allowing you to download and use a pre-trained model just by knowing its URL, which can be found on the Hub website.

The `hub.KerasLayer` function not only allows you to download and load a pre-trained model but also offers the capability of doing both transfer learning and fine-tuning by toggling the `trainable` flag.

In the *Transfer Learning* and *Fine-Tuning* sections, we developed our classification models and trained them using a custom training loop. TensorFlow Datasets has been used to easily download, process, and get the `tf.data.Dataset` objects that have been used to utilize the processing hardware in its entirety, by defining high-efficiency data input pipelines.

The final part of this chapter was dedicated to exercises: most of the code in the chapter has been left incomplete deliberately, so as to allow you to get your hands dirty and learn more effectively.

Classification models built using convolutional architectures are used everywhere, from industry to smartphone applications. Classifying an image by looking at its whole content is useful, but sometimes its usage is limited (images more often than not contain more than one object). For this reason, other architectures that use convolutional neural networks as building blocks have been developed. These architectures can localize and classify more than one object per image, and these are the architectures that are used in self-driving cars and many other exciting applications!

In the next chapter, `Chapter 7`, *Introduction to Object Detection*, object localization and classification problems are analyzed and a model able to localize objects in images is built from scratch using TensorFlow 2.0.

Exercises

1. Describe the concept of transfer learning.
2. When can the transfer learning process bring good results?
3. What are the differences between transfer learning and fine-tuning?
4. If a model has been trained on a small dataset with low variance (similar examples), is it an excellent candidate to be used as a fixed-feature extractor for transfer learning?
5. The flower classifier built in the *transfer learning* section has no performance evaluation on the test dataset: add it.
6. Extend the flower classifier source code, making it log the metrics on TensorBoard. Use the summary writers that are already defined.
7. Extend the flower classifier to save the training status using a checkpoint (and its checkpoint manager).
8. Create a second checkpoint for the model that reached the highest validation accuracy.
9. Since the model suffers from overfitting, a good test is to reduce the number of neurons of the classification layer; try and see whether this reduces the overfitting problem.
10. Add a dropout layer after the first fully connected layer and measure the performance on several runs using different dropout keep probability. Select the model that reached the highest validation accuracy.

11. Using the same model defined for the flower classifier, create a new training script that uses the Keras training loop: do not write the custom training loop, but use Keras instead.

12. Convert the Keras model created in the previous point (11) to an estimator. Train and evaluate the model.

13. Use the TensorFlow Hub website to find a lightweight pre-trained model for image classification, trained on a high-variance dataset. Use the feature extractor version to build a fashion-MNIST classifier.

14. Was the idea of using a model trained on a complex dataset as the feature extractor for a fashion-MNIST classifier a good one? Are the extracted features meaningful?

15. Apply fine-tuning to the previously built fashion-MNIST classifier.

16. Did the process of fine-tuning a complex dataset to a simple one help us to achieve better results with respect to the ones obtained using transfer learning? If yes, why? If not, why?

17. What happens if a higher learning rate is used to fine-tune a model? Try it.

Introduction to Object Detection 7

Detecting and classifying objects in images is a challenging problem. So far, we have treated the issue of image classification on a simple level; in a real-life scenario, we are unlikely to have pictures containing just one object. In industrial environments, it is possible to set up cameras and mechanical supports to capture images of single objects. However, even in constrained environments, such as an industrial one, it is not always possible to have such a strict setup. Smartphone applications, automated guided vehicles, and, more generally, any real-life application that uses images captured in a non-controlled environment require the simultaneous localization and classification of several objects in the input images. Object detection is the process of localizing an object into an image by predicting the coordinates of a bounding box that contains it, while at the same time correctly classifying it.

State-of-the-art methods to tackle object detection problems are based on convolutional neural networks that, as we will see in this chapter, can be used not only to extract meaningful classification features but also to regress the coordinates of the bounding box. Being a challenging problem, it is better to start with the foundations. Detecting and classifying more than one object at the same time requires the convolutional architecture to be designed and trained in a more complicated way than the one needed to solve the same problem with a single object. The tasks of regressing the bounding box coordinates of a single object and classifying the content are called **localization and classification**. Solving this task is the starting point to develop more complicated architectures that address the object detection task.

In this chapter, we will look at both problems; we start from the foundations, developing a regression network completely, and then extending it to perform both regression and classification. The chapter ends with an introduction to anchor-based detectors, since a complete implementation of an object detection network goes beyond the scope of this book.

The dataset used throughout the chapter is the PASCAL Visual Object Classes Challenge 2007.

In this chapter, we will cover the following topics:

- Getting the data
- Object localization
- Classification and localization

Getting the data

Object detection is a supervised learning problem that requires a considerable amount of data to reach good performance. The process of carefully annotating images by drawing bounding boxes around the objects and assigning them the correct labels is a time-consuming process that requires several hours of repetitive work.

Fortunately, there are already several datasets for object detection that are ready to use. The most famous is the ImageNet dataset, immediately followed by the PASCAL VOC 2007 dataset. To be able to use ImageNet, dedicated hardware is required since its size and number of labeled objects per image makes the object detection task hard to tackle.

PASCAL VOC 2007, instead, consists of only 9,963 images in total, each of them with a different number of labeled objects belonging to the 20 selected object classes. The twenty object classes are as follows:

- **Person**: Person
- **Animal**: Bird, cat, cow, dog, horse, sheep
- **Vehicle**: Airplane, bicycle, boat, bus, car, motorbike, train
- **Indoor**: Bottle, chair, dining table, potted plant, sofa, tv/monitor

As described in the official dataset page (http://host.robots.ox.ac.uk/pascal/VOC/voc2007/), the dataset already comes with three splits (train, validation, and test) ready to use. The data has been split into 50% for training/validation and 50% for testing. The distributions of images and objects by class are approximately equal across the training/validation and test sets. In total there are 9,963 images, containing 24,640 annotated objects.

TensorFlow datasets allow us to download the whole dataset with a single line of code (approximately 869 MiB) and to obtain the `tf.data.Dataset` object of every split:

```
(tf2)

    import tensorflow as tf
    import tensorflow_datasets as tfds
```

```
# Train, test, and validation are datasets for object detection: multiple
objects per image.
(train, test, validation), info = tfds.load(
 "voc2007", split=["train", "test", "validation"], with_info=True
)
```

As usual, TensorFlow datasets give us a lot of useful information about the dataset format. The output that follows is the result of `print(info)`:

```
tfds.core.DatasetInfo(
    name='voc2007',
    version=1.0.0,
    description='This dataset contains the data from the PASCAL Visual
Object Classes Challenge
2007, a.k.a. VOC2007, corresponding to the Classification and Detection
competitions.
A total of 9,963 images are included in this dataset, where each image
contains
a set of objects, out of 20 different classes, making a total of 24,640
annotated objects.
In the Classification competition, the goal is to predict the set of labels
contained in the image, while in the Detection competition the goal is to
predict the bounding box and label of each individual object.
',
    urls=['http://host.robots.ox.ac.uk/pascal/VOC/voc2007/'],
    features=FeaturesDict({
        'image': Image(shape=(None, None, 3), dtype=tf.uint8),
        'image/filename': Text(shape=(), dtype=tf.string, encoder=None),
        'labels': Sequence(shape=(None,), dtype=tf.int64,
feature=ClassLabel(shape=(), dtype=tf.int64, num_classes=20)),
        'labels_no_difficult': Sequence(shape=(None,), dtype=tf.int64,
feature=ClassLabel(shape=(), dtype=tf.int64, num_classes=20)),
        'objects': SequenceDict({'label': ClassLabel(shape=(),
dtype=tf.int64, num_classes=20), 'bbox': BBoxFeature(shape=(4,),
dtype=tf.float32), 'pose': ClassLabel(shape=(), dtype=tf.int64,
num_classes=5), 'is_truncated': Tensor(shape=(), dtype=tf.bool),
'is_difficult'
: Tensor(shape=(), dtype=tf.bool)})
    },
    total_num_examples=9963,
    splits={
        'test': <tfds.core.SplitInfo num_examples=4952>,
        'train': <tfds.core.SplitInfo num_examples=2501>,
        'validation': <tfds.core.SplitInfo num_examples=2510>
    },
    supervised_keys=None,
    citation='"""
        @misc{pascal-voc-2007,
```

```
        author = "Everingham, M. and Van~Gool, L. and Williams, C. K. I.
and Winn, J. and Zisserman, A.",
        title = "The {PASCAL} {V}isual {O}bject {C}lasses {C}hallenge
2007 {(VOC2007)} {R}esults",
        howpublished =
"http://www.pascal-network.org/challenges/VOC/voc2007/workshop/index.html"}
    """,
    redistribution_info=,
)
```

For every image, there is a `SequenceDict` object that contains the information of every labeled object present. Something handy when working with any data related project is to visualize the data. In this case in particular, since we are trying to solve a computer vision problem, visualizing the images and the bounding boxes can help us to have a better understanding of the difficulties the network should face during the training.

To visualize the labeled images, we use `matplotlib.pyplot` together with the usage of the `tf.image` package; the former is used to display the images, and the latter is used to draw the bounding boxes and to convert them to `tf.float32` (thus scaling the values in the [0,1] range). Moreover, how to use the `tfds.ClassLabel.int2str` method is shown; this method is convenient since it allows us to get the text representation of a label from its numerical representation:

`(tf2)`

```
import matplotlib.pyplot as plt
```

From the training set, take five images, draw the bounding box, and then print the class:

```
with tf.device("/CPU:0"):
    for row in train.take(5):
        obj = row["objects"]
        image = tf.image.convert_image_dtype(row["image"], tf.float32)

        for idx in tf.range(tf.shape(obj["label"])[0]):
            image = tf.squeeze(
                tf.image.draw_bounding_boxes(
                    images=tf.expand_dims(image, axis=[0]),
                    boxes=tf.reshape(obj["bbox"][idx], (1, 1, 4)),
                    colors=tf.reshape(tf.constant((1.0, 1.0, 0, 0)), (1,
4)),
                ),
                axis=[0],
            )

            print(
```

```
        "label: ",
info.features["objects"]["label"].int2str(obj["label"][idx])
        )
```

Then, plot the image using the following code:

```
plt.imshow(image)
plt.show()
```

The following images are a collage of the five images produced by the code snippet:

 Please note that since TensorFlow dataset shuffles the data when it creates the TFRecords, it is unlikely that the same execution on a different machine will produce the same sequence of images.

It is also worth noting that partial objects are annotated as full objects; for instance, the human hand on the bottom-left image is labeled as a person, and the rear wheel of a motorbike present in the bottom right of the picture is marked as a motorbike .

The object detection task is challenging by its nature, but looking at the data, we can see that the data itself is hard to use. In fact, the labels printed to the standard output for the bottom-right image are:

- Person
- Bird

Thus, the dataset contains full objects annotated and labeled (bird) and also partial objects annotated and labeled as the whole object (for example, the human hand is labeled as a person). This small example shows how difficult object detection is: the network should be able to classify and localize, for example, people from their attributes (a hand) or from their complete shape while dealing with the problem of occlusion.

Looking at the data gives us a better idea of how challenging the problem is. However, before facing the challenge of object detection, it is better to start from the foundations by tackling the problem of localization and classification. Therefore, we have to filter the dataset objects to extract only the images that contain a single labeled object. For this reason, a simple function that accepts a `tf.data.Dataset` object as input and applies a filter on it can be defined and used. Create a subset of the dataset by filtering the elements: we are interested in creating a dataset for object detection and classification, that is, a dataset of images with a single object annotated:

```
(tf2)

def filter(dataset):
    return dataset.filter(lambda row:
tf.equal(tf.shape(row["objects"]["label"])[0], 1))

train, test, validation = filter(train), filter(test), filter(validation)
```

Using the same snippet as earlier, we can visualize some of the images to check if everything goes as we expect:

We can see images that contain only a single object, sampled from the training set, drawn using the previous code snippet after applying the `filter` function. The `filter` function returns a new dataset that contains only the elements of the input dataset that contain a single bounding box, hence the perfect candidates to train a single network for classification and localization.

Object localization

Convolutional neural networks (CNNs) are extremely flexible objects—so far, we have used them to solve classification problems, making them learn to extract features specific to the task. As shown in `Chapter 6`, *Image Classification Using TensorFlow Hub*, the standard architecture of CNNs designed to classify images is made of two parts—the feature extractor, which produces a feature vector, and a set of fully connected layers that classifies the feature vector in the (hopefully) correct class:

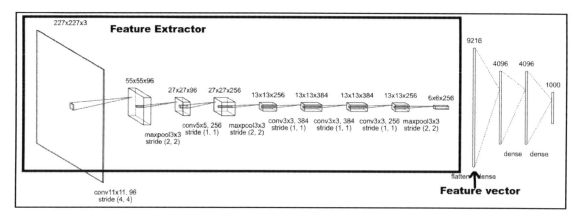

The classifier placed on top of the feature vector can also be seen as the head of the network

The fact that, so far, CNNs have only been used to solve classification problems should not mislead us. These types of networks are extremely powerful, and, especially in their multilayer setting, they can be used to solve many different kinds of problems, extracting information from the visual input.

For this reason, solving the localization and classification problem is just a matter of adding a new head to the network, the localization head.

The input data is an image that contains a single object together with the four coordinates of the bounding box. So the idea is to use this information to solve the classification and localization problem at the same time by treating the localization as a regression problem.

Localization as a regression problem

Ignoring for a moment the classification problem and focusing only on the localization part, we can think about the localization as the problem of regressing the four coordinates of the bounding box that contains the subject of the input image.

In practice, there is not much difference between training a CNN to solve a classification task or a regression task: the architecture of the feature extractor remains the same, while the classification head changes and becomes a regression head. In the very end, this only means to change the number of output neurons from the number of classes to 4, one neuron per coordinate of the bounding box.

The idea is that the regression head should learn to output the correct coordinates when certain input features are present.

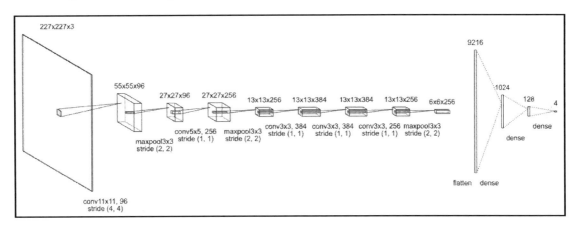

The AlexNet architecture used as a feature extractor and the classification head replaced with a regression head with four output neurons

To make the network learn to regress the coordinates of the bounding box of an object, we have to express the input/output relationship between the neurons and the labels (that is, the four coordinates of the bounding box, present in the dataset) using a loss function.

The L2 distance can be effectively used as the loss function: the goal is to regress correctly all the four coordinates and thus minimize the distance between the predicted values and the real one, making it tend to zero:

$$L_2\left((x_1, y_1, x_2, y_2), (x_1', y_1', x_2', y_2')\right)$$

Where the first tuple (x_1, y_1, x_2, y_2) is the regression head output, and the second tuple (x_1', y_1', x_2', y_2') represents the ground truth bounding box coordinates.

Implementing a regression network in TensorFlow 2.0 is straightforward. As shown in Chapter 6, *Image Classification Using TensorFlow Hub*, TensorFlow Hub can be used to speed up the training phase by using it to download and embed a pretrained feature extractor in our model.

A detail that is worth pointing out is the format that TensorFlow uses to represent the bounding box coordinates (and the coordinates in general)—the format used is `[ymin, xmin, ymax, xmax]`, and the coordinates are normalized in the [0,1] range, in order not to depend on the original image resolution.

Using TensorFlow 2.0 and TensorFlow Hub, we can define and train a coordinate regression network on the PASCAL VOC 2007 dataset in a few lines of code.

Using the Inception v3 network from TensorFlow Hub as the backbone of the coordinate regression network, defining the regression model is straightforward. Although the network has a sequential structure, we define it using the functional API since this will allow us to extend the model easily without the need to rewrite it:

(tf2)

```
import tensorflow_hub as hub

inputs = tf.keras.layers.Input(shape=(299,299,3))
net = hub.KerasLayer(
"https://tfhub.dev/google/tf2-preview/inception_v3/feature_vector/2",
        output_shape=[2048],
        trainable=False,
    )(inputs)
net = tf.keras.layers.Dense(512)(net)
net = tf.keras.layers.ReLU()(net)
coordinates = tf.keras.layers.Dense(4, use_bias=False)(net)

regressor = tf.keras.Model(inputs=inputs, outputs=coordinates)
```

Moreover, since we decided to use the inception network that needs a 299 x 299 input image resolution with values in the [0,1] range, we have to add an additional step to the input pipeline to prepare the data:

(tf2)

```
def prepare(dataset):
    def _fn(row):
        row["image"] = tf.image.convert_image_dtype(row["image"],
tf.float32)
        row["image"] = tf.image.resize(row["image"], (299, 299))
        return row

    return dataset.map(_fn)

train, test, validation = prepare(train), prepare(test),
prepare(validation)
```

As previously introduced, the loss function to use is the standard L2 loss, which already comes implemented in TensorFlow as a Keras loss that can be found in the `tf.losses` package. However, instead of using `tf.losses.MeanSquaredError`, it is worth defining the loss function ourselves since there is a detail to highlight.

If we decide to use the implemented **Mean Squared Error** (MSE) function, we have to take into account that under the hood, the `tf.subtract` operation is used. This operation simply computes the subtraction of the left-hand operation with the right-hand operand. This behavior is what we are looking for, of course, but the subtraction operation in TensorFlow follows the NumPy broadcasting semantic (as almost any mathematical operation). This particular semantic broadcasts the value of the left-side tensor to the right-side tensor, and if the right-side tensor has a dimension of 1 where the value of the left-side tensor is copied.

Since we selected the images with only one object inside, we have a single bounding box present in the `"bbox"` attribute. Hence, if we pick a batch size of 32, the tensor that contains the bounding box will have a shape of `(32, 1, 4)`. The 1 in the second position can cause problems in the loss computation and preventing the model from converging .

Thus, we have two options:

- Define the loss function using Keras, removing the unary dimension by using `tf.squeeze`
- Define the loss function manually

In practice, defining the loss function manually allows us to place the `tf.print` statements in the body function, which can be used for a raw debugging process and, more importantly, to define the training loop in the standard way, making the loss function itself taking care of squeezing the unary dimension where needed:

```
(tf2)

    # First option -> this requires to call the loss l2, taking care of
    squeezing the input
    # l2 = tf.losses.MeanSquaredError()

    # Second option, it is the loss function iself that squeezes the input
    def l2(y_true, y_pred):
        return tf.reduce_mean(
            tf.square(y_pred - tf.squeeze(y_true, axis=[1]))
        )
```

The training loop is straightforward, and it can be implemented in two different ways:

- Writing a custom training loop (thus using the `tf.GradientTape` object)
- Using the `compile` and `fit` methods of the Keras model, since this is a standard training loop that Keras can build for us

However, since we are interested in extending this solution in the next sections, it is better to start using the custom training loop, as it gives more freedom for customization. Moreover, we are interested in visualizing the ground truth and the predicted bounding box, by logging them on TensorBoard.

Therefore, before defining the training loop, it is worth defining a `draw` function that takes a dataset, the model, and the current step, and using them to draw both the ground truth and the predicted boxes:

```
(tf2)
```

```python
def draw(dataset, regressor, step):
    with tf.device("/CPU:0"):
        row = next(iter(dataset.take(3).batch(3)))
        images = row["image"]
        obj = row["objects"]
        boxes = regressor(images)
        tf.print(boxes)

        images = tf.image.draw_bounding_boxes(
            images=images, boxes=tf.reshape(boxes, (-1, 1, 4))
        )
        images = tf.image.draw_bounding_boxes(
            images=images, boxes=tf.reshape(obj["bbox"], (-1, 1, 4))
        )
        tf.summary.image("images", images, step=step)
```

The training loop for our coordinate regressor (that can also be thought of as a region proposal, since it is now aware of the label of the object it's detecting in the images), which also logs on TensorBoard the training loss value and the prediction on three images sampled from the training and validation set (using the `draw` function), can be easily defined:

1. Define the `global_step` variable, used to keep track of the training iterations, followed by the definition of the file writers, used to log the train and validation summaries:

```python
optimizer = tf.optimizers.Adam()
epochs = 500
```

```
batch_size = 32

global_step = tf.Variable(0, trainable=False, dtype=tf.int64)

train_writer, validation_writer = (
    tf.summary.create_file_writer("log/train"),
    tf.summary.create_file_writer("log/validation"),
)
with validation_writer.as_default():
    draw(validation, regressor, global_step)
```

2. Following the TensorFlow 2.0 best practice, we can define the training step as a function and convert it to its graph representation using `tf.function`:

```
@tf.function
def train_step(image, coordinates):
    with tf.GradientTape() as tape:
        loss = l2(coordinates, regressor(image))
    gradients = tape.gradient(loss, regressor.trainable_variables)
    optimizer.apply_gradients(zip(gradients,
regressor.trainable_variables))
    return loss
```

3. Define the training loop over the batches and invoke the `train_step` function on every iteration:

```
train_batches = train.cache().batch(batch_size).prefetch(1)
with train_writer.as_default():
    for _ in tf.range(epochs):
        for batch in train_batches:
            obj = batch["objects"]
            coordinates = obj["bbox"]
            loss = train_step(batch["image"], coordinates)
            tf.summary.scalar("loss", loss, step=global_step)
            global_step.assign_add(1)
            if tf.equal(tf.mod(global_step, 10), 0):
                tf.print("step ", global_step, " loss: ", loss)
                with validation_writer.as_default():
                    draw(validation, regressor, global_step)
                with train_writer.as_default():
                    draw(train, regressor, global_step)
```

Although the Inception network is used as a fixed feature extractor, the training process can take a few hours on a CPU and almost half an hour on a GPU.

The following screenshot shows the visible trend of the loss function during the training:

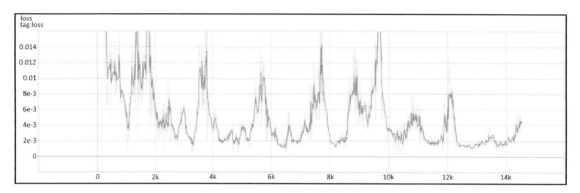

We see that from the early training steps, the loss value is close to zero, although oscillations are present during the whole training process.

During the training process, in the images tab of TensorBoard, we can visualize the images with the regressed and ground truth bounding boxes drawn. Since we created two different summary writers (one for the training logs and the other for the validation logs), TensorFlow visualizes for us the images logged for the two different splits:

The preceding images are samples from the training (first row) and validation (second row) set, with the ground truth and regressed bounding boxes. The regressed bounding boxes in the training set are close to the ground truth boxes, while the regressed boxes on the validation images are different.

The training loop previously defined has various problems:

- The only measured metric is the L2 loss
- The validation set is never used to measure any numerical score
- No check for overfitting is present
- There is a complete lack of a metric that measures how good the regression of the bounding box is, measured on both the training and the validation set

The training loop can, therefore, be improved by measuring an object detection metric; measuring the metric also reduces the training time since we can stop the training earlier. Moreover, from the visualization of the results, it is pretty clear that the model is overfitting the training set, and a regularization layer, such as dropout, can be added to address this problem. The problem of regressing a bounding box can be treated as a binary classification problem. In fact, there are only two possible outcomes: ground truth bounding box matched or not matched.

Of course, having a perfect match is not an easy task; for this reason, a function that measures how good the detected bounding box is with a numerical score (with respect to the ground truth) is needed. The most widely used function to measure the goodness of localization is the **Intersection over Union (IoU)**, which we will explore in the next section.

Intersection over Union

Intersection over Union (IoU) is defined as the ratio between the area of overlap and the area of union. The following image is a graphical representation of IoU:

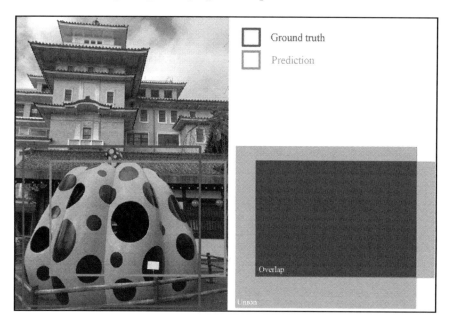

Credits: Jonathan Hui (https://medium.com/@jonathan_hui/map-mean-average-precision-for-object-detection-45c121a31173)

In practice, the IoU measures *how much* the predicted bounding box overlaps with the ground truth. Since IoU is a metric that uses the areas of the objects, it can be easily expressed treating the ground truth and the detected area like sets. Let A be the set of the proposed object pixels and B the set of true object pixels; then IoU is defined as:

$$IoU = \frac{A \cap B}{A \cup B}$$

The IoU value is in the [0,1] range, where 0 is a no-match (no overlap), and 1 is the perfect match. The IoU value is used as an overlap criterion; usually, an IoU value greater than 0.5 is considered as a true positive (match), while any other value is regarded as a false positive. There are no true negatives.

Implementing the IoU formula in TensorFlow is straightforward. The only subtlety to take into account is that de-normalizing the coordinates is needed since the area should be computed in pixels. The conversion in pixel coordinates together with the coordinate swapping in a more friendly representation is implemented in the _swap closure:

(tf2)

```
def iou(pred_box, gt_box, h, w):
    """
    Compute IoU between detect box and gt boxes
    Args:
        pred_box: shape (4,): y_min, x_min, y_max, x_max - predicted box
        gt_boxes: shape (4,): y_min, x_min, y_max, x_max - ground truth
        h: image height
        w: image width
    """
```

Transpose the coordinates from y_min, x_min, y_max, and x_max in absolute coordinates to x_min, y_min, x_max, and y_max in pixel coordinates:

```
    def _swap(box):
        return tf.stack([box[1] * w, box[0] * h, box[3] * w, box[2] * h])

    pred_box = _swap(pred_box)
    gt_box = _swap(gt_box)

    box_area = (pred_box[2] - pred_box[0]) * (pred_box[3] - pred_box[1])
    area = (gt_box[2] - gt_box[0]) * (gt_box[3] - gt_box[1])
    xx1 = tf.maximum(pred_box[0], gt_box[0])
    yy1 = tf.maximum(pred_box[1], gt_box[1])
    xx2 = tf.minimum(pred_box[2], gt_box[2])
    yy2 = tf.minimum(pred_box[3], gt_box[3])
```

Then, compute the width and height of the bounding box:

```
w = tf.maximum(0, xx2 - xx1)
h = tf.maximum(0, yy2 - yy1)

inter = w * h
return inter / (box_area + area - inter)
```

Average precision

A value of IoU greater than a specified threshold (usually 0.5) allows us to treat the bounding box regressed as a match.

In the case of single class prediction, having the number of **true positives** (TP) and **false positives** (FP) measured on the dataset allows us to compute the average precision as follows:

$$AP = \frac{|TP|}{|TP| + |FP|}$$

In the object detection challenges, the **Average Precision** (AP) is often measured for different values of IoU. The minimum requirement is to measure the AP for an IoU value of 0.5, but achieving good results with a half overlap is not sufficient in most real-life scenarios. Usually, in fact, a bounding box prediction is required to match at least a value of IoU of 0.75 or 0.85 to be useful.

So far we have treated the AP for the single-class case, but it is worth it to treat the more general multi-class object detection scenario.

Mean Average Precision

In the case of a multi-class detection, where every bounding box regressed can contain one of the available classes, the standard metric used to evaluate the performance of the object detector is the **Mean Average Precision** (mAP).

Computing it is straightforward—the mAP is the average precision for each class in the dataset:

$$mAP = \frac{1}{|\text{classes}|} \sum_{c \in classes} \frac{|TP_c|}{|FP_c| + |FP_c|}$$

Knowing the metrics to use for object detection, we can improve the training script by adding this measurement on the validation set at the end of every training epoch and measuring it on a batch of training data every ten steps. Since the model defined so far is just a coordinate regressor without classes, the measured metric will be the AP.

Implementing the mAP in TensorFlow is trivial since in the `tf.metrics` package there is an implementation ready to use. The first parameter of the `update_state` method is the true labels; the second parameter is the predicted labels. For instance, for a binary classification problem, a possible scenario can be as follows:

(tf2)

```
m = tf.metrics.Precision()

m.update_state([0, 1, 1, 1], [1, 0, 1, 1])
print('Final result: ', m.result().numpy()) # Final result: 0.66
```

It should also be noted that the average precision and the IoU are not object-detection-specific metrics, but they can be used whenever a localization task is performed (the IoU) and the precision of the detection is measured (the mAP).

In `Chapter 8`, *Semantic Segmentation and Custom Dataset Builder*, dedicated to the semantic segmentation task, the same metrics are used to measure the segmentation model performance. The only difference is that the IoU is measured at the pixel level and not using a bounding box. The training loop can be improved; in the next section, a draft of an improved training script is presented, but the real improvement is left as an exercise.

Improving the training script

Measuring the mean average precision (over a single class) requires you to fix a threshold for the IoU measurement and to define the `tf.metrics.Precision` object that computes the mean average precision over the batches.

In order not to change the whole code structure, the `draw` function is used not only to draw the ground truth and regressed boxes, but also to measure the IoU and log the mean average precision summary:

(tf2)

```
# IoU threshold
threshold = 0.75
# Metric object
```

```
precision_metric = tf.metrics.Precision()

def draw(dataset, regressor, step):
    with tf.device("/CPU:0"):
        row = next(iter(dataset.take(3).batch(3)))
        images = row["image"]
        obj = row["objects"]
        boxes = regressor(images)

        images = tf.image.draw_bounding_boxes(
            images=images, boxes=tf.reshape(boxes, (-1, 1, 4))
        )
        images = tf.image.draw_bounding_boxes(
            images=images, boxes=tf.reshape(obj["bbox"], (-1, 1, 4))
        )
        tf.summary.image("images", images, step=step)

        true_labels, predicted_labels = [], []
        for idx, predicted_box in enumerate(boxes):
            iou_value = iou(predicted_box, tf.squeeze(obj["bbox"][idx]),
299, 299)
            true_labels.append(1)
            predicted_labels.append(1 if iou_value >= threshold else 0)

        precision_metric.update_state(true_labels, predicted_labels)
        tf.summary.scalar("precision", precision_metric.result(),
step=step)
```

As an exercise (see the *Exercises* section), you can use this code as a baseline and restructure them, in order to improve the code organization. After improving the code organization, you are also invited to retrain the model and analyze the precision plot.

Object localization alone, without the information about the class of the object being localized, has a limited utility, but, in practice, it is the basis of any object detection algorithm.

Classification and localization

An architecture like the one defined so far that has no information about the class of the object it's localizing is called a **region proposal**.

It is possible to perform object detection and localization using a single neural network. In fact, there is nothing stopping us adding a second head on top of the feature extractor and training it to classify the image and at the same time training the regression head to regress the bounding box coordinates.

Solving multiple tasks at the same time is the goal of multitask learning.

Multitask learning

Rich Caruna defines multi-task learning in his paper *Multi-task learning* (1997):

> *"Multitask Learning is an approach to inductive transfer that improves generalization by using the domain information contained in the training signals of related tasks as an inductive bias. It does this by learning tasks in parallel while using a shared representation; what is learned for each task can help other tasks be learned better."*

In practice, multi-task learning is a machine learning subfield with the explicit goal of solving multiple different tasks, exploiting commonalities and differences across tasks. It has been empirically shown that using the same network to solve multiple tasks usually results in improved learning efficiency and prediction accuracy compared to the performance achieved by the same network trained to solve the same tasks separately.

Multi-task learning also helps to fight the overfitting problem since the neural network is less likely to adapt its parameters to solve a specific task, so it has to learn how to extract meaningful features that can be useful to solve different tasks.

Double-headed network

In the past few years, several architectures for object detection and classification have been developed using a two-step process. The first process was to use a region proposal to get regions of the input image that are likely to contain an object. The second step was to use a simple classifier on the proposed regions to classify the content.

Using a double-headed neural network allows us to have faster inference time, since only a single forward pass of a single model is needed to achieve better performance overall.

From the architectural side, supposing for simplicity that our feature extractor is AlexNet (when, instead, it is the more complex network Inception V3), adding a new head to the network changes the model architecture as shown in the following screenshot:

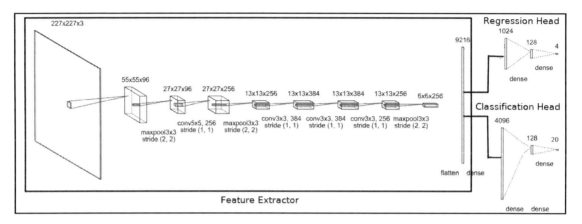

The preceding screenshot is a representation of what a classification and localization network looks like. The feature extract part should be able to extract features general enough to make the two heads solve the two different tasks, using the same shared features.

From the code side, as we used the Keras functional style model definition, adding the additional output to the model is straightforward. In fact, it is only a matter of adding the desired numbers of layers that compose the new head and adding the final layer to the outputs list of the Keras model definition. As may be obvious at this point in the book, this second head must end with a number of neurons equal to the number of classes the model will be trained to classify. In our case, the PASCAL VOC 2007 dataset contains 20 different classes. Therefore, we only have to define the model as follows:

(tf2)

1. First, start with the input layer definition:

```
inputs = tf.keras.layers.Input(shape=(299, 299, 3))
```

2. Then, using TensorFlow Hub, we define the fixed (non-trainable) feature extractor:

```
net = hub.KerasLayer(
"https://tfhub.dev/google/tf2-preview/inception_v3/feature_vector/2
",
    output_shape=[2048],
    trainable=False,
)(inputs)
```

3. Then, we define the regression head, which is just a stack of fully connected layers that end with four linear neurons (one per bounding box coordinate):

```
regression_head = tf.keras.layers.Dense(512)(net)
regression_head = tf.keras.layers.ReLU()(regression_head)
coordinates = tf.keras.layers.Dense(4,
use_bias=False)(regression_head)
```

4. Next, we define the classification head, which is just a stack of fully connected layers that is trained to classify the features extracted by the fixed (non-trainable) feature extractor:

```
classification_head = tf.keras.layers.Dense(1024)(net)
classification_head = tf.keras.layers.ReLU()(classificatio_head)
classification_head = tf.keras.layers.Dense(128)(net)
classification_head = tf.keras.layers.ReLU()(classificatio_head)
num_classes = 20
classification_head = tf.keras.layers.Dense(num_classes,
use_bias=False)(
    classification_head
)
```

5. Finally, we can define the Keras model that will perform classification and localization. Please note that the model has a single input and two outputs:

```
model = tf.keras.Model(inputs=inputs, outputs=[coordinates,
classification_head])
```

Using TensorFlow datasets, we have all the information needed to perform both the classification and localization easily since every row is a dictionary that contains the label for every bounding box present in the image. Moreover, since we filtered the dataset in order to have only images with a single object inside, we can treat the training of the classification head exactly as the training of the classification model, as shown in Chapter 6, *Image Classification Using TensorFlow Hub*.

The implementation of the training script is left as an exercise for you (see the *Exercises* section). The only peculiarity of the training process is the loss function to use. In order to effectively train the network to perform different tasks at the same time, the loss function should contain different terms for each different task.

Usually, the weighted sum of different terms is used as a loss function. In our case, one term is the classification loss that can easily be the sparse categorical cross-entropy loss, and the other is the regression loss (the L2 loss previously defined):

$$\lambda_1 \, classification\_loss + \lambda_2 \, regression\_loss$$

The multiplicative factors (λ_1, λ_2) are hyperparameters used to give more or less *importance* (strength of the gradient update) to the different tasks.

Classifying images with a single object inside and regressing the coordinate of the only bounding box present can be applied only in limited real-life scenarios. More often, instead, given an input image, it is required to localize and classify multiple objects at the same time (the real object detection problem).

Over the years, several models for object detection have been proposed, and the ones that recently outperformed all the others are all based on the concept of anchor. We will explore anchor-based detectors in the following section.

Anchor-based detectors

Anchor-based detectors rely upon the concept of anchor boxes to detect objects in images in a single pass, using a single architecture.

The intuitive idea of the anchor-based detectors is to split the input image into several regions of interests (the anchor boxes) and apply a localization and regression network to each of them. The idea is to make the network learn not only to regress the coordinates of a bounding box and classify its content, but also to use the same network to look at different regions of the image in a single forward pass.

To train these models, it is required not only to have a dataset with the annotated ground truth boxes, but also to add to every input image a new collection of boxes that overlap (with the desired amount of IoU) the ground truth boxes.

Anchor-boxes

Anchor-boxes are a discretization of the input image in different regions, also called **anchors** or **bounding boxes prior**. The idea behind the concept of anchor-boxes is that the input can be discretized in different regions, each of them with a different appearance. An input image could contain big and small objects, and therefore the discretization should be made at different scales in order to detect the same time objects at different resolutions.

When discretizing the input in anchor boxes, the important parameters are as follows:

- **The grid size:** How the input is evenly divided
- **The box scale levels**: Given the parent box, how to resize the current box
- **The aspect ratio levels**: For every box, the ratio between width and height

The input image can be divided into a grid with cells of equal dimensions, for instance, a 4 x 4 grid. Each cell of this grid can then be resized with different scales (0.5, 1, 2, ...) and each of them with different levels of aspect ratios (0.5, 1, 2, ...). As an example, the following image shows how an image can be "covered" by anchor boxes:

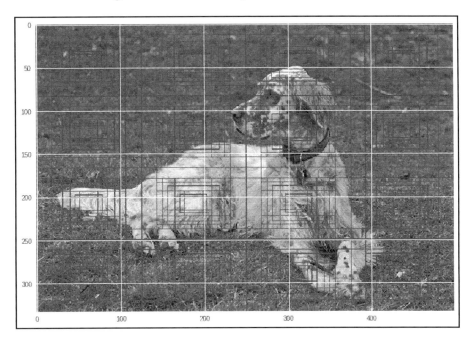

The generation of the anchor boxes influences the network performance—the dimension of the smaller box represents the dimension of the smaller objects the network is able to detect. The same reasoning applies to the larger box as well.

In the last few years, anchor-based detectors have demonstrated they are capable of reaching astonishing detection performance, being not only accurate, but also faster.

The most famous anchor-based detector is **You Only Look Once (YOLO)**, followed by **Single Shot MultiBox Detector (SSD)**. The following YOLO image detects multiple objects in the image, at different scales, with a single forward pass:

The implementation of an anchor-based detector goes beyond the scope of this book due to the theory needed to understand the concepts and the complexity of these models. Therefore, only an intuitive idea of what happens when these models are used has been presented.

Summary

In this chapter, the problem of object detection was introduced and some basic solutions were proposed. We first focused on the data required and used TensorFlow datasets to get the PASCAL VOC 2007 dataset ready to use in a few lines of code. Then, the problem of using a neural network to regress the coordinate of a bounding box was looked at, showing how a convolutional neural network can be easily used to produce the four coordinates of a bounding box, starting from the image representation. In this way, we build a region proposal, that is, a network able to suggest where in the input image a single object can be detected, without producing other information about the detected object.

After that, the concept of multi-task learning was introduced and how to add a classification head next to the regression head was shown by using the Keras functional API. Then, we covered a brief introduction about the anchor-based detectors. These detectors are used to solve the problem of object detection (the detection and classification of multiple objects in a single image) by discretizing the input in thousands of regions (anchors).

We used TensorFlow 2.0 and TensorFlow Hub together, allowing us to speed up the training process by using the Inception v3 model as a fixed feature extractor. Moreover, thanks to the quick execution, mixing pure Python and TensorFlow code simplified the way of defining the whole training process.

In the next chapter, we will learn about semantic segmentation and dataset builder.

Exercises

You can answer all the theoretical questions and, perhaps more importantly, struggle to solve all the code challenges that each exercise contains:

1. In the *Getting the data* section, a filtering function was applied to the PASCAL VOC 2007 dataset to select only the images with a single object inside. The filtering process, however, doesn't take into account the class balancement. Create a function that, given the three filtered datasets, merges them first and then creates three balanced splits (with a tolerable class imbalance, if it is not possible to have them perfectly balanced).

2. Use the splits created in the previous point to retrain the network for localization and classification defined in the chapter. How and why do the performances change?

3. What measures the Intersection over Union metric?

4. What does an IoU value of 0.4 represent? A good or a bad match?

5. What is the Mean Average Precision? Explain the concept and write the formula.

6. What is multi-task learning?

7. Does multi-task learning improve or worsen the model performance on single tasks?

8. In the domain of object detection, what is an anchor?

9. Describe how an anchor-based detector looks at the input image during training and inference.

10. Are mAP and IoU object detection metrics only?

11. To improve the code of the object detection and localization network, add the support saving the model at the end of every epoch into a checkpoint and to restore the model (and the global step variable) status to continue the training process.

12. The code of the localization and regression networks explicitly use a `draw` function that not only draws the bounding boxes but also measures the mAP. Improve the code quality by creating different functions for each different feature.

13. The code that measures network performance only uses three samples. This is wrong, can you explain the reason? Change the code in order to use a single training batch during the training and the whole validation set at the end of every epoch.

14. Define a training script for the model defined in the "Multi-Headed Network and Multi-Task learning": train the regression and classification head at the same time and measure the training and validation accuracy at the end of every training epoch.

15. Filter the PASCAL VOC train, validation, and test datasets to produce only images with at least a person inside (there can be other labeled objects present in the picture).

16. Replace the regression and classification head of the trained localization and classification network with two new heads. The classification head should now have a single neuron that represents the probability of the image to contain a person. The regression head should regress the coordinates of the objects labeled as a person.

17. Apply transfer learning to train the previously defined network. Stop the training process when the mAP on the person class stops increasing (with a tolerance of +/- 0.2) for 50 steps.

18. Create a Python script that generates anchor boxes at different resolutions and scales.

8
Semantic Segmentation and Custom Dataset Builder

In this chapter, we'll analyze semantic segmentation and the challenges that come with it. Semantic segmentation is the challenging problem of classifying every single pixel of an image with the correct semantic label. The first part of this chapter presents the problem itself, why it is important, and what are the possible applications. At the end of the first part, we will discuss the well-known U-Net architecture for semantic segmentation, and we will implement it as a Keras model in pure TensorFlow 2.0 style. The model implementation is preceded by the introduction of the deconvolution operation required to implement semantic segmentation networks successfully.

The second part of this chapter starts with dataset creation—since, at the time of writing, there is no `tfds` builder for semantic segmentation, we take advantage of this to introduce the TensorFlow Datasets architecture and show how to implement a custom DatasetBuilder. After getting the data, we'll perform the training process of U-Net step by step, showing how straightforward it is to train this model using Keras and Keras callbacks. This chapter ends with the usual exercise section, perhaps the most crucial part of this whole chapter. The only way to understand a concept is to get your hands dirty.

In this chapter, we will cover the following topics:

- Semantic segmentation
- Create a TensorFlow DatasetBuilder
- Model training and evaluation

Semantic segmentation

Different from object detection, where the goal is to detect objects in rectangular regions, and image classification, which has the purpose of classifying the whole image with a single label, semantic segmentation is a challenging computer vision task, the goal of which is to assign the correct label to every pixel of the input image:

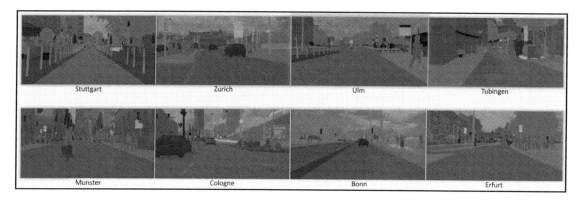

Examples of semantically annotated images from the CityScapes dataset. Every single pixel of the input image has a corresponding pixel-label. (Source: https://www.cityscapes-dataset.com/examples/)

The applications of semantic segmentation are countless, but perhaps the most important ones are in the autonomous driving and medical imaging domains.

Automated guided vehicles and self-driving cars can take advantage of semantic segmentation results, getting a complete understanding of the whole scene captured by the cameras mounted on the vehicle. For example, having the pixel-level information of the road can help the driving software have better control of the position of the car. Localizing the road using a bounding box is far less accurate than having a pixel-level classification that localizes the road pixels independently from the perspective.

In the medical imaging domain, the bounding boxes predicted by an object detector are sometimes useful and other times not. In fact, if the task is the detection of a specific type of cell, a bounding box can give the user enough information. But if, instead, the task is to localize blood vessels, then using a bounding box is not enough. As it is easy to imagine, a fine-grained classification is not an easy task, and there are several challenges to face from both the theoretical and practical points of view.

Challenges

One of the tough challenges is to get the correct data. There are several enormous datasets of labeled images since the process of classifying an image by its main content is relatively fast. A team of professional annotators can easily label thousands of images a day since the task only consists of looking at the picture and selecting a label.

There are also a lot of object detection datasets, where multiple objects have been localized and classified. The process requires more annotation time with respect to the classification alone, but as it is something that does not require extreme accuracy, it is a relatively fast process.

The semantic segmentation dataset, instead, requires specialized software and very patient annotators that are extremely accurate in their work. In fact, the process of labeling with pixel-level accuracy is perhaps the most time-consuming process of all of the annotation types. For this reason, the number of semantic segmentation datasets is low, and their number of images is limited. As we will see in the next section, dedicated to dataset creation, PASCAL VOC 2007, which contains 24,640 annotated objects for the image classification and localization task, only contains approximately 600 labeled images.

Another challenge that semantic segmentation brings is technical. Classifying every single pixel of an image requires designing convolutional architectures in a different way with respect to the ones seen so far. All of the architectures described so far followed the same structure:

- One input layer, which defines the input resolution expected by the network
- The feature extractor part, which is a stack of several convolution operations with different strides or with pooling operations in between, which, layer-by-layer, reduce the spatial extent of the feature maps until it is reduced to a vector

- The classification part which, given the feature vector produced by the feature extractor, is trained to classify this low-dimensional representation to a fixed number of classes
- Optionally, a regression head, which uses the same features to produce a set of four coordinates

The task of semantic segmentation, however, cannot follow this structure since, if the feature extractor only reduces the input resolution layer-by-layer, how can the network produce a classification for every pixel in the input image?

One of the proposed solutions is the deconvolution operation.

Deconvolution – transposed convolution

Let's start this section by saying that the term deconvolution is misleading. In fact, in mathematics and engineering, the deconvolution operation exists but has very little in common with what deep learning practitioners intend with this term.

In this domain, a deconvolution operation is a transposed convolution operation, or even an image resize, followed by a standard convolution operation. Yes, two different implementations are named in the same way.

The deconvolution operation in deep learning just guarantees that, if a feature map is a result of a convolution between an input map and a kernel with a certain size and stride, the deconvolution operation will produce a feature map with the same spatial extent of the input, if applied with the same kernel size and stride.

To do that, a standard convolution is performed with a pre-processed input where a zero padding is added not only at the borders but also within the feature map cells. The following diagram should help to clarify the process:

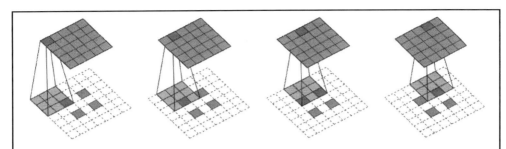

Figure 4.5: The transpose of convolving a 3×3 kernel over a 5×5 input using 2×2 strides (i.e., $i = 5$, $k = 3$, $s = 2$ and $p = 0$). It is equivalent to convolving a 3×3 kernel over a 2×2 input (with 1 zero inserted between inputs) padded with a 2×2 border of zeros using unit strides (i.e., $i' = 2$, $\tilde{i}' = 3$, $k' = k$, $s' = 1$ and $p' = 2$).

Image and caption source: A guide to convolution arithmetic for deep learning—Vincent Dumoulin and Francesco Visin

TensorFlow, through the `tf.keras.layers` package, offers a ready-to-use deconvolution operation: `tf.keras.layers.Conv2DTranspose`.

Another possible way of performing the deconvolution is to resize the input to the desired resolution and make this operation learnable by adding a standard 2D convolution with same padding on top of the resized image.

In short, what really matters in the deep learning context is creating a learnable layer that reconstructs the original spatial resolution and performs a convolution. This is not the mathematical inverse of the convolution operation, but the practice has shown that it is enough to achieve good results.

One of the semantic segmentation architectures that used the deconvolution operation extensively and achieved impressive results in the task of the segmentation of medical images is the U-Net architecture.

The U-Net architecture

U-Net is a convolutional architecture for semantic segmentation introduced by Olaf Ronnerberg et al. in *Convolutional Networks for Biomedical Image Segmentation* with the explicit goal of segmenting biomedical images.

The architecture revealed itself to be general enough to be applied in every semantic segmentation task since it has been designed without any constraints about the datatypes.

The U-Net architecture follows the typical encoder-decoder architectural pattern with skip connections. This way of designing the architecture has proven to be very effective when the goal is to produce an output with the same spatial resolution of the input since it allows the gradients to propagate between the output and the input layer in a better way:

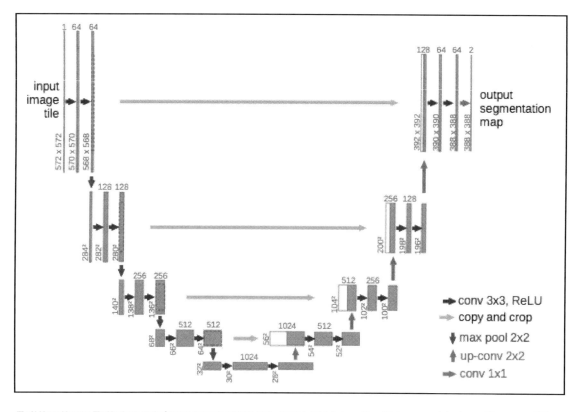

The U-Net architecture. The blue boxes are the feature maps produced by the blocks, denoted with their shapes. The white boxes are copied and cropped feature maps. Different arrows indicate different operations. Source: Convolutional Networks for Biomedical Image Segmentation—Olaf Ronnerberg et al.

The left side of the U-Net architecture is an encoder that, layer-by-layer, reduces the input size from 572 x 572 to 32 x 32 in the lowest resolution. The right side contains the encoder part of the architecture, which mixes information extracted from the encoding part to the information learned by the up-convolution (deconvolution) operations.

The original U-Net architecture does not produce an output with the same resolution of the input, but it has been designed to produce a slightly lower resolution output. A final 1 x 1 convolution is used as the final layer to map each feature vector (with a depth of 64) to the desired number of classes. For a complete assessment of the original architecture, carefully read the original U-Net paper by Olaf Ronnerberg et al. in *Convolutional Networks for Biomedical Image Segmentation*.

Instead of implementing the original U-net architecture, we are going to show how to implement a slightly modified U-Net that produces an output with the same resolution of the input and that follows the same original block organization.

As can be seen from the screenshot of the architecture, there are two main blocks:

- **Encoding blocks**: There are three convolutions followed by a downsampling operation.
- **Decoding blocks**: This is a deconvolution operation, followed by the concatenation of its output with the corresponding input feature, and two convolution operations.

It is possible and really easy to use the Keras functional API to define this model and connect these logical blocks. The architecture we are going to implement differs a little from the original one, since this is a custom U-Net variation, and it shows how Keras allows the use of models as layers (or building blocks).

The `upsample` and `downsample` functions are implemented as a `Sequential` model, which is nothing but a convolution or deconvolution operation, with a stride of 2, followed by an activation function:

```
(tf2)

    import tensorflow as tf
    import math


    def downsample(depth):
        return tf.keras.Sequential(
            [
                tf.keras.layers.Conv2D(
                    depth, 3, strides=2, padding="same",
    kernel_initializer="he_normal"
```

```
            ),
            tf.keras.layers.LeakyReLU(),
        ]
    )


def upsample(depth):
    return tf.keras.Sequential(
        [
            tf.keras.layers.Conv2DTranspose(
                depth, 3, strides=2, padding="same",
    kernel_initializer="he_normal"
            ),
            tf.keras.layers.ReLU(),
        ]
    )
```

The model definition function supposes a minimum input resolution of 256 x 256, and it implements the encoding, decoding, and concatenate (skip connection) blocks of the architecture:

```
(tf2)

    def get_unet(input_size=(256, 256, 3), num_classes=21):
        # Downsample from 256x256 to 4x4, while adding depth
        # using powers of 2, startin from 2**5. Cap to 512.
        encoders = []
        for i in range(2, int(math.log2(256))):
            depth = 2 ** (i + 5)
            if depth > 512:
                depth = 512
            encoders.append(downsample(depth=depth))

        # Upsample from 4x4 to 256x256, reducing the depth
        decoders = []
        for i in reversed(range(2, int(math.log2(256)))):
            depth = 2 ** (i + 5)
            if depth < 32:
                depth = 32
            if depth > 512:
                depth = 512
            decoders.append(upsample(depth=depth))

        # Build the model by invoking the encoder layers with the correct input
        inputs = tf.keras.layers.Input(input_size)
        concat = tf.keras.layers.Concatenate()

        x = inputs
```

```
# Encoder: downsample loop
skips = []
for conv in encoders:
    x = conv(x)
    skips.append(x)

skips = reversed(skips[:-1])

# Decoder: input + skip connection
for deconv, skip in zip(decoders, skips):
    x = deconv(x)
    x = tf.keras.layers.Concatenate()([x, skip])

# Add the last layer on top and define the model
last = tf.keras.layers.Conv2DTranspose(
    num_classes, 3, strides=2, padding="same",
kernel_initializer="he_normal")

outputs = last(x)
return tf.keras.Model(inputs=inputs, outputs=outputs)
```

Using Keras, it is possible to visualize not only the tabular summary of the model (by using the summary() method of a Keras model), but also to get a graphical representation of the created model, which is often a blessing when designing complex architectures:

(tf2)

```
from tensorflow.keras.utils import plot_model
model = get_unet()
plot_model(model, to_file="unet.png")
```

These three lines of code, generate this great graphical representation:

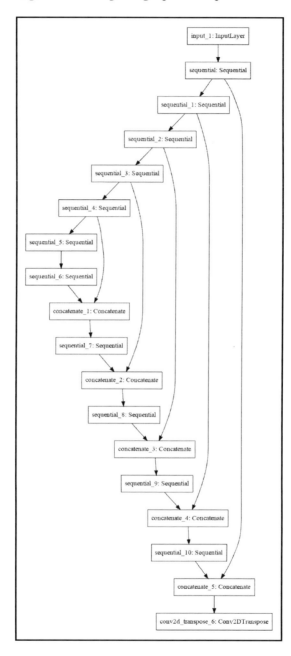

Graphical representation of the U-Net-like structure defined. Keras allows this kind of visualization to help the architecture design process.

The generated image looks like the horizontally flipped version of the U-net architecture, and this is the architecture we are going to use to tackle the semantic segmentation problem in this chapter.

Now that we have understood the problem and defined a deep architecture, we can move forward and gather the required data.

Create a TensorFlow DatasetBuilder

In the same way as any other machine learning problem, the first step is getting the data. Since semantic segmentation is a supervised learning task, we need a classification dataset of images and corresponding labels. The peculiarity is that the label in itself is an image.

At the time of writing, there is no semantic dataset ready to use in TensorFlow Datasets. For this reason, we use this section not only to create `tf.data.Dataset` with the data that we need, but also to have a look at the process required to develop a `tfds` DatasetBuilder.

Since, in the previous section dedicated to the object detection, we used the PASCAL VOC 2007 dataset, we are going to reuse the downloaded files to create the semantic segmentation version of the PASCAL VOC 2007 dataset. The following screenshot shows how the dataset is provided. Each picture has a corresponding label, where the pixel color identifies a different class:

A pair (image, label) sampled from the dataset. The top image is the original image, while the bottom image contains the semantic segmentation class of the known objects. Every not know class is marked as background (color black), while the objects are delimited using the color white.

The dataset previously downloaded comes not only with the annotated bounding boxes but also with the semantic segmentation annotation for many images. TensorFlow Datasets downloaded the raw data in the default directory (`~/tensorflow_datasets/downloads/`) and placed the extracted archive in the `extracted` subfolder. We can, therefore, re-use the downloaded data to create a new dataset for semantic segmentation.

Before doing it, it is worth looking at the TensorFlow dataset organization to understand what we need to do to achieve our goal.

Hierarchical organization

The whole TensorFlow Datasets API has been designed to be as extensible as possible. To do that, the architecture of TensorFlow Datasets is organized in several abstraction layers that transform the raw dataset data to the `tf.data.Dataset` object. The following diagram, from the TensorFlow Dataset GitHub page (`https://github.com/tensorflow/datasets/`), shows the logical organization of the project:

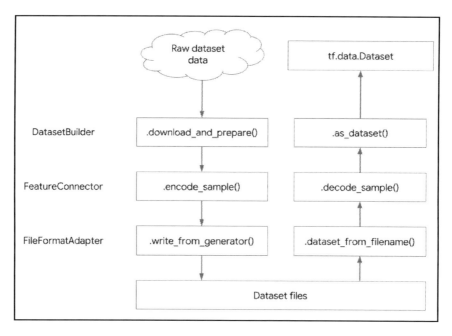

The logical organization of the TensorFlow Datasets project. The raw data flows from several abstraction layers that apply transformation and standardizations, in order to define the TFRecord structure and obtain a tf.data.Dataset object at the end.

Usually, the `FeatureConnector` and `FileFormatAdapter` classes are ready to use, while the `DatasetBuilder` class must be correctly implemented since it is the data-specific part of the pipeline.

Each dataset creation pipeline starts from a subclass of a `DatasetBuilder` object that must implement the following methods:

- `_info` is used to build the `DatasetInfo` object that describes the dataset (and produces the human-readable representation that is extremely useful to have a complete understanding of the data).
- `_download_and_prepare` is used to download the data from a remote location (if any) and do some basic preprocessing (such as extracting the compressed archives). Moreover, it creates the serialized (TFRecord) representation.
- `_as_dataset`: This is the final step, to produce a `tf.data.Dataset` object from the serialized data.

Subclassing directly, the `DatasetBuilder` class is often not needed since `GeneratorBasedBuilder` is a ready-to-use subclass of `DatasetBuilder` that simplifies the dataset definition. The methods to implement by subclassing it are as follows:

- `_info` is the same method of `DatasetBuilder` (see the `_info` method description of the previous bullet list).
- `_split_generators` is used to download the raw data and do some basic preprocessing but without the need to worry about TFRecord creation.
- `_generate_examples` is used to create a Python iterator. This method yields examples in the dataset from the raw data, where every example will be automatically serialized as a row in a TFRecord.

Therefore, by subclassing `GeneratorBasedBuilder`, there are only three simple methods to implement, and we can hence start implementing them.

The dataset class and DatasetInfo

Subclassing a model and implementing the required methods is straightforward. The first step is to define the skeleton of our class and then start by implementing the methods in the order of complexity. Moreover, since our goal is to create a dataset for semantic segmentation that uses the same downloaded files of the PASCAL VOC 2007 dataset, we can override the methods of the `tfds.image.Voc2007` DatasetBuilder to reuse all of the information already present in the parent class:

```
(tf2)
```

```python
    import tensorflow as tf
    import tensorflow_datasets as tfds
    import os

    class Voc2007Semantic(tfds.image.Voc2007):
        """Pasval VOC 2007 - semantic segmentation."""

        VERSION = tfds.core.Version("0.1.0")

        def _info(self):
            # Specifies the tfds.core.DatasetInfo object
            pass   # TODO

        def _split_generators(self, dl_manager):
            # Downloads the data and defines the splits
            # dl_manager is a tfds.download.DownloadManager that can be used to
            # download and extract URLs
            pass   # TODO

        def _generate_examples(self):
            # Yields examples from the dataset
            pass   # TODO
```

The most straightforward, but perhaps the most important method, to implement is `_info`, which contains all of the dataset information and the definition of the structure of a single example.

Since we are extending the `tfds.image.Voc2007` dataset, it is possible to reuse certain common information. The only thing to note is that the semantic segmentation requires a label, which is a single-channel image (and not a color image as we are used to seeing).

Implementing the _info method is hence straightforward:

(tf2)

```
    def _info(self):
        parent_info = tfds.image.Voc2007().info
        return tfds.core.DatasetInfo(
            builder=self,
            description=parent_info.description,
            features=tfds.features.FeaturesDict(
                {
                    "image": tfds.features.Image(shape=(None, None, 3)),
                    "image/filename": tfds.features.Text(),
                    "label": tfds.features.Image(shape=(None, None, 1)),
                }
            ),
            urls=parent_info.urls,
            citation=parent_info.citation,
        )
```

It is worth noting that TensorFlow Datasets already comes with a predefined set of feature connectors that have been used to define FeatureDict. For example, the correct way of defining an image feature with a fixed depth (4 or 1) and an unknown height and width is to use tfds.features.Image(shape=(None, None, depth)).

The description, urls, and citation fields have been kept from the parent, although this is not fully correct since the description and citation fields of the parent are about the object detection and classification challenges.

The second method to implement is _split_generators.

Creating the dataset splits

The _split_generators method is used to download the raw data and do some basic preprocessing without needing to worry about TFRecord creation.

Since we are inheriting from tfds.image.Voc2007, there is no need to reimplement it, but it is, instead, required to have a look at the parent source code:

(tf2)

```
    def _split_generators(self, dl_manager):
        trainval_path = dl_manager.download_and_extract(
            os.path.join(_VOC2007_DATA_URL, "VOCtrainval_06-Nov-2007.tar"))
        test_path = dl_manager.download_and_extract(
```

```
                  os.path.join(_VOC2007_DATA_URL, "VOCtest_06-Nov-2007.tar"))
        return [
            tfds.core.SplitGenerator(
                name=tfds.Split.TEST,
                num_shards=1,
                gen_kwargs=dict(data_path=test_path, set_name="test")),
            tfds.core.SplitGenerator(
                name=tfds.Split.TRAIN,
                num_shards=1,
                gen_kwargs=dict(data_path=trainval_path, set_name="train")),
            tfds.core.SplitGenerator(
                name=tfds.Split.VALIDATION,
                num_shards=1,
                gen_kwargs=dict(data_path=trainval_path, set_name="val")),
        ]
```

 The source code is from `https://github.com/tensorflow/datasets/blob/master/tensorflow_datasets/image/voc.py`, released under the Apache License, 2.0.

As it can be easily seen, the method uses a `dl_manager` object to download (and cache) and extract the archive from some remote location. The dataset split definition in `"train"`, `"test"`, and `"val"` is performed in the return line.

The most important part of every `tfds.core.SplitGeneratro` call is the `gen_kwargs` parameter. In fact, at this line, we are instructing how the `_generate_exaples` function is going to be called.

In short, this function creates three splits, by calling the `_generate_examples` function, passing the `data_path` parameters set to the current dataset path (`test_path` or `trainval_path`), and setting `set_name` to the correct dataset name.

The `set_name` parameter value comes from the PASCAL VOC 2007 directory and file organization. As we will see in the next section, where the `_generate_example` method is implemented, knowing the dataset structure and content is needed to create the splits correctly.

Generating the example

The `_generate_example` method can be defined with any signature. This method is called only by the `_split_generators` method, and therefore, it is up to this method to correctly invoke `_generate_example` with the correct parameters.

Since we haven't overwritten the parent `_split_generators` method, we have to use the same signature required by the parent. Hence, we have the `data_path` and `set_name` parameters to use, in addition to all of the other information that is available in the PASCAL VOC 2007 documentation.

To goal of `_generate_examples` is to yield an example every time it is invoked (behaving like a standard Python iterator).

From the dataset structure, we know that, inside `VOCdevkit/VOC2007/ImageSets/Segmentation/`, there are three text files—one for each split: `"train"`, `"test"`, and `"val"`. Every file contains the name of the labeled image for every split.

Therefore, it is straightforward to use the information contained in these files to create the three splits. We only have to open the file and read it line-by-line to know which are the images to read.

TensorFlow Datasets constrains us from using the Python file operations, but it explicitly requires the usage of the `tf.io.gfile` package. This constraint is necessary, since there are datasets that are too huge to be processed on a single machine, and `tf.io.gfile` can be easily used by TensorFlow Datasets to read and process remote and distributed datasets.

From the PASCAL VOC 2007 documentation, we can also extract a **Look-Up Table (LUT)** to create a mapping between the RGB values and the scalar labels:

```
(tf2)

    LUT = {
        (0, 0, 0): 0, # background
        (128, 0, 0): 1, # aeroplane
        (0, 128, 0): 2, # bicycle
        (128, 128, 0): 3, # bird
        (0, 0, 128): 4, # boat
        (128, 0, 128): 5, # bottle
        (0, 128, 128): 6, # bus
        (128, 128, 128): 7, # car
        (64, 0, 0): 8, # cat
        (192, 0, 0): 9, # chair
        (64, 128, 0): 10, # cow
        (192, 128, 0): 11, # diningtable
        (64, 0, 128): 12, # dog
        (192, 0, 128): 13, # horse
        (64, 128, 128): 14, # motorbike
        (192, 128, 128): 15, # person
        (0, 64, 0): 16, # pottedplant
```

```
            (128, 64, 0): 17, # sheep
            (0, 192, 0): 18, # sofa
            (128, 192, 0): 19, # train
            (0, 64, 128): 20, # tvmonitor
            (255, 255, 255): 21, # undefined / don't care
        }
```

After creating this look-up table, we can use only TensorFlow operations to read the images, check for their existence (because there is no guarantee that the raw data is perfect and we have to prevent failures during the dataset creation), and create the single-channel image that contains the numerical value associated with the RGB color.

Read the source code carefully since it may be hard to understand the first read. In particular, the loop over the look-up table where we look for correspondences between the RGB colors and the colors available may be not easy to understand at first glance. The following code not only creates the single-channel image with the numerical values associated with the RGB colors, using tf.Variable, but also checks whether the RGB values are correct:

(tf2)

```
    def _generate_examples(self, data_path, set_name):
        set_filepath = os.path.join(
            data_path,
  "VOCdevkit/VOC2007/ImageSets/Segmentation/{}.txt".format(set_name),
        )
        with tf.io.gfile.GFile(set_filepath, "r") as f:
            for line in f:
                image_id = line.strip()

                image_filepath = os.path.join(
                    data_path, "VOCdevkit", "VOC2007", "JPEGImages",
  f"{image_id}.jpg"
                )
                label_filepath = os.path.join(
                    data_path,
                    "VOCdevkit",
                    "VOC2007",
                    "SegmentationClass",
                    f"{image_id}.png",
                )

                if not tf.io.gfile.exists(label_filepath):
                    continue

                label_rgb = tf.image.decode_image(
                    tf.io.read_file(label_filepath), channels=3
```

```
                    )
                    label = tf.Variable(
                        tf.expand_dims(
                            tf.zeros(shape=tf.shape(label_rgb)[:-1],
dtype=tf.uint8), -1
                        )
                    )

                    for color, label_id in LUT.items():
                        match = tf.reduce_all(tf.equal(label_rgb, color),
axis=[2])
                        labeled = tf.expand_dims(tf.cast(match, tf.uint8),
axis=-1)
                        label.assign_add(labeled * label_id)

                    colored = tf.not_equal(tf.reduce_sum(label), tf.constant(0,
tf.uint8))
                    # Certain labels have wrong RGB values
                    if not colored.numpy():
                        tf.print("error parsing: ", label_filepath)
                        continue
                    yield image_id, {
                        # Declaring in _info "image" as a tfds.feature.Image
                        # we can use both an image or a string. If a string is
detected
                        # it is supposed to be the image path and tfds take
care of the
                        # reading process.
                        "image": image_filepath,
                        "image/filename": f"{image_id}.jpg",
                        "label": label.numpy(),
                    }
```

The _generate_examples method not only yields single examples, but it must yield a pair, (id, example), where id—in this case, image_id—should uniquely identify the record; this field is used to shuffle the dataset globally and to avoid having repeated elements in the generated dataset.

Having implemented this last method, everything is correctly set up, and we can use the brand-new Voc2007Semantic loader.

Use the builder

TensorFlow Datasets can automatically detect whether a class visible in the current scope is a `DatasetBuilder` object. Therefore, having implemented the class by subclassing an existing `DatasetBuilder`, the `"voc2007_semantic"` builder is already ready to use:

```
dataset, info = tfds.load("voc2007_semantic", with_info=True)
```

At the first execution, the splits are created and the `_generate_examples` method is classed three times to create the TFRecord representation of the examples.

By inspecting the `info` variable, we can see some dataset statistics:

```
[...]
    features=FeaturesDict({
        'image': Image(shape=(None, None, 3), dtype=tf.uint8),
        'image/filename': Text(shape=(), dtype=tf.string, encoder=None),
        'label': Image(shape=(None, None, 1), dtype=tf.uint8)
    },
    total_num_examples=625,
    splits={
        'test': <tfds.core.SplitInfo num_examples=207>,
        'train': <tfds.core.SplitInfo num_examples=207>,
        'validation': <tfds.core.SplitInfo num_examples=211>
    }
```

The features are described by implementing the `_info` method, and the dataset size is relatively small, containing only 207 images each for train and test split and 211 for the validation split.

Implementing `DatasetBuilder` is a relatively straightforward operation that you are invited to do every time you start working with a new dataset—in this way, a high-efficiency pipeline can be used during the training and evaluation processes.

Model training and evaluation

Although the network architecture is not that of an image classifier and the labels are not scalars, semantic segmentation can be seen as a traditional classification problem and therefore the training and evaluation processes can be the same.

For this reason, instead of writing a custom training loop, we can use the `compile` and `fit` Keras models to build the training loop and execute it respectively.

Data preparation

To use the Keras `fit` model, the `tf.data.Dataset` object should generate tuples in the `(feature, label)` format, where `feature` is the input image and `label` is the image label.

Therefore, it is worth defining some functions that can be applied to the elements produced by `tf.data.Dataset`, which transforms the data from a dictionary to a tuple, and, at the same time, we can apply some useful preprocessing for the training process:

(tf2)

```
def resize_and_scale(row):
    # Resize and convert to float, [0,1] range
    row["image"] = tf.image.convert_image_dtype(
        tf.image.resize(
            row["image"],
            (256,256),
            method=tf.image.ResizeMethod.NEAREST_NEIGHBOR),
        tf.float32)
    # Resize, cast to int64 since it is a supported label type
    row["label"] = tf.cast(
        tf.image.resize(
            row["label"],
            (256,256),
            method=tf.image.ResizeMethod.NEAREST_NEIGHBOR),
        tf.int64)
    return row
def to_pair(row):
    return row["image"], row["label"]
```

It is now easy to get the validation and training sets from the `dataset` object obtained from the `tfds.load` call and apply to them the required transformations:

(tf2)

```
batch_size= 32

train_set = dataset["train"].map(resize_and_scale).map(to_pair)
train_set = train_set.batch(batch_size).prefetch(1)

validation_set = dataset["validation"].map(resize_and_scale)
validation_set = validation_set.map(to_pair).batch(batch_size)
```

The datasets are ready to be used in the `fit` method, and since we are developing a pure Keras solution, we can configure the hidden training loop using the Keras callbacks.

Training loop and Keras callbacks

The `compile` method is used to configure the training loop. We can specify the optimizer, the loss, the metrics to measure, and some useful callbacks.

Callbacks are functions that are executed at the end of every training epoch. Keras comes with a long list of predefined callbacks that are ready to use. In the next code snippet, two of the most common are going to be used, the `ModelCheckpoint` and `TensorBoard` callbacks. As it can be easily guessed, the former saves a checkpoint at the end of the epoch, while the latter logs the metrics using `tf.summary`.

Since semantic segmentation can be treated as a classification problem, the loss used is `SparseCategoricalCrossentropy`, configured to apply the sigmoid to the output layer of the network when computing the loss value (in the depth dimension), as stated by the `from_logits=True` parameter. This configuration is required since we haven't added an activation function to the last layer of the custom U-Net:

(tf2)

```
# Define the model
model = get_unet()

# Choose the optimizer
optimizer = tf.optimizers.Adam()

# Configure and create the checkpoint callback
checkpoint_path = "ckpt/pb.ckpt"
cp_callback = tf.keras.callbacks.ModelCheckpoint(checkpoint_path,
                                                 save_weights_only=True,
                                                 verbose=1)
# Enable TensorBoard loggging
TensorBoard = tf.keras.callbacks.TensorBoard(write_images=True)

# Cofigure the training loop and log the accuracy
model.compile(optimizer=optimizer,
loss=tf.losses.SparseCategoricalCrossentropy(from_logits=True),
              metrics=['accuracy'])
```

The datasets and the callbacks are passed to the `fit` method, which performs the effective training loop for the desired number of epochs:

(tf2)

```
num_epochs = 50
model.fit(train_set, validation_data=validation_set, epochs=num_epochs,
          callbacks=[cp_callback, TensorBoard])
```

The training loop will train the model for 50 epochs, measuring the loss and the accuracy during the training and, at the end of every epoch, the accuracy and loss value on the validation set. Moreover, having passed two callbacks, we have a checkpoint with the model parameters logged in the ckpt directory, and we have the logging of the metrics not only on the standard output (that is, the Keras default) but also on TensorBoard.

Evaluation and inference

During the training, we can open TensorBoard and look at the plots of the losses and metrics. At the end of the 50th epoch, we get the plots shown in the following screenshot:

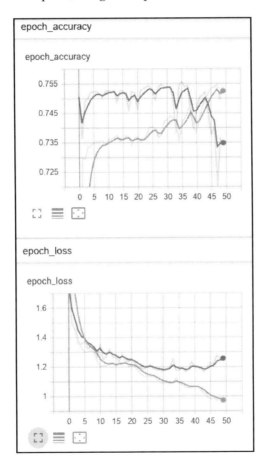

The accuracy and loss values on the training set (orange) and validation set (blue). The summary usage and configuration is hidden to the user by Keras.

Moreover, since we have all of the parameters of the model in our `model` variable, we can try to feed it an image downloaded from the internet and see whether the segmentation works as expected.

Let's suppose that we downloaded the following image from the internet and saved it as `"author.jpg"`:

Greetings!

We expect the model to produce a segmentation of the only known class contained in this image, that is, `"person"`, while producing the `"background"` label everywhere else.

Once we've downloaded the image, we convert it into the same format expected by the model (a float with values between *[0,1]*) and resize it to *512*. Since the model works on a batch of images, a unary dimension to the `sample` variable has to be added. Now, running the inference is as easy as `model(sample)`. After that, we use the `tf.argmax` function on the last channel to extract the predicted labels for every pixel position:

`(tf2)`

```
sample = tf.image.decode_jpeg(tf.io.read_file("author.jpg"))
sample = tf.expand_dims(tf.image.convert_image_dtype(sample, tf.float32),
axis=[0])
sample = tf.image.resize(sample, (512,512))
pred_image = tf.squeeze(tf.argmax(model(sample), axis=-1), axis=[0])
```

In the `pred_image` tensor, we have the dense predictions that are pretty much useless for visualization. In fact, this tensor has values in the *[0, 21]* range, and these values are indistinguishable once visualized (they all look black).

Hence, we can use the LUT created for the dataset to apply the inverse mapping from label to color. In the end, we can use the TensorFlow `io` package to convert the image and JPEG format and store it on the disk for easy visualization:

```
(tf2)

    REV_LUT = {value: key for key, value in LUT.items()}

    color_image = tf.Variable(tf.zeros((512,512,3), dtype=tf.uint8))
    pixels_per_label = []
    for label, color in REV_LUT.items():
        match = tf.equal(pred_image, label)
        labeled = tf.expand_dims(tf.cast(match, tf.uint8), axis=-1)
        pixels_per_label.append((label, tf.math.count_nonzero(labeled)))
        labeled = tf.tile(labeled, [1,1,3])
        color_image.assign_add(labeled * color)

    # Save
    tf.io.write_file("seg.jpg", tf.io.encode_jpeg(color_image))
```

Here's the result of the segmentation after training a simple model for only 50 epochs on a small dataset:

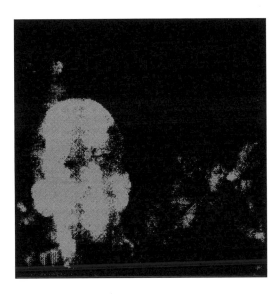

The result of the segmentation after mapping the predicted labels to the corresponding colors.

Although coarse, because the architecture hasn't been optimized, model selection hasn't been performed, and the dataset size is small, the segmentation results already look promising!

It is possible to inspect the predicted labels by counting the number of matches per label. In the `pixels_per_label` list, we saved the pair (`label`, `match_count`) and by printing it, we can verify if the predicted class is "`person`" (id 15) as expected:

(tf2)

```
for label, count in pixels_per_label:
  print(label, ": ", count.numpy())
```

That produces the following:

```
0: 218871
1: 0
3: 383
[...]
15: 42285
[...]
```

This is as expected. Of course, there is still room for improvement, and this is left to the reader as an exercise.

Summary

In this chapter, we introduced the problem of semantic segmentation and implemented U-Net: a deep encoder-decoder architecture used to tackle this problem. A short introduction about the possible use cases and the challenges this problem poses has been presented, followed by an intuitive introduction of the deconvolution (transposed convolution) operation, used to build the decoder part of the architecture. Since, at the time of writing, there is not a dataset for semantic segmentation that's ready to use in TensorFlow Datasets, we took the advantage of this to show the architecture of TensorFlow Datasets and show how to implement a custom `DatasetBuilder`. Implementing it is straightforward, and it is something that's recommended to every TensorFlow user since it is a handy way of creating a high-efficiency data input pipeline (`tf.data.Dataset`). Moreover, by implementing the `_generate_examples` method, the user is forced to "have a look" at the data, and this is something that's highly recommended when doing machine learning and data science.

After that, we learned the implementation of the training loop for the semantic segmentation network by treating this problem as a classification problem. This chapter showed how to use the Keras `compile` and `fit` methods and presented how to customize the training loop using Keras callbacks. This chapter ended with a quick example of how to use the trained model for inference and how to save the resulting image using only the TensorFlow methods.

In the next chapter, `Chapter 9`, *Generative Adversarial Networks*, an introduction to **Generative Adversarial Networks (GANs)** and the adversarial training process is shown, and, obviously, we explain how to implement them using TensorFlow 2.0.

Exercises

The following exercises are of fundamental importance and you are invited to answer to every theoretical question and solve all of the code challenges presented:

1. What is the semantic segmentation?
2. Why is semantic segmentation a difficult problem?
3. What is deconvolution? Is the deconvolution operation in deep learning a real deconvolution operation?
4. It is possible to use Keras models as layers?
5. Is it possible to use a single Keras `Sequential` model to implement a model architecture with skip connections?
6. Describe the original U-Net architecture: what are the differences between the custom implementation presented in this chapter and the original one?
7. Implement, using Keras, the original U-Net architecture.
8. What is a DatasetBuilder?
9. Describe the hierarchical organization of TensorFlow Datasets.
10. The `_info` method contains the description of every single example of the dataset. How is this description related to the `FeatureConnector` object?
11. Describe the `_generate_splits` and `_generate_examples` methods. Explain how these methods are connected and the role of the `gen_kwargs` parameter of `tfds.core.SplitGenerator`.
12. What is a LUT? Why is it a useful data structure when creating a dataset for semantic segmentation?
13. Why it is required to use `tf.io.gfile` when developing a custom DatasetBuilder?

14. (Bonus): Add a missing dataset for semantic segmentation to the TensorFlow Datasets project! Submit a Pull Request to `https://github.com/tensorflow/datasets`, and in the message, feel free to share this exercise section and this book.

15. Train the modified U-Net architecture as shown in this chapter.

16. Change the loss function and add a term of reconstruction loss, where the goal of the minimization process is to both minimize the cross-entropy and make the predicted label similar to the ground truth label.

17. Measure the mean intersection over union using the Keras callback. The Mean IOU is already implemented in the `tf.metrics` package.

18. Try to improve the model's performance, on the validation set, by adding dropout layers in the encoder.

19. During the training, start by dropping neurons with a probability of 0.5 and, at every epoch, increase this value of 0.1. Stop the training when the validations mean IOU stops increasing.

20. Use the trained model to run inference on a random image downloaded from the internet. Postprocess the result segmentation in order to detect a bounding box around different elements of different classes. Draw the bounding boxes, using TensorFlow, on the input image.

Generative Adversarial Networks

9

In this chapter, **Generative Adversarial Networks (GANs)** and the adversarial training process will be presented. In the first section, we will go over a theoretical overview of the GAN framework, while highlighting the strengths of the adversarial training process and the flexibility that was introduced by using neural networks as the model of choice for creating GANs. The theoretical part will give you an intuitive idea about which part of the GAN value function is being optimized during the adversarial training process and show you why the non-saturating value function should be used instead of the original one.

We will then go through a step-by-step implementation of GAN models and their training, with a visual explanation of what happens during this process. You will become familiar with the concept of target and learned distributions, which happens by watching the model learn.

The natural extension of the GAN framework to the conditional version is presented in the second part of this chapter, and how to create a conditional image generator will be shown. This chapter, just like the previous ones, will end with an exercise section that you are encouraged not to skip.

In this chapter, we will cover the following topics:

- Understanding GANs and their applications
- Unconditional GANs
- Conditional GANs

Understanding GANs and their applications

Introduced in 2014 by *Ian Goodfellow et a*l. in the paper *Generative Adversarial Networks*, GANs have revolutionized the field of generative models, opening the road to incredible applications.

GANs are frameworks that are used for the estimation of generative models via an adversarial process in which two models, the Generator and the Discriminator, are trained simultaneously.

The goal of the generative model (Generator) is to capture the data distribution contained in the training set, while the discriminative model acts as a binary classifier. Its goal is to estimate the probability of a sample to come from the training data rather than from the Generator. In the following diagram, the general architecture of adversarial training is shown:

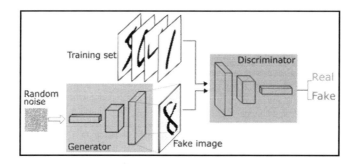

Graphical representation of the adversarial training process. The generator goal is used to fool the Discriminator by learning to generate samples that are more and more similar to the training set. (Image source: https://www.freecodecamp.org/news/an-intuitive-introduction-to-generative-adversarial-networks-gans-7a2264a81394/—by Thalles Silva)

The idea is to train a generative model without explicitly defining a loss function. Instead, we use a signal coming from another network as feedback. The Generator's aim is to fool the Discriminator, while the Discriminator's aim is to correctly classify whether the input samples are real or fake. The power of adversarial training comes from the fact that both the Generator and the Discriminator can be non-linear, parametric models such as neural networks. It is therefore possible to use gradient descent to train them.

To learn about generator distribution over the data, the generator builds a *mapping* from a **prior noise distribution**, $p_z(z)$, to a data space $G(z)$.

The Discriminator, $D(x)$, is a function (neural network) that outputs a single scalar representing the probability that x came from the real data distribution rather than $G(z)$.

The original GAN framework is expressed by using a game-theory approach to the problem and poses it as a min-max game in which two players, the Generator and the Discriminator, compete against each other.

Value function

The value function is a mathematical way of representing the goals of the players in terms of expected returns. The GAN game is expressed by the following value function:

$$\min_{G} \max_{D} V_{GAN}(D, G) = \mathbb{E}_{x \sim p_{data}(x)}[\log D(x)] + \mathbb{E}_{z \sim p_z(z)}[\log(1 - D(G(z)))]$$

This value function represents the game that the two players are playing, along with their respective long-term goals.

The Discriminator's goal is to correctly classify the real and fake samples, and this goal is expressed as the **maximization** of both the $\mathbb{E}_{x \sim p_{data}(x)}[\log D(x)]$ and $\mathbb{E}_{z \sim p_z(z)}[\log(1 - D(G(z)))]$ terms. The former represents the correct classification of the samples coming from the real data distribution (therefore, the goal is to get $D(x) = 1$), while the latter is the correct classification of fake samples (and in this case, the goal is to get $D(G(z)) = 0$).

The generator, on the other hand, is trained to fool the Discriminator, and its goal is to **minimize** $\mathbb{E}_{z \sim p_z(z)}[\log(1 - D(G(z)))]$. The way you minimize this term is by producing samples that are more and more similar to the real ones, thereby trying to fool the Discriminator.

A subtlety worth noting is that the min-max game is played only in the second term of the value function since, in the first term, only the Discriminator plays. It does this by learning to correctly classify the data coming from the real data distribution.

Although clear and pretty easy to understand, this formulation has a practical disadvantage. In the early training steps, the Discriminator can easily learn how to correctly classify fake data by maximizing $\mathbb{E}_{z \sim p_z(z)}[\log(1 - D(G(z)))]$ because the generated samples are too different from the real ones. Since learning from the quality of the generated samples is poor, the Discriminator can reject samples with high confidence because they are clearly different from the training data. This rejection consists of classing the correct classification of the generated samples as fake ($D(G(z)) = 0$), making the term $\mathbb{E}_{z \sim p_z(z)}[\log(1 - D(G(z)))]$ saturate. It follows that the previous equation may not provide a sufficient gradient for G to learn well. The solution to this practical problem is the definition of a new value function that does not saturate.

Non-saturating value function

The proposed solution is to train G to **maximize** $\log D(G(z))$ instead of minimizing $\log(1 - D(G(z)))$. Intuitively, we can see the proposed solution as a way of playing the same min-max game in a different manner.

The Discriminator's goal is to maximize the probability of correctly classifying the real and fake samples, with no changes with respect to the previous formulation. The Generator's goal, on the other hand, is to minimize the Discriminator's probability of correctly classifying the generated samples as fake but to explicitly fool the Discriminator by making it classify the fake samples as real.

The value function of the same game, which is played in a different manner by the two players, can be expressed as follows:

$$V_{GAN}(D, G) = \begin{cases} D: & \max_D \mathbb{E}_{x \sim p_{data}(x)}[\log D(x)] + \mathbb{E}_{z \sim p_z(z)}[\log(1 - D(G(z)))] \\ G: & \max_G \mathbb{E}_{z \sim p_z(z)}[\log(D(G(z)))] \end{cases}$$

As we stated previously, the power of the adversarial training frameworks comes from the fact that both G and D can be neural networks and that they can both be trained via gradient descent.

Model definition and training phase

Defining the Generator and the Discriminator as neural networks allows us to tackle the problem using all the neural network architectures that have been developed over the years, with each one specialized to work with a certain data type.

There are no constraints in the model's definition; in fact, it is possible to define their architecture in a completely arbitrary manner. The only constraints are given by the structure of the data we are working on; the architectures depend on the data type, all of which are as follows:

- **Images**: Convolutional neural networks
- **Sequences, Text**: Recurrent neural networks
- **Numerical, Categorical values**: Fully connected networks

Once we've defined the model's architecture as a function of the data type, it is possible to use them to play the min-max game.

Adversarial training consists of alternating the execution of training steps. Every training step is a player action, and the Generator and Discriminator compete against each other in turn. The game follows the following rules:

- **Discriminator**: The Discriminator plays first and can repeat the following three steps from 1 to k times, where k is a hyperparameter (often, k equals 1):

  1. Sample a minibatch of m noise samples, $z^{(1)}, \ldots, z^{(m)}$, from the noise prior to $p_z(z)$
  2. Sample a minibatch of m samples, $x^{(1)}, \ldots, x^{(m)}$, from the real data distribution, $p_{\text{data}}(x)$
  3. Train the Discriminator via stochastic gradient ascent:

  $$J = \frac{1}{m} \sum_{i=1}^{m} \log D(x^{(i)}) + \log(1 - D(G(z^{(i)})))$$

  $$\theta_D = \theta_D + \lambda \nabla_{\theta_D} J$$

  Here, θ_D is the Discriminator's parameters

- **Generator**: The Generator always plays after the Discriminator's turn, and it plays only once:

  1. Sample a minibatch of m noise samples, $z^{(1)}, \ldots, z^{(m)}$, from the noise prior to $p_z(z)$
  2. Train the Generator via stochastic gradient ascent (this is a maximization problem since the game is targeted the non-saturating value function):

  $$J = \frac{1}{m} \sum_{i=1}^{m} \log(D(G(z^{(i)})))$$

  $$\theta_g = \theta_g + \lambda \nabla_{\theta_g} J$$

  Here, θ_G is the Generator's parameters

Just like any other neural network that's trained via gradient descent, the updates can use any standard optimization algorithm (Adam, SGD, SGD with Momentum, and so on). The game should go on until the Discriminator isn't completely fooled by the Generator, that is, when the Discriminator always predicts a probability of 0.5 for every input sample. The value of 0.5 may sound strange, but intuitively, this means that the Generator is now able to generate samples that are similar to the real ones and the Discriminator can now only make random guesses.

Applications of GANs

At first glance, Generative models have a limited utility. What is the purpose of having a model that generates something similar to what we already have (the real sample dataset)?

In practice, learning from a data distribution is extremely useful in the anomaly detection domain and in "human-only" fields such as art, painting, and music generation. Moreover, the applications of GANs in their conditional formulation are astonishing and used to create applications with a great market value (see the *Conditional GANs* section of this chapter for more information).

With GANs, it is possible to make a machine generate extremely realistic faces, starting from random noise. The following image shows applying GAN to the face generation problem. These results were obtained in the paper titled *Progressive Growing of GANs for Improved Quality, Stability, and Variation* (T. Karras et al. 2017, NVIDIA):

These people do not exist. Every image, although super realistic, is GAN generated. You can try this out for yourself by going to https://thispersondoesnotexist.com/ (Image source, the paper titled *Progressive Growing of GANs for Improved Quality, Stability, and Variation*).

Another astonishing application from before GANs were introduced that was practically impossible to achieve was domain translation, which is where you use a GAN to go from one domain to another, for example, from sketches to a realistic image or from an aerial view to a map.

The following image, which was retrieved from the paper *Image-to-Image Translation with Conditional Adversarial Networks* (Isola et al., 2017) shows how (conditional) GANs are able to solve tasks that were considered impossible only some years ago:

GANs allow you to solve the domain translation problem. Colorizing a black and white image or generating photos only from sketches is now possible. Image source: *Image-to-Image Translation with Conditional Adversarial Networks* (Isola et al., 2017).

GAN applications are astonishing and their practical applications are always being discovered. Starting from the next section, we'll learn how to implement some of them in pure TensorFlow 2.0.

Unconditional GANs

It isn't common to see GANs mentioned as unconditional since this is the default and original configuration. In this book, however, we decided to stress this characteristic of the original GAN formulation in order to make you aware of the two main GAN classifications:

- Unconditional GANs
- Conditional GANs

The generative model that we described in the previous section falls under the category of unconditional GANs. The generative model is trained to capture the training data distribution and to generate samples that have been randomly sampled from the captured distribution. The conditional configuration is a slightly modified version of the framework and is presented in the next section.

Thanks to TensorFlow 2.0's eager-by-default style, the implementation of adversarial training is straightforward. In practice, to implement the adversarial training loop as described in the Goodfellow et al. paper (*Generative Adversarial Networks*), it is required to implement it as it is defined, line by line. Of course, the best way to create a custom training loop that requires the alternate training steps of two different models is not to use Keras, but to implement it manually.

Just like in any other machine learning problem, we have to start with the data. In this section, we will define a generative model, with the goal of learning about the random normal data distribution, centered at 10 and with a small standard deviation.

Preparing the data

Since the goal of this section is to learn about data distribution, we will start from the foundations in order to build a strong intuition of the adversarial training process. The most simple and the easiest way to visualize data distribution is by looking at the random normal distribution. We can, therefore, pick a Gaussian (or normal) centered at 10 and with a standard deviation of 0.1 as our target data distribution:

$$\mathcal{N}(\mu = 10, \sigma = 0.1)$$

Thanks to the eager execution process, we can use TensorFlow 2.0 itself to sample a value from the target distribution. We do this by using the `tf.random.normal` function. The following code snippet shows a function that samples (2,000) data points from the target distribution:

(tf2)

```
import tensorflow as tf

def sample_dataset():
    dataset_shape = (2000, 1)
    return tf.random.normal(mean=10., shape=dataset_shape, stddev=0.1,
dtype=tf.float32)
```

To have a better understanding of what a GAN can learn, and of what happens during the adversarial training itself, we use `matplotlib` to visualize the data on a histogram:

(tf2)

```
import matplotlib.pyplot as plt

counts, bin, ignored = plt.hist(sample_dataset().numpy(), 100)
axes = plt.gca()
axes.set_xlim([-1,11])
axes.set_ylim([0, 60])
plt.show()
```

This displays the target distribution that's shown in the following image. As expected, if we have a small standard deviation, the histogram peaks at the mean value:

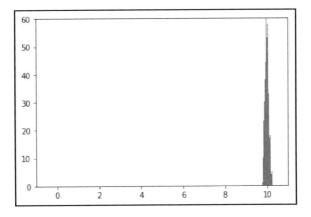

The histogram of the target distribution – 5,000 data points sampled from a Gaussian distribution with a mean of 10 and a stddev of 0.1

Now that we've defined the target data distribution and we have a function that samples from it (`sample_dataset`), we are ready to define the Generator and Discriminator networks.

As we stated at the beginning of this chapter, the power of the adversarial training process is that both the Generator and the Discriminator can be neural networks, and the models can be trained using gradient descent.

Defining the Generator

The Generator's goal is to behave like the target distribution. For this reason, we have to define it as a network with a single neuron. We can sample one number at a time from the target distribution, and the same should be possible from the Generator.

There is no guideline or constraint for the model architecture definition. The only restrictions are given from the nature of the problem, and these are the input and output dimensions. The output dimension, as we explained previously, depends on the target distribution, while the input dimension is the arbitrary dimension of the noise prior, which is often set to 100.

To solve this problem, we are going to define a simple three-layer neural network, with two hidden layers with 64 neurons each:

(tf2)

```python
def generator(input_shape):
    """Defines the generator keras.Model.
    Args:
        input_shape: the desired input shape (e.g.: (latent_space_size))
    Returns:
        G: The generator model
    """
    inputs = tf.keras.layers.Input(input_shape)
    net = tf.keras.layers.Dense(units=64, activation=tf.nn.elu,
name="fc1")(inputs)
    net = tf.keras.layers.Dense(units=64, activation=tf.nn.elu,
name="fc2")(net)
    net = tf.keras.layers.Dense(units=1, name="G")(net)
    G = tf.keras.Model(inputs=inputs, outputs=net)
    return G
```

The `generator` function returns a Keras model. The Keras functional API has been used to define the model, although a Sequential was enough.

Defining the Discriminator

Just like the Generator, the Discriminator architecture depends on the target distribution. The goal is to classify samples into two categories. The input layer, therefore, depends on the size of the samples that have been sampled from the target distribution; in our case, it is one. The output layer is a single linear neuron that's used to classify the sample into two categories.

The activation function is linear because the Keras loss function applies the sigmoid:

(tf2)

```python
def disciminator(input_shape):
    """Defines the Discriminator keras.Model.
    Args:
        input_shape: the desired input shape (e.g.: (the generator output
shape))
    Returns:
        D: the Discriminator model
    """
    inputs = tf.keras.layers.Input(input_shape)
    net = tf.keras.layers.Dense(units=32, activation=tf.nn.elu,
```

```
name="fc1")(inputs)
    net = tf.keras.layers.Dense(units=1, name="D")(net)
    D = tf.keras.Model(inputs=inputs, outputs=net)
    return D
```

After defining the Generator and Discriminator architecture, we only have to instantiate the Keras models by specifying the correct input shapes:

(tf2)

```
# Define the real input shape
input_shape = (1,)

# Define the Discriminator model
D = disciminator(input_shape)

# Arbitrary set the shape of the noise prior
latent_space_shape = (100,)
# Define the input noise shape and define the generator
G = generator(latent_space_shape)
```

The models and the target data distribution have been defined; the only thing that's missing is expressing the relationships between them, which is done by defining the loss functions.

Defining the loss functions

As shown in the previous section, the Discriminator's output is linear because the `loss` function we are going to use applies the nonlinearity for us. To implement the adversarial training process by following the original formulation, the `loss` function to use is binary cross-entropy:

(tf2)

```
bce = tf.keras.losses.BinaryCrossentropy(from_logits=True)
```

The `bce` object is used to compute the binary cross-entropy between two distributions:

- The learned distribution, which is represented by the Discriminator's output, is squashed into the [0,1] range (by applying it the sigmoid σ function, since the `from_logits` parameter is set to `True`). This produces a value closer to one if the Discriminator classifies the input as coming from the real data distribution.
- The conditional empirical distribution over class labels, that is, a discrete probability distribution where the probability of it being a real sample, is labeled as 1 and is 0 otherwise.

Mathematically, the binary cross-entropy between the conditional empirical distribution over class labels (y) and the generator output squashed in $[0,1]$ ($\hat{y} = \sigma(D(x))$) is expressed as follows:

$$\mathcal{L}_{BCE} = y \log(\hat{y}) - (1 - y) \log(1 - \hat{y}).$$

We want to train the Discriminator to correctly classify real and fake data: correctly classifying the real data can be seen as the maximization of $\mathbb{E}_{x \sim p_{data}(x)}[\log D(x)]$, while the correct classification of the fake data is the maximization of $\mathbb{E}_{z \sim p_z(z)}[\log(1 - D(G(z)))]$.

By replacing the expected value with the empirical mean over a batch of m samples, it is possible to express the maximization of the log probability of correctly classifying a sample as the sum of two BCEs:

$$\frac{1}{m}\sum_{i=1}^{m} -\log\sigma(D(x^{(i)})) + \frac{1}{m}\sum_{i=1}^{m} -\log(1 - \sigma(D(G(z^{(i)})))$$

The first term is the BCE between the label $y = 1$ and the Discriminator output when given a real sample as input, while the second term is the BCE between the label $y = 0$ and the Discriminator output when given a fake sample as input.

Implementing this loss function in TensorFlow is straightforward:

(tf2)

```
def d_loss(d_real, d_fake):
    """The disciminator loss function."""
    return bce(tf.ones_like(d_real), d_real) + bce(tf.zeros_like(d_fake),
d_fake)
```

The same `bce` object we created previously is used inside the `d_loss` function since it is a stateless object that only computes the binary cross-entropy between its inputs.

 Please note that there is no need to add a minus sign in front of the `bce` invocations to maximize them; the mathematical formulation of the BCE already contains the minus sign.

The generator loss function follows on from this theory. Implementing the non-saturating value function only consists of the TensorFlow implementation of the following formula:

$$-\frac{1}{m} \sum_{i=1}^{m} \sigma(\log(D(G(z)))).$$

This formula is the binary cross-entropy between the log probability of the generated images and the distribution of the real images (labeled with 1). In practice, we want to maximize the log probability of the generated samples, updating the Generator parameters in order to make the Discriminator classify them as real (label 1).

The TensorFlow implementation is trivial:

(tf2)

```
def g_loss(generated_output):
    """The Generator loss function."""
    return bce(tf.ones_like(generated_output), generated_output)
```

Everything is set up to implement the adversarial training process.

Adversarial training process in unconditional GANs

As we explained at the beginning of this chapter, the adversarial training process is where we alternate the execution of the training steps for the Discriminator and Generator. The Generator requires the value that's computed by the Discriminator to perform its parameter update, while the Discriminator requires the generated samples (also known as fake input) and the real samples.

TensorFlow allows us to define a custom training loop easily. The `tf.GradientTape` object, in particular, is extremely useful for computing the gradient of a specific model, even when there are two models interacting. In fact, thanks to the `trainable_variables` property of every Keras model, it is possible to compute the gradient of a certain function, but only with respect to these variables.

The training process is exactly like the one that's described in the GAN paper (*Generative Adversarial Networks - Ian Goodfellow et al.*), thanks to the eager mode. Moreover, since this training process can be computationally intensive (especially on big datasets where the data distribution that we want to capture is complex), it is worth decorating the training step function with `@tf.function` in order to speed up the computation by converting it into a graph:

(tf2)

```
def train():
    # Define the optimizers and the train operations
    optimizer = tf.keras.optimizers.Adam(1e-5)
    @tf.function
    def train_step():
        with tf.GradientTape(persistent=True) as tape:
            real_data = sample_dataset()
            noise_vector = tf.random.normal(
                mean=0, stddev=1,
                shape=(real_data.shape[0], latent_space_shape[0]))
            # Sample from the Generator
            fake_data = G(noise_vector)
            # Compute the D loss
            d_fake_data = D(fake_data)
            d_real_data = D(real_data)
            d_loss_value = d_loss(d_real_data, d_fake_data)
            # Compute the G loss
            g_loss_value = g_loss(d_fake_data)
        # Now that we comptuted the losses we can compute the gradient
        # and optimize the networks
        d_gradients = tape.gradient(d_loss_value, D.trainable_variables)
        g_gradients = tape.gradient(g_loss_value, G.trainable_variables)
        # Deletng the tape, since we defined it as persistent
        # (because we used it twice)
        del tape
        optimizer.apply_gradients(zip(d_gradients, D.trainable_variables))
        optimizer.apply_gradients(zip(g_gradients, G.trainable_variables))
        return real_data, fake_data, g_loss_value, d_loss_value
```

In order to visualize what the Generator is learning during the training process, we plot the same graph values that were sampled from the target distribution (in orange), as well as the values that were sampled from the Generator (in blue):

(tf2)

```
    fig, ax = plt.subplots()
    for step in range(40000):
        real_data, fake_data,g_loss_value, d_loss_value = train_step()
```

```
    if step % 200 == 0:
        print("G loss: ", g_loss_value.numpy(), " D loss: ",
d_loss_value.numpy(), " step: ", step)

        # Sample 5000 values from the Generator and draw the histogram
        ax.hist(fake_data.numpy(), 100)
        ax.hist(real_data.numpy(), 100)
        # these are matplotlib.patch.Patch properties
        props = dict(boxstyle='round', facecolor='wheat', alpha=0.5)

        # place a text box in upper left in axes coords
        textstr = f"step={step}"
        ax.text(0.05, 0.95, textstr, transform=ax.transAxes,
fontsize=14,
                verticalalignment='top', bbox=props)

        axes = plt.gca()
        axes.set_xlim([-1,11])
        axes.set_ylim([0, 60])
        display.display(pl.gcf())
        display.clear_output(wait=True)
        plt.gca().clear()
```

Now that we've defined the whole training loop as a function, we can execute it by calling `train()`.

The `train_step` function is the most important of the whole snippet since it contains the implementation of the adversarial training. A peculiarity that is worth highlighting is how, by using `trainable_variables`, it has been possible to compute the gradients of the loss function with respect to the model parameters we are interested in, while considering everything else constant.

The second peculiarity has been the usage of a persistent gradient tape object. Using a persistent tape allowed us to keep track of the execution while allocating a single object in memory (the tape) and using it twice. If the tape had been created non-persistently, we couldn't reuse it since it would be automatically destroyed after the first `.gradient` invocation.

Instead of visualizing the data using TensorBoard (this is left as an exercise for you), we followed the matplotlib approach we've used so far and sampled 5,000 data points every 200 training steps from both the target and the learned distributions, and then visualized them by plotting the corresponding histograms.

During the initial training steps, the learned distribution is different from the target one, as shown in the following graph:

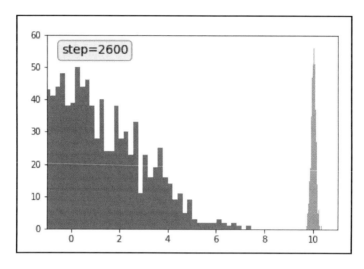

Data visualization at the 2,600th training step. The target distribution is a random normal distribution with a mean of 10 and a standard deviation of 0.1. The values that were sampled from the learned distribution are slowly shifting toward the target distribution.

During the training phase, it is possible to appreciate how the Generator is learning to approximate the target distribution:

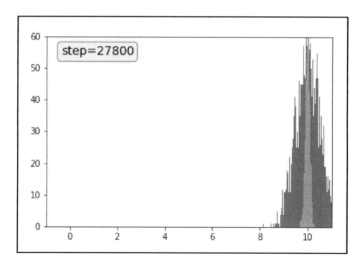

Data visualization at the 27,800th training step. The learned distribution is approaching the mean value of 10 and is reducing its variance.

In the late training stages, the two distributions almost completely overlap and the training process can be stopped:

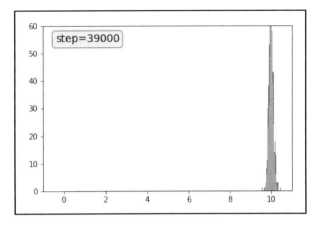

Data visualization at the 39,000th training step. The target distribution and the learned distribution overlap.

Thanks to the expressive power of the Keras model and the ease of usage of the TensorFlow eager mode (plus the graph-conversion via `tf.function`), defining two models and training them by manually implementing the adversarial training process has been almost trivial.

Although trivial, this is the very same training loop that we use when working with different data types. In fact, the same training loop can be used to train image, text, and even audio generators, except that we use different Generator and Discriminator architectures in those cases.

A slightly modified version of the GAN framework allows you to collect a conditional generation of samples; for example, the Generator is trained to generate specific samples when given a condition.

Conditional GANs

Mirza et al. in their paper, *Conditional Generative Adversarial Nets*, introduced a conditional version of the GAN framework. This modification is extremely easy to understand and is the foundation of amazing GAN applications that are widely used in today's world.

Some of the most astonishing GAN applications, such as the generation of a street scene from a semantic label to the colorization of an image given a grayscale input, pass through image super-resolution as specialized versions of the conditional GAN idea.

Conditional GANs are based on the idea that GANs can be extended to a conditional model if both G and D are conditioned on some additional information, y. This additional information can be any kind of additional information, from class labels to semantic maps, or data from other modalities. It is possible to perform this conditioning by feeding the additional information into both the Generator and the Discriminator as an additional input layer. The following diagram, which was taken from the *Conditional Generative Adversarial Nets* paper, clearly shows how the Generator and Discriminator models can be extended to support the conditioning:

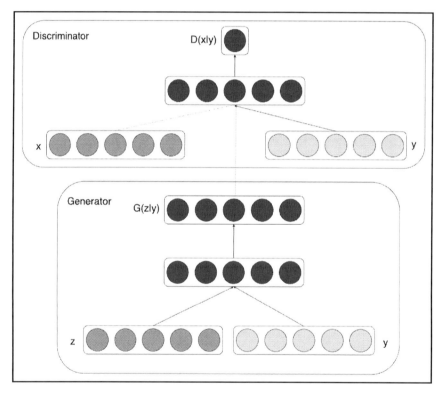

Conditional GANs. The Generator and the Discriminator have one additional input, y, which represents the auxiliary information that conditions the models (Image source: *Conditional Generative Adversarial Nets*, Mirza et al., 2014).

The generator architecture is extended to combine the joint hidden representation of the noise prior to the condition. There are no constraints on how to feed the condition to the Generator network. You can simply concatenate the condition to the noise vector. Alternatively, if the condition is complex, you can encode it using a neural network and concatenate its output to one layer of the Generator. The same reasoning applies to the Discriminator.

Conditioning the models changes the value's function since the data distributions that we sample from are now conditioned:

$$\min_{G} \max_{D} V_{GAN}(D, G) = \mathbb{E}_{x \sim p_{data}(x|y)}[\log D(x, y)] + \mathbb{E}_{z \sim p_z(z)}[\log(1 - D(G(z|y), y))]$$

There are no other changes in regards to the adversarial training process, and the same considerations about the non-saturating value function still apply.

In this section, we are going to implement a conditional Fashion-MNIST generator.

Getting the data for a conditional GAN

By using TensorFlow Datasets, getting the data is straightforward. Since the goal is to create a Fashion-MNIST generator, we will use the class labels as a condition. The data that's returned from the `tfds.load` call is in a dictionary format. Therefore, we need to define a function that maps the dictionary to a tuple that contains only the image and the corresponding label. In this phase, we can also prepare the whole data input pipeline:

```
(tf2)
```

```python
import tensorflow as tf
import tensorflow_datasets as tfds
import matplotlib.pyplot as plt

dataset = tfds.load("fashion_mnist", split="train")

def convert(row):
    image = tf.image.convert_image_dtype(row["image"], tf.float32)
    label = tf.cast(row["label"], tf.float32)
    return image, label

batch_size = 32
dataset = dataset.map(convert).batch(batch_size).prefetch(1)
```

Defining the Generator in a conditional GAN

Since we are working with images, the natural choice is to use a convolutional neural network. In particular, using the deconvolution operation we introduced in Chapter 8, *Semantic Segmentation and Custom Dataset Builder*, it is possible to easily define a decoder-like network that generates images, starting from a latent representation and a condition:

(tf2)

```
def get_generator(latent_dimension):
    # Condition subnetwork: encode the condition in a hidden representation
    condition = tf.keras.layers.Input((1,))
    net = tf.keras.layers.Dense(32, activation=tf.nn.elu)(condition)
    net = tf.keras.layers.Dense(64, activation=tf.nn.elu)(net)
    # Concatenate the hidden condition representation to noise and upsample
    noise = tf.keras.layers.Input(latent_dimension)
    inputs = tf.keras.layers.Concatenate()([noise, net])
    # Convert inputs from (batch_size, latent_dimension + 1)
    # To a 4-D tensor, that can be used with convolutions
    inputs = tf.keras.layers.Reshape((1,1, inputs.shape[-1]))(inputs)
    depth = 128
    kernel_size= 5
    net = tf.keras.layers.Conv2DTranspose(
        depth, kernel_size,
        padding="valid",
        strides=1,
        activation=tf.nn.relu)(inputs) # 5x5
    net = tf.keras.layers.Conv2DTranspose(
        depth//2, kernel_size,
        padding="valid",
        strides=2,
        activation=tf.nn.relu)(net) #13x13
    net = tf.keras.layers.Conv2DTranspose(
        depth//4, kernel_size,
        padding="valid",
        strides=2,
        activation=tf.nn.relu,
        use_bias=False)(net) # 29x29
    # Standard convolution with a 2x2 kernel to obtain a 28x28x1 out
    # The output is a sigmoid, since the images are in the [0,1] range
    net = tf.keras.layers.Conv2D(
        1, 2,
        padding="valid",
        strides=1,
        activation=tf.nn.sigmoid,
        use_bias=False)(net)
```

```
model = tf.keras.Model(inputs=[noise, condition], outputs=net)
return model
```

Defining the Discriminator in a conditional GAN

The Discriminator architecture is straightforward. A standard way of conditioning the Discriminator consists of concatenating the encoded representation of the image, with the encoded representation of the condition being placed in a unique vector. Doing this requires the definition of two subnetworks – the first one encodes the image in a feature vector, while the second one encodes the condition in another vector. The following code clarifies this concept:

(tf2)

```
def get_Discriminator():
    # Encoder subnetwork: feature extactor to get a feature vector
    image = tf.keras.layers.Input((28,28,1))
    depth = 32
    kernel_size=3
    net = tf.keras.layers.Conv2D(
        depth, kernel_size,
        padding="same",
        strides=2,
        activation=tf.nn.relu)(image) #14x14x32
    net = tf.keras.layers.Conv2D(
        depth*2, kernel_size,
        padding="same",
        strides=2,
        activation=tf.nn.relu)(net) #7x7x64
    net = tf.keras.layers.Conv2D(
        depth*3, kernel_size,
        padding="same",
        strides=2,
        activation=tf.nn.relu)(net) #4x4x96
    feature_vector = tf.keras.layers.Flatten()(net) # 4*4*96
```

After defining the encoder subnetwork that encoded the image into a feature vector, we are ready to create a hidden representation of the condition and concatenate it with the feature vector. After doing it, we can create the Keras model and return it:

(tf2)

```
# Create a hidden representation of the condition
condition = tf.keras.layers.Input((1,))
hidden = tf.keras.layers.Dense(32, activation=tf.nn.elu)(condition)
hidden = tf.keras.layers.Dense(64, activation=tf.nn.elu)(hidden)
# Concatenate the feature vector and the hidden label representation
out = tf.keras.layers.Concatenate()([feature_vector, hidden])
# Add the final classification layers with a single linear neuron
out = tf.keras.layers.Dense(128, activation=tf.nn.relu)(out)
out = tf.keras.layers.Dense(1)(out)
model = tf.keras.Model(inputs=[image, condition], outputs=out)
return model
```

Adversarial training process

The adversarial training process is the same as what we presented for the unconditional GAN. The `loss` functions are exactly the same:

(tf2)

```
bce = tf.keras.losses.BinaryCrossentropy(from_logits=True)

def d_loss(d_real, d_fake):
    """The disciminator loss function."""
    return bce(tf.ones_like(d_real), d_real) + bce(tf.zeros_like(d_fake),
d_fake)
def g_loss(generated_output):
    """The Generator loss function."""
    return bce(tf.ones_like(generated_output), generated_output)
```

The only difference is that our models now accept two input parameters.

After deciding on the noise's prior dimension and instantiated the G and D models, defining the train function requires a slight modification of the previous training loop. As for the unconditional GAN training loop definition, matplotlib has been used to log the images. Improving this script is left as an exercise for you to carry out:

(tf2)

```
latent_dimension = 100
G = get_generator(latent_dimension)
```

```
D = get_Discriminator()


def train():
    # Define the optimizers and the train operations
    optimizer = tf.keras.optimizers.Adam(1e-5)
    @tf.function
    def train_step(image, label):
        with tf.GradientTape(persistent=True) as tape:
            noise_vector = tf.random.normal(
            mean=0, stddev=1,
            shape=(image.shape[0], latent_dimension))
            # Sample from the Generator
            fake_data = G([noise_vector, label])
            # Compute the D loss
            d_fake_data = D([fake_data, label])
            d_real_data = D([image, label])
            d_loss_value = d_loss(d_real_data, d_fake_data)
            # Compute the G loss
            g_loss_value = g_loss(d_fake_data)
        # Now that we comptuted the losses we can compute the gradient
        # and optimize the networks
        d_gradients = tape.gradient(d_loss_value, D.trainable_variables)
        g_gradients = tape.gradient(g_loss_value, G.trainable_variables)
        # Deletng the tape, since we defined it as persistent
        del tape
        optimizer.apply_gradients(zip(d_gradients, D.trainable_variables))
        optimizer.apply_gradients(zip(g_gradients, G.trainable_variables))
        return g_loss_value, d_loss_value, fake_data[0], label[0]
    epochs = 10
    epochs = 10
    for epoch in range(epochs):
        for image, label in dataset:
            g_loss_value, d_loss_value, generated, condition =
train_step(image, label)

        print("epoch ", epoch, "complete")
        print("loss:", g_loss_value, "d_loss: ", d_loss_value)
        print("condition ", info.features['label'].int2str(
                tf.squeeze(tf.cast(condition, tf.int32)).numpy()))
        plt.imshow(tf.squeeze(generated).numpy(), cmap='gray')
        plt.show()
```

The training loop loops over the training set for 10 epochs and displays an image of a generated Fashion-MNIST element, along with its label. After a few epochs, the generated images become more and more realistic and they start matching the label, as shown in the following screenshot:

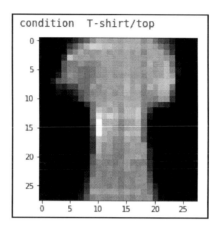

A generated sample feeding in input to the Generator's random noise and the condition T-shirt/top

Summary

In this chapter, we looked at GANs and the adversarial training process. In the first section, a theoretical explanation of the adversarial training process was presented, with a focus on the value function, which is used to formulate the problem as a min-max game. We also showed how the non-saturating value function is, in practice, the solution to making the Generator learn how to solve the saturation problem.

We then looked at implementing the Generator and Discriminator models that are used to create an unconditional GAN in pure TensorFlow 2.0. In this section, the expressive power of TensorFlow 2.0 and the definition of custom training loops was presented. In fact, it has been shown how straightforward it is to create Keras models and write the custom training loop that implements the adversarial training process, just by following the steps described in the GAN paper (*Generative Adversarial Networks - Ian Goodfellow et al.*).

The Keras functional API has been also extensively used, where a conditional generator of Fashion-MNIST-like images has been implemented. The implementation showed us how, by using the Keras functional API, it is possible to feed a second input (the condition) to both the Generator and Discriminator and define a flexible neural network architecture easily.

The GAN universe is rich in terms of very complex architectures and clever ideas for astonishing applications. This chapter aims to explain the GAN framework without claiming to be complete; there's enough material out there about GANs for me to write more than a whole book.

This chapter ends with an exercise section, which contains a challenge for you (questions 16 and 17): can you create a conditional GAN that generates realistic images, starting from a semantic label?

So far, we've focused on how to train various models, from simple classifiers to generative models, without worrying about the deployment stage.

In the next chapter, Chapter 10, *Bringing a Model to Production*, the final step of every real-life machine learning application will be presented – the deployment of learned models.

Exercises

Try answering and working on the following exercises to expand the knowledge that you've gained from this chapter:

1. What is the adversarial training process?
2. Write the value function of the min-max game that the Discriminator and Generator are playing.
3. Explain why the min-max value function formulation can saturate in the early training step of training.
4. Write and explain the non-saturating value function.
5. Write the rules of the adversarial training process.
6. Are there any recommendations on how to feed a condition to a GAN?
7. What does it mean to create a conditional GAN?
8. Can only the fully connected neural networks be used to create GANs?
9. Which neural network architecture works better for the image generation problem?
10. Update the code of the Unconditional GAN: Log the Generator and Discriminator loss value on TensorBoard, and also log matplotlib plots.
11. Unconditional GAN: Save the model parameter in a checkpoint at every epoch. Add support for the model's restoration, restarting from the latest checkpoint.

12. Extend the code of the unconditional GAN by making it conditional. Given the condition of 0, the Generator must behave like the normal distribution, with a mean of 10 and a standard deviation of 0.1. Given the condition of 1, the Generator must produce a value that has been sampled from a Gaussian distribution with a mean of 100 and a standard deviation of 1.

13. Log the magnitude of the Gradient that was computed to update the Discriminator and Generator in TensorBoard. Apply gradient clipping if the magnitude is greater than 1 in an absolute value.

14. Repeat exercises 1 and 2 for the conditional GAN.

15. Conditional GAN: Do not use matplotlib to plot the images; use `tf.summary.image` and TensorBoard.

16. Using the dataset we created in the previous chapter, `Chapter 8`, *Semantic Segmentation and Custom Dataset Builder*, create a conditional GAN that performs domain translation, from the semantic label to an image.

17. Use TensorFlow Hub to download a pre-trained feature extractor and use it as a building block to create the Discriminator for a conditional GAN that generates realistic scenes from semantic labels.

Bringing a Model to Production **10**

In this chapter, the ultimate goal of any real-life machine learning application will be presented—the deployment and inference of a trained model. As we saw in the previous chapters, TensorFlow allows us to train models and save their parameters in checkpoint files, making it possible to restore the model's status and continue with the training process, while also running the inference from Python.

The checkpoint files, however, are not in the right file format when the goal is to use a trained machine learning model with low latency and a low memory footprint. In fact, the checkpoint files only contain the models' parameters value, without any description of the computation; this forces the program to define the model structure first and then restore the model parameters. Moreover, the checkpoint files contain variable values that are only useful during the training process. However, they are a complete waste of resources during inference (for instance, all the variables created by the optimizers). The correct representation to use is the SavedModel serialization format, which is described in the next section. After analyzing the SavedModel serialization format, and seeing how a `tf.function` decorated function can be graph-converted and serialized, we will deep dive into the TensorFlow deployment ecosystem to see how TensorFlow 2.0 speeds up the deployment of a graph on a wide number of platforms and how it is designed for serving at scale.

In this chapter, we will cover the following topics:

- The SavedModel serialization format
- Python deployment
- Supported deployment platforms

The SavedModel serialization format

As we explained in `Chapter 3`, *TensorFlow Graph Architecture*, representing computations using DataFlow graphs has several advantages in terms of model portability since a graph is a language-agnostic representation of the computation.

SavedModel is a universal serialization format for TensorFlow models that extends the TensorFlow standard graph representation by creating a language-agnostic representation for the computation that is recoverable and hermetic. This representation has been designed not only to carry the graph description and values (like the standard graph) but also to offer additional features that were designed to simplify the usage of the trained models in heterogeneous production environments.

TensorFlow 2.0 has been designed with simplicity in mind. This design choice is visible in the following diagram, where it is possible to appreciate how the SavedModel format is the only bridge between the research and development phases (on the left) and the deployment phase (on the right):

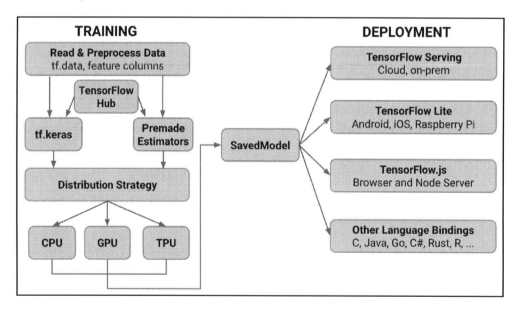

The TensorFlow 2.0 training and deployment ecosystem. Image source: `https://medium.com/tensorflow/whats-coming-in-tensorflow-2-0-d3663832e9b8`—the TensorFlow Team

Being the bridge between the model's training and its deployment, the SavedModel format must offer a broad set of features to satisfy the wide spectrum of deployment platforms available, thereby providing excellent support for different software and hardware platforms.

Features

A SavedModel contains a complete computational graph, including model parameters and everything else that's specified during its creation. SavedModel objects that are created using the TensorFlow 1.x API only contain a flat graph representation of the computation; in TensorFlow 2.0, a SavedModel contains a serialized representation of `tf.function` objects.

Creating a SavedModel is straightforward when you're using the TensorFlow Python API (as shown in the next section), but its configuration requires that you understand its main features, which are as follows:

- **Graph tagging**: In a production environment, you often need to put a model into production, while at the same time continuing the development of the same model after getting new data. Another possible scenario is the parallel training of two or more identical models, trained with different techniques or with different data, with the desire to put them all in production to test which performs better. The SavedModel format allows you to have multiple graphs that share the same set of variables and assets in the same file. Each graph is associated with one or more tags (user-defined strings) that allow us to identify it during the load operation.
- **SignatureDefs**: When defining a computational graph, we are aware of the model's inputs and outputs; this is called a **Model Signature**. The SavedModel serialization format uses `SignatureDefs` to allow generic support for signatures that may need to be saved within `graph`. `SignatureDefs` are nothing but a set of named Model Signatures that defines from which nodes the model can be called and which is the output node, given a certain input.
- **Assets**: To allow the models to rely upon external files for initialization, SavedModel supports the concept of assets. The assets are copied to the SavedModel location during its creation, and they can be read by the model initialization procedure safely.

- **Device cleanup**: The computational graph, which we looked at in Chapter 3, *TensorFlow Graph Architecture*, contains the device name of where the computation must be executed. To generate generic graphs that can run on any hardware platform, SavedModel supports clearing devices before its generation.

These features allow you to create hardware that's independent and self-contained objects that specify how the model should be called, the output nodes, given a specific input, and which particular model to use among the ones available (via tags).

Creating a SavedModel from a Keras model

In TensorFlow 1.x, creating a SavedModel requires that we know what the input nodes are, what the output nodes are, and that we have successfully loaded the graph representation of the model we want to save inside a tf.Session function.

TensorFlow 2.0 simplified the way of creating a SavedModel a lot. Since Keras is the only way of defining models, and there are no more sessions, the process of creation of SavedModel consists of a single line of code:

(tf2)

This is as follows:

```
# model is a tf.keras.Model model
path = "/tmp/model/1"
tf.saved_model.save(model, path)
```

The path variable follows a good practice that consists of adding a version number to the model directly in the export path (/1). The only tag associated with the model is the default tag: "serve".

The tf.saved_model.save call creates the following directory structure in the specified path variable

```
assets/
variables/
    variables.data-?????-of-?????
    variables.index
saved_model.pb
```

The directory contains the following:

- `assets` contains auxiliary files. These files were described in the previous section.
- `variables` contains the model variables. These variables are created from a TensorFlow Saver object in the same way they are created for the checkpoint files.
- `saved_model.pb` is the compiled Protobuf. This is a binary representation of the computation the Keras model describes.

The Keras model already specifies what the model input and outputs are; therefore, there is no need to worry about which is which. The SignatureDef that's exported by a Keras model (it is worth recalling from the previous section that they are just named functions that describe how to call the model) is the invocation of the `call` method of the Keras model (its forward pass), and it is exported under the `serving_default` signature key.

Creating a SavedModel from a Keras model is straightforward since the description of the forward pass is contained in its `call` method. This function is then automatically converted by TensorFlow into its graph equivalent using AutoGraph. The input parameters of the `call` method become the input signature of the graph and the outputs of the Keras model.

However, we may not be interested in exporting a Keras model. What if we just want to deploy and serve a generic computational graph?

Converting a SavedModel from a generic function

In TensorFlow 1.x, there is no difference between exporting a generic graph and a model: select the input and output nodes, create a session, define the signature, and save it.

In TensorFlow 2.0, since graphs are hidden, the conversion of a generic TensorFlow computation to a SavedModel (graph) requires some additional attention.

The description of the first parameter of the `tf.saved_model.save(obj, export_dir, signatures=None)` function clearly states that `obj` must be a trackable *object*.

A trackable object is an object derived from the `TrackableBase` class (private, which means it's not visible in the `tensorflow` package)—almost every object in TensorFlow 2.0 derives from this class. These objects are the objects that can be stored inside a checkpoint file, and among them, we find the Keras models, the optimizers, and so on.

For this reason, it is not possible to export a function like the following one without creating an object that inherits from a `TrackableBase` object:

(tf2)

```
def pow(x, y):
    return tf.math.pow(x, y)
```

The most generic class in the TensorFlow API that, once instantiated, creates a trackable object is the `tf.Module` class. A module is a named container for `tf.Variable` objects, other modules, and functions that apply to user input. Subclassing `tf.Module` is a straightforward way to create a trackable object and satisfying the requirement of the `tf.saved_model.save` function:

(tf2)

```
class Wrapper(tf.Module):

    def pow(self, x, y):
        return tf.math.pow(x, y)
```

Not being a Keras model, `tf.saved_model.save` doesn't know which one of the `Wrapper` class methods applies to graph conversion. There are two different ways of instructing the `save` function to convert only the methods we are interested in. They are as follows:

- **Specify the signature**: The third parameter of the `save` function optionally accepts a dictionary. The dictionary must contain the name of the method to export and the input description. It does so by using the `tf.TensorSpec` object.
- **Use** `tf.function`: The `save` mode, when the `signature` parameter is omitted, searches inside the `obj` for a `@tf.function` decorated method. If exactly one method is found, that method will be used as the default signature for the SavedModel. Also, in this case, we have to describe the input type and shape by using `tf.TensorSpec` objects that are manually passed to the `tf.function` `input_signature` parameter.

The second method is the handiest, and it also brings the advantage of having defined and converted to graph the current Python program. When used, this could speed up computation.

```
(tf2)

    class Wrapper(tf.Module):

        @tf.function(
            input_signature=[
                tf.TensorSpec(shape=None, dtype=tf.float32),
                tf.TensorSpec(shape=None, dtype=tf.float32),
            ]
        )
        def pow(self, x, y):
            return tf.math.pow(x, y)


    obj = Wrapper()
    tf.saved_model.save(obj, "/tmp/pow/1")
```

Therefore, the way of exporting a generic function to its SavedModel representation is to wrap the function into a trackable object, decorate the method with `tf.function`, and specify the input signature to use during the conversion.

This is all we need to do to export a generic function, that is, a generic computational graph, or a Keras model to its self-contained and language-agnostic representation, so that it's ready to use in every programming language.

The easiest way to use a SavedModel object is to use the TensorFlow Python API, since it's the more complete high-level API for TensorFlow and offers convenient methods to load and use a SavedModel.

Python deployment

Using Python, it is straightforward to load the computational graphs stored inside a SavedModel and use them as native Python functions. This is all thanks to the TensorFlow Python API. The `tf.saved_model.load(path)` method deserializes the SavedModel located in `path` and returns a trackable object with a `signatures` attribute that contains the mapping from the signature keys to Python functions that are ready to be used.

The `load` method is capable of deserializing the following:

- Generic computational graphs, such as the ones we created in the previous section
- Keras models
- SavedModel created using TensorFlow 1.x or the Estimator API

Generic computational graph

Let's say we are interested in loading the computational graph of the `pow` function we created in the previous section and using it inside a Python program. Doing this is straightforward in TensorFlow 2.0. Follow these steps to do so:

1. Import the model:

   (tf2)

   ```
   path = "/tmp/pow/1"
   imported = tf.saved_model.load(path)
   ```

2. The `imported` object has a `signatures` attribute we can inspect to see the available functions. In this case, since we didn't specify a signature when we exported the model, we expect to find only the default signature, `"serving_default"`:

   (tf2)

   ```
   assert "serving_default" == list(imported.signatures)[0]
   assert len(imported.signatures) == 1
   ```

   The computational graph of the power function can be made available by accessing `imported.signatures["serving_default"]`. Then, it is ready to be used.

    Using the imported computational graphs requires you to have good understanding of the TensorFlow graph structure, as explained in Chapter 3, *TensorFlow Graph Architecture*. In fact, the `imported.signatures["serving_default"]` function is a static graph, and as such, it requires some additional attention to be used.

3. Calling the graph but passing a wrong input type will make it raise an exception since the static graph is strictly statically typed. Moreover, the object returned by the `tf.saved_model.load` function forces the usage of named parameters only, and not positional ones (which is different to the `pow` function's original definition, which used only positional arguments). Thus, once the inputs with the correct shape and input type are defined, it is possible to invoke the function easily:

(tf2)

```
pow = imported.signatures["serving_default"]
result = pow(x=tf.constant(2.0), y=tf.constant(5.0))
```

The `result` variable, as opposed to what you might expect, does not contain a `tf.Tensor` object with a value of `32.0`; it is a dictionary. Using a dictionary to return the result of a computation is a good design choice. In fact, this forces the caller (the Python program using the imported computational graph) to explicitly access a key that indicates the desired return value.

4. In the case of the `pow` function, where the return value is a `tf.Tensor` and not a Python dictionary, the returned dictionary has keys that follow a naming convention—the key name is always the `"output_"` string, followed by the position (starting from zero) of the returned argument. The following code snippet clarifies this concept:

(tf2)

```
assert result["output_0"].numpy() == 32
```

If the `pow` function is updated as follows, the dictionary keys will be `"output_0"`, `"output_1"`:

(tf2)

```
def pow(self, x, y):
    return tf.math.pow(x, y), tf.math.pow(y, x)
```

Of course, falling back on the default naming convention is not a good or maintainable solution (what does `output_0` represent?). Therefore, when designing functions that will be exported in a SavedModel, it's good practice to make the function return a dictionary so that the exported SavedModel will use the same dictionary as the return value when invoked. Thus, a better design of the `pow` function could be as follows:

(tf2)

```
class Wrapper(tf.Module):

class Wrapper(tf.Module):
    @tf.function(
        input_signature=[
            tf.TensorSpec(shape=None, dtype=tf.float32),
            tf.TensorSpec(shape=None, dtype=tf.float32),
        ]
    )
    def pow(self, x, y):
        return {"pow_x_y":tf.math.pow(x, y), "pow_y_x":
tf.math.pow(y, x)}


obj = Wrapper()
tf.saved_model.save(obj, "/tmp/pow/1")
```

Once imported and executed, the following code will produce a dictionary with meaningful names:

(tf2)

```
path = "/tmp/pow/1"

imported = tf.saved_model.load(path)
print(imported.signatures["serving_default"](
        x=tf.constant(2.0),y=tf.constant(5.0)))
```

The resultant output is the following dictionary:

```
{
   'pow_x_y': <tf.Tensor: id=468, shape=(), dtype=float32,
numpy=32.0>,
   'pow_y_x': <tf.Tensor: id=469, shape=(), dtype=float32,
numpy=25.0>
   }
```

The TensorFlow Python API simplifies not only the loading of a generic computational graph, but also the usage of a trained Keras model.

Keras models

Being the official TensorFlow 2.0 way of defining machine learning models, the Keras models, when serialized, contain more than just the serialized `call` method. The object returned by the `load` function is similar to the object that's returned when you're restoring a generic computational graph, but with more attributes and peculiarities:

- The `.variables` attribute: The non-trainable variables attached to the original Keras model have been serialized and stored inside the SavedModel.
- The `.trainable_variables` attribute: In the same manner as the `.variables` attribute, the trainable variables of the model have also been serialized and stored inside the SavedModel.
- The `__call__` method: Instead of exposing a `signatures` attribute with a single key, `"serving_default"`, the returned object exposes a `__call__` method that accepts inputs just like the original Keras model.

All of these features allow not only the use of the SavedModel as a standalone computational graph, as shown in the following code snippet, but they also allow you to completely restore the Keras model and continue to train it:

`(tf2)`

```
imported = tf.saved_model.load(path)
# inputs is a input compatible with the serialized model
outputs = imported(inputs)
```

As we mentioned previously, all these additional features (variables that are trainable and not trainable, plus the serialized representation of the computation) allow for a complete restore of a Keras model object from a SavedModel, making it possible to use them as checkpoint files. The Python API offers the `tf.keras.models.load_model` function to do that, and, as usual, in TensorFlow 2.0, it is really handy:

`(tf2)`

```
model = tf.keras.models.load_model(path)
# models is now a tf.keras.Model object!
```

Here, `path` is the path of the SavedModel, or the `h5py` file. The `h5py` serialization format is not considered in this book since it is a Keras representation and has no additional advantages with respect to the SavedModel serialization format.

The Python API is also backward-compatible with the TensorFlow 1.x SavedModel format, and so you can restore flat graphs instead of `tf.function` objects.

Flat graphs

The SavedModel objects created by the `tf.estimator` API or using the SavedModel 1.x API contain a rawer representation of the computation. This representation is known as **flat graph**.

In this representation, the flat graph inherits no signatures from a `tf.function` object in order to simplify the restoration process. It only takes the computational graph as is, along with its node names and variables (see `Chapter 3`, *TensorFlow Graph Architecture*, for details).

These SavedModels have functions that correspond to their signatures (defined manually before the serialization process) in the `.signatures` attribute, but more importantly, the restored SavedModel that uses the new TensorFlow 2.0 API has a `.prune` method that allows you to extract functions from arbitrary subgraphs just by knowing the input and output node names.

Using the `.prune` method is the equivalent of restoring the SavedModel in the default graph and putting it in a TensorFlow 1.x Session; then, the input and output nodes can be accessed by using the `tf.Graph.get_tensor_by_name` method.

TensorFlow 2.0, through the `.prune` method, simplified this process, making it just as easy, as shown in the following code snippet:

```
(tf2)

    imported = tf.saved_model.load(v1savedmodel_path)
    pruned = imported.prune("input_:0", "cnn/out/identity:0")
    # inputs is an input compatible with the flat graph
    out = pruned(inputs)
```

Here, `input_` is a placeholder of any possible input node, and `"cnn/out/identity:0"` is the output node.

After the SavedModel has been loaded inside the Python program, it is possible to use the trained model (or the generic computational graph) as a building block for any standard Python application. For instance, once you've trained a face detection model, it is straightforward to use OpenCV (the most famous open source computer vision library) to open the webcam stream and feed it to the face detection model. The applications of trained models are countless and you can develop your own Python application that uses a trained machine learning model as a building block.

Although Python is the language of data science, it isn't the perfect candidate for the deployment of machine learning models on different platforms. There are programming languages that are the de facto standard for certain tasks or environments; for example, Javascript for client-side web development, C++ and Go for data centers and cloud services, and so on.

Being a language-agnostic representation, it is, in theory, possible to load and execute (deploy) a SavedModel using every programming language; this is a huge advantage since there are cases in which Python is not usable, or it is not the best choice.

TensorFlow supports many different deployment platforms: it offers tools and frameworks in many different languages in order to satisfy a wide range of use cases.

Supported deployment platforms

As shown in the diagram at the beginning of this chapter, SavedModel is the input for a vast ecosystem of deployment platforms, with each one being created to satisfy a different range of use cases:

- **TensorFlow Serving**: This is the official Google solution for serving machine learning models. It supports model versioning, multiple models can be deployed in parallel, and it ensures that concurrent models achieve high throughput with low latency thanks to its complete support for hardware accelerators (GPUs and TPUs). TensorFlow Serving is not merely a deployment platform, but an entire ecosystem built around TensorFlow and written in highly efficient C++ code. Currently, this is the solution Google itself uses to run tens of millions of inferences per second on Google Cloud's ML platform.

- **TensorFlow Lite**: This is the deployment platform of choice for running machine learning models on mobile and embedded devices. TensorFlow Lite is a whole new ecosystem and has its own training and deployment tools. It is designed to optimize the trained models for size, thereby creating a small binary representation of the original model that's optimized for fast inference and low power consumption. Moreover, the TensorFlow Lite framework also offers the tools to build a new model and retrain an existing one (thus it allows you to do transfer learning/fine-tuning) directly from the embedded device or smartphone. TensorFlow Lite comes with a Python toolchain that's used to convert the SavedModel into its optimized representation, the .tflite file.
- **TensorFlow.js**: This is a framework similar to TensorFlow Lite but designed to train and deploy TensorFlow models in the browser and Node.js. Like TensorFlow Lite, the framework comes with a Python toolchain that can be used to convert a SavedModel into a JSON readable format by the TensorFlow Javascript library. TensorFlow.js can be used to fine-tune or train models from scratch, which it does by using sensor data coming from the browser or any other client-side data.
- **Other language bindings**: TensorFlow Core is written in C++, and there are bindings for many different programming languages, most of which are automatically generated. The structure of the binding is often very low-level and similar to the TensorFlow Graph structure used in the TensorFlow 1.x Python API and under the hood of the TensorFlow C++ API.

Supporting many different deployment platforms, TensorFlow is ready to deploy on a broad range of platforms and devices. In the following sections, you will learn how to deploy a trained model on a browser using TensorFlow.js and how to run inferences using the Go programming language.

TensorFlow.js

TensorFlow.js (https://www.tensorflow.org/js/) is a library that's used for developing and training machine learning models on JavaScript and deploying them in browsers or in Node.js.

To be used inside TensorFlow.js, a trained model must be converted into a format TensorFlow.js can load. The target format is a directory containing a model.json file and a set of binary files containing the model parameters. The model.json file contains the graph description and information about the binary files, to make it possible to restore the trained model successfully.

Although it is fully compatible with TensorFlow 2.0, it is good practice to create an isolated environment for TensorFlow.js, as explained in the *Environment setup* section of `Chapter 3`, *TensorFlow Graph Architecture*. The TensorFlow.js dedicated environment is, from now on, displayed using the (`tfjs`) notation, before the code snippets.

The first step in developing a TensorFlow.js application is to install TensorFlow.js inside the isolated environment. You need to do this so that you can use all the provided command-line tools and the library itself via Python:

(`tfjs`)

```
pip install tensorflowjs
```

TensorFlow.js has tight integration with TensorFlow 2.0. In fact, it is possible to convert a Keras model into a TensorFlow.js representation directly using Python. Moreover, it offers a command-line interface for converting a generic SavedModel that could contain any computational graph into its supported representation.

Converting a SavedModel into model.json format

Since it is not possible to use a SavedModel directly from TensorFlow.js, we need to convert it into a compatible version and then load it in the TensorFlow.js runtime. The `tensorflowjs_converter` command-line application makes the conversion process straightforward. This tool not only performs the conversion between the SavedModel and the TensorFlow.js representation but also automatically quantizes the model, thereby reducing its dimensions when necessary.

Let's say we are interested in converting the SavedModel of the computational graph we exported in the previous section into TensorFlow format via the serialized `pow` function. Using `tensorflowjs_converter`, we only need to specify the input and output file formats (in this case, the input is a SavedModel, and the output is a TensorFlow.js graph model) and location, and then we are ready to go:

(`tfjs`)

```
tensorflowjs_converter \
    --input_format "tf_saved_model" \
    --output_format "tfjs_graph_model" \
    /tmp/pow/1 \
    exported_js
```

The preceding command reads the SavedModel present in `/tmp/pow/1` and places the result of the conversion in the current directory, `exported_js` (creating it if it doesn't exist). Since the SavedModel has no parameters, in the `exported_js` folder, we only find the `model.json` file that contains the description of the computation.

We are now ready to go – we can define a simple web page or a simple Node.js application that imports the TensorFlow.js runtime and then successfully import and use the converted SavedModel. The following code creates a one-page application with a form inside it; by using the click event of the **pow** button, the exported graph is loaded, and the computation is executed:

```
<html>
    <head>
        <title>Power</title>
        <!-- Include the latest TensorFlow.js runtime -->
        <script
src="https://cdn.jsdelivr.net/npm/@tensorflow/tfjs@latest"></script>
    </head>
    <body>
        x: <input type="number" step="0.01" id="x"><br>
        y: <input type="number" step="0.01" id="y"><br>
        <button id="pow" name="pow">pow</button><br>
        <div>
            x<sup>y</sup>: <span id="x_to_y"></span>
        </div>
        <div>
            y<sup>x</sup>: <span id="y_to_x"></span>
        </div>

        <script>
            document.getElementById("pow").addEventListener("click", async
function() {
                // Load the model
                const model = await
tf.loadGraphModel("exported_js/model.json")
                // Input Tensors
                let x = tf.tensor1d([document.getElementById("x").value],
dtype='float32')
                let y = tf.tensor1d([document.getElementById("y").value],
dtype='float32')
                let results = model.execute({"x": x, "y": y})
                let x_to_y = results[0].dataSync()
                let y_to_x = results[1].dataSync()

                document.getElementById("x_to_y").innerHTML = x_to_y
                document.getElementById("y_to_x").innerHTML = y_to_x
            });
```

```
        </script>
    </body>
</html>
```

TensorFlow.js follows different conventions in regards to how to use a loaded SavedModel. As we can see in the preceding code snippet, the signature defined inside the SavedModel has been preserved, and the function is being invoked by passing the named parameters `"x"` and `"y"`. Instead, the return value format has been changed: the `pow_x_y` and `pow_y_x` keys have been discarded, and the return values are now positional; in the first position (`results[0]`), we found the value of the `pow_x_y` key, and in the second position, the value of the `pow_y_x` key.

Moreover, with JavaScript being a language with strong support for asynchronous operations, the TensorFlow.js API uses it a lot—the model loading is asynchronous and defined inside an `async` function. Even fetching the results from the model is asynchronous by default. But in this case, we forced the call to be synchronous using the `dataSync` method.

Using Python, we can now launch a simple HTTP server and see the application inside the browser:

```
(tfjs)

    python -m http.server
```

By visiting the `http://localhost:8000/` address using a web browser and opening the HTML page containing the previously written code, we can see and use the deployed graph, directly in the browser:

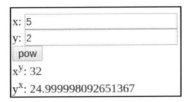

The TensorFlow.js API, although similar to the Python one, is different and follows different rules; a complete analysis of TensorFlow.js is beyond the scope of this book, and so you should have a look at the official documentation to gain a better understanding of the TensorFlow.js API.

Compared to the preceding procedure, which involves the usage of `tensorflowjs_converter`, the deployment of a Keras model is simplified, and it is possible to integrate the conversion from a Keras model to a `model.json` file directly in the TensorFlow 2.0 Python script that's used to train the model.

Converting a Keras Model into model.json format

As shown at the beginning of this chapter, a Keras model can be exported as a SavedModel, and therefore, the procedure explained earlier to convert a SavedModel into a `model.json` file can still be used. However, since the Keras models are particular objects in the TensorFlow 2.0 framework, it is possible to directly embed the deployment into TensorFlow.js at the end of the training pipeline:

```
(tfjs)

    import tensorflowjs as tfjs
    from tensorflow import keras

    model = keras.models.Sequential() # for example
    # create the model by adding layers

    # Standard Keras way of defining and executing the training loop
    # (this can be replaced by a custom training loop)
    model.compile(...)
    model.fit(...)

    # Convert the model to the model.json in the exported_js dir
    tfjs_target_dir = "exported_js"
    tfjs.converters.save_keras_model(model, tfjs_target_dir)
```

The conversion is straightforward since it only consists of a single line, `tfjs.converters.save_keras_model(model, tfjs_target_dir)`. For this reason, the practical application is left as an exercise to you (see the *Exercises* section for more information).

Among the available deployment platforms, there is a long list of programming languages whose support to TensorFlow is given by bindings, which are usually automatically generated.

Supporting different programming languages is a great advantage since it allows developers to embed machine learning models that have been developed and trained using Python in their applications. If, for instance, we are Go developers and we want to embed a machine learning model in our application, we can use the TensorFlow Go bindings or a simplified interface built upon them called **tfgo**.

Go Bindings and tfgo

The TensorFlow bindings for the Go programming language are almost entirely automatically generated from the C++ API, and as such, they implement only primitive operations. There's no Keras models, no eager execution, nor any other TensorFlow 2.0 new features; in fact, almost no changes were made to the Python API. Moreover, the Go API is not covered by the TensorFlow API satabilty guarantee, which means that everything can change between minor releases. However, this API is particularly useful for loading models that are created with Python and running them within a Go application.

Setup

Setting up the environment is more complex compared to Python since it is necessary to download and install the TensorFlow C library and clone the whole TensorFlow repository to create the Go TensorFlow package at the correct version.

The following `bash` script shows how to download, configure, and install the TensorFlow Go API, with no GPU, at version 1.13:

```bash
#!/usr/bin/env bash

# variables
TF_VERSION_MAJOR=1
TF_VERSION_MINOR=13
TF_VERSION_PATCH=1

curl -L
"https://storage.googleapis.com/tensorflow/libtensorflow/libtensorflow-cpu-
linux-x86_64-
""$TF_VERSION_MAJOR"."$TF_VERSION_MINOR"."$TF_VERSION_PATCH"".tar.gz" |
sudo tar -C /usr/local -xz
sudo ldconfig
git clone https://github.com/tensorflow/tensorflow
$GOPATH/src/github.com/tensorflow/tensorflow/
pushd $GOPATH/src/github.com/tensorflow/tensorflow/tensorflow/go
git checkout r"$TF_VERSION_MAJOR"."$TF_VERSION_MINOR"
go build
```

Once installed, it is possible to build and run an example program that only uses the Go bindings.

Go bindings

Refer to the example program available at `https://www.tensorflow.org/install/lang_go` for this section.

As you will see from the code, using TensorFlow in Go is very different compared to Python or even JavaScript. In particular, the operations that are available are really low-level and there is still the graph definition and session execution pattern to follow. A detailed explanation of the TensorFlow Go API is beyond the scope of this book; however, you can read the *Understanding TensorFlow using GO* article (`https://pgaleone.eu/tensorflow/go/2017/05/29/understanding-tensorflow-using-go/`), which explains the basics of the Go API.

A `Go` package that simplifies the usage of Go bindings is `tfgo`. In the following section, we are going to use it to restore and execute the computational graph of the `pow` operation from the previously exported SavedModel.

Working with tfgo

Installing `tfgo` is straightforward; just use the following code after installing the TensorFlow Go package:

```
go get -u github.com/galeone/tfgo
```

Since the goal is to use Go to deploy the SavedModel of the previously defined `pow` function, we are going to use the `tfgo LoadModel` function, which was created to load a SavedModel given the path and the desired tag.

TensorFlow 2.0 comes with the `saved_model_cli` tool, which can be used to inspect a SavedModel file. This tool is fundamental to correctly using a SavedModel using the Go bindings or `tfgo`. In fact, contrary to Python or TensorFlow.js, the Go API requires the name of the operations of input and output, and not the high-level names given during the SavedModel's creation.

By using `saved_model_cli show`, it is possible to have all the information about the inspect SavedModel and thus be able to use them in Go:

```
saved_model_cli show --all --dir /tmp/pow/1
```

This produces the following list of information:

```
MetaGraphDef with tag-set: 'serve' contains the following SignatureDefs:

signature_def['__saved_model_init_op']:
  The given SavedModel SignatureDef contains the following input(s):
  The given SavedModel SignatureDef contains the following output(s):
    outputs['__saved_model_init_op'] tensor_info:
        dtype: DT_INVALID
        shape: unknown_rank
        name: NoOp
  Method name is:

signature_def['serving_default']:
  The given SavedModel SignatureDef contains the following input(s):
    inputs['x'] tensor_info:
        dtype: DT_FLOAT
        shape: unknown_rank
        name: serving_default_x:0
    inputs['y'] tensor_info:
        dtype: DT_FLOAT
        shape: unknown_rank
        name: serving_default_y:0
  The given SavedModel SignatureDef contains the following output(s):
    outputs['pow_x_y'] tensor_info:
        dtype: DT_FLOAT
        shape: unknown_rank
        name: PartitionedCall:0
    outputs['pow_y_x'] tensor_info:
        dtype: DT_FLOAT
        shape: unknown_rank
        name: PartitionedCall:1
  Method name is: tensorflow/serving/predict
```

The most important parts are as follows:

- **The tag name**: `serve` is the only tag present in this SavedModel object.
- **The SignatureDefs**: There are two different SignatureDefs in this SavedModel: `__saved_model_init_op` which, in this case, does nothing; and `serving_default`, which contains all the necessary information about the input and output nodes of the exported computational graph.
- **The inputs and outputs**: Every SignatureDef section contains a list of input and outputs. As we can see, for every node, the dtype, shape, and name of the operation that generates the output Tensor are available.

Since the Go bindings support the flat graph structure, we have to use the operation names and not the names that were given during the SavedModel's creation to access the input/output nodes.

Now that we have all this information, it is easy to use `tfgo` to load and execute the model. The following code contains information about how the model is loaded and its usage so that it only executes the output node that computes x^y:

(go)

```
package main

import (
"fmt"
tg "github.com/galeone/tfgo"
tf "github.com/tensorflow/tensorflow/tensorflow/go"
)
```

In the following code snippet, you restore the model from the SavedModel tag, `"serve"`. Define the input tensors, that is, x=2, y=5. Then, compute the result. The output is the first node, `"PartitionedCall:0"`, which corresponds to *x_to_y*. The input names are `"serving_default_{x,y}"` and correspond to x and y. The predictions need to be converted back into the correct type, which is `float32` in this case:

```
func main() {
 model := tg.LoadModel("/tmp/pow/1", []string{"serve"}, nil)
 x, _ := tf.NewTensor(float32(2.0))
 y, _ := tf.NewTensor(float32(5.0))

results := model.Exec([]tf.Output{
 model.Op("PartitionedCall", 0),
 }, map[tf.Output]*tf.Tensor{
 model.Op("serving_default_x", 0): x,
 model.Op("serving_default_y", 0): y,
 })

 predictions := results[0].Value().(float32)
 fmt.Println(predictions)
 }
```

As expected, the program produces *32* as the output.

The process of inspecting a SavedModel using `saved_model_cli` and using it in a Go program or in any other supported deployment platform is always the same, no matter what the content of the SavedModel is. This is one of the greatest advantages of using the standardized SavedModel serialization format as the unique connection point between the training/graph definition and the deployment.

Summary

In this chapter, we looked at the SavedModel serialization format. This standardized serialization format was designed with the goal of simplifying the deployment of machine learning models on many different platforms.

SavedModel is a language-agnostic, self-contained representation of the computation, and the whole TensorFlow ecosystem supports it. Deploying a trained machine learning model on embedded devices, smartphones, browsers, or using many different languages is possible thanks to the conversion tools based on the SavedModel format or the native support offered by the TensorFlow bindings for other languages.

The easiest way to deploy a model is by using Python since the TensorFlow 2.0 API has complete support for the creation, restoration, and manipulation of SavedModel objects. Moreover, the Python API offers additional features and integrations between the Keras models and the SavedModel objects, making it possible to use them as checkpoints.

We saw how all the other deployment platforms supported by the TensorFlow ecosystem are based on the SavedModel file format or on some of its transformations. We used TensorFlow.js to deploy a model in a browser and in Node.js. We learned that we require an additional conversion step, but doing this is straightforward thanks to the Python TensorFlow.js package and the native support for Keras models. The automatically generated language bindings are close to the C++ API, and so they are more low-level and difficult to use. We also learned about Go bindings and `tfgo`, which is a simplified interface for the TensorFlow Go API. Together with the command-line tools that are used to analyze a SavedModel object, you've seen how to read the information contained inside a SavedModel and use it to deploy a SavedModel in Go.

We've reached the end of this book. By looking back at the previous chapters, we can see all the progress that we've made. Your journey into the world of neural networks shouldn't end here; in fact, this should be a starting point so that you can create your own neural network applications in TensorFlow 2.0. Throughout this journey, we learned about the basics of machine learning and deep learning while emphasizing the graph representation of the computation. In particular, we learned about the following:

- Machine learning basics, from the dataset's importance to the most common machine learning algorithm families (supervised, unsupervised, and semi-supervised).
- The most common neural network architectures, how to train a machine learning model, and how to fight the overfitting problem through regularization.
- The TensorFlow graph architecture that's explicitly used in TensorFlow 1.x and still present in TensorFlow 2.0. In this chapter, we started to write TensorFlow 1.x code, which we found to be extremely useful when working with `tf.function`.
- The TensorFlow 2.0 architecture with its new way of programming, the TensorFlow 2.0 Keras implementation, eager execution, and many other new features, which were also explained in previous chapters.
- How to create efficient data input pipelines and how to use the new **TensorFlow datasets (tfds)** project to quickly get a common benchmark dataset. Moreover, the Estimator API was presented, although it still uses the old graph representation.
- How to use TensorFlow Hub and Keras to fine-tune a pre-trained model or do transfer learning. By doing this, we learned how to quickly prototype a classification network, thereby speeding up the training time by reusing the work made by the tech giant.
- How to define a simple classification and regression network, with the goal of introducing the topic of object detection and showing how easy it is to train a multi-headed network using TensorFlow eager execution.
- After object detection, we focused on the more difficult task (but easier to implement) of performing semantic segmentation on images, and we developed our own version of U-Net to solve it. Since a dataset of semantic segmentation is not presented in TensorFlow datasets (tfds), we also learned how to add a custom DatasetBuilder to add a new datset.
- The **Generative Adversarial Networks (GANs)** theory and how to implement the adversarial training loop using TensorFlow 2.0. Moreover, by using the fashion-MNIST dataset, we also learned how to define and train a conditional GAN.

- Finally, in this chapter, we learned how to bring a trained model (or a generic computational graph) to production by leveraging the SavedModel serialization format and the TensorFlow 2.0 Serving ecosystem.

Although this is the last chapter, there are exercises to do and, as usual, you shouldn't skip them!

Exercises

The following exercises are programming challenges, combining the expressive power of the TensorFlow Python API and the advantages brought by other programming languages:

1. What is a checkpoint file?
2. What is a SavedModel file?
3. What are the differences between a checkpoint and a SavedModel?
4. What is a SignatureDef?
5. Can a checkpoint have a SignatureDef?
6. Can a SavedModel have more than one SignatureDef?
7. Export a computational graph as a SavedModel that computes the batch matrix multiplication; the returned dictionary must have a meaningful key value.
8. Convert the SavedModel defined in the previous exercise into its TensorFlow.js representation.
9. Use the `model.json` file we created in the previous exercise to develop a simple web page that computes the multiplication of matrices chosen by the user.
10. Restore the semantic segmentation model defined in `Chapter 8`, *Semantic Segmentation and Custom Dataset Builder*, from its latest checkpoint and use `tfjs.converters.save_keras_model` to convert it into a `model.json` file.
11. Use the semantic segmentation model we exported in the previous exercise to develop a simple web page that, given an image, performs semantic segmentation. Use the `tf.fromPixels` method to get the input model. A complete reference for the TensorFlow.js API is available at `https://js.tensorflow.org/api/latest/`.
12. Write a Go application using the TensorFlow Go bindings that computes the convolution between one image and a 3 x 3 kernel.

13. Rewrite the Go application that you wrote in the previous exercise using tfgo. Use the "image" package. Read the documentation at `https://github.com/galeone/tfgo` for more information.

14. Restore the semantic segmentation model we defined in `Chapter 8`, *Semantic Segmentation and Custom Dataset Builder,* to its latest checkpoint and export it as a SavedModel object.

15. Use `tg.LoadModel` to load the Semantic Segmentation model into a Go program and use it to produce a segmentation map for an input image whose path is passed as a command-line parameter.

Other Books You May Enjoy

If you enjoyed this book, you may be interested in these other books by Packt:

Hands-On Computer Vision with TensorFlow 2
Benjamin Planche, Eliot Andres

ISBN: 9781788830645

- Create your own neural networks from scratch
- Classify images with modern architectures including Inception and ResNet
- Detect and segment objects in images with YOLO, Mask R-CNN, and U-Net
- Tackle problems faced when developing self-driving cars and facial emotion recognition systems
- Boost your application's performance with transfer learning, GANs, and domain adaptation
- Use recurrent neural networks (RNNs) for video analysis
- Optimize and deploy your networks on mobile devices and in the browser

What's New in TensorFlow 2.0
Ajay Baranwal, Tanish Baranwal and Alizishaan Khatri

ISBN: 9781838823856

- Implement tf.keras APIs in TF 2.0 to build, train, and deploy production-grade models
- Build models with Keras integration and eager execution
- Explore distribution strategies to run models on GPUs and TPUs
- Perform what-if analysis with TensorBoard across a variety of models
- Discover Vision Kit, Voice Kit, and the Edge TPU for model deployments
- Build complex input data pipelines for ingesting large training datasets

Leave a review - let other readers know what you think

Please share your thoughts on this book with others by leaving a review on the site that you bought it from. If you purchased the book from Amazon, please leave us an honest review on this book's Amazon page. This is vital so that other potential readers can see and use your unbiased opinion to make purchasing decisions, we can understand what our customers think about our products, and our authors can see your feedback on the title that they have worked with Packt to create. It will only take a few minutes of your time, but is valuable to other potential customers, our authors, and Packt. Thank you!

Index

69689489R00199

Made in the USA
Middletown, DE
21 September 2019